MAR 1 2 2010

Working in the Shadows

ALSO BY GABRIEL THOMPSON

There's No José Here

Calling All Radicals

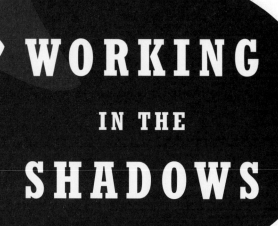

WORKING

IN THE

SHADOWS

A Year of Doing the Jobs
(Most) Americans Won't Do

Gabriel Thompson

NATION
BOOKS

New York

Published by
Nation Books, A Member of the Perseus Books Group
116 East 16th Street, 8th Floor
New York, NY 10003

Nation Books is a co-publishing venture of the Nation Institute and
the Perseus Books Group.

Books published by Nation Books are available at special discounts for
bulk purchases in the United States by corporations, institutions, and
other organizations. For more information, please contact the Special
Markets Department at the Perseus Books Group, 2300 Chestnut
Street, Suite 200, Philadelphia, PA 19103, or call (800) 810–4145,
extension 5000, or e-mail special.markets@perseusbooks.com.

Designed by Timm Bryson

Library of Congress Cataloging-in-Publication Data
Thompson, Gabriel.
  Working in the shadows : a year of doing the jobs (most) Americans
won't do / Gabriel Thompson.
    p. cm.
  Includes bibliographical references.
  ISBN 978–1-56858–408–9 (alk. paper)
1. Foreign workers—United States. 2. Immigrants—United States. 3.
Immigrants—Employment—Economic aspects—United States. 4.
Minimum wage—United States. I. Title.
  HD6300.T46 2010
  331.6'20973—dc22
                                                  2009032055

ISBN: 978–1–56858–408–9
10 9 8 7 6 5 4 3 2

For Daniella, who was with me every step of the way

CONTENTS

AUTHOR'S NOTE

For privacy reasons, the names of workers and supervisors have been changed, and in the case of one worker I altered identifying characteristics. To deal with the challenge of reporting while undercover, I took detailed notes upon arriving home after each shift. During shifts, I used the breaks to disappear whenever possible to jot down scenes or bits of dialogue in a small notebook. I should clarify: Those were the good days. Often, the notebook remained stuffed in my pocket throughout the entire shift. On those days, during breaks, I rested.

INTRODUCTION

I wake up staring into the bluest blue I've ever seen. I must have fallen into a deep sleep during the short break because I need several seconds to realize that I'm looking at the sky, that the pillow beneath my head is a large clump of dirt, and that Manuel is standing over me and smiling. I pull myself to a sitting position. To my left, in the distance, a Border Patrol helicopter is hovering. To my right is Mexico, separated by only a few fields of lettuce.

"*Buenos días.*"

"How much time left?"

Manuel checks his watch. "Four minutes."

I stand up gingerly. It's only my third day in the fields, but already my thirty-year-old body is failing me. I feel like someone has dropped a log on my back. And then piled that log onto a truck with many other logs, and driven that truck over my thighs. I reach down and grab two 32-ounce bottles of Gatorade, both empty. This is nothing new: Yesterday I finished four bottles. A few people on the crew have already suggested that I see a doctor about my sweating problem.

"Let's go," I say to Manuel, trying to sound energetic. I fall in line behind him, stumbling across rows of lettuce and thinking about the five-day rule. The five-day rule, according to Manuel, is simple: Survive the first five days and you'll be fine. He's been a farmworker for almost two decades, so he should know. I'm on day three of five—the goal is within sight. Of course, another way to look at my situation is that I'm on day three of what I promised myself would be a two-month job. Or that this is only the first in a series of jobs that I hope to survive over the course of the year. But that kind of thinking doesn't benefit anyone. *Day three of five.*

"I've been thinking," Manuel calls over his shoulder. "When you showed up, I could tell right away that you had money." On the first day I was wearing jeans and a hooded sweatshirt I've had since high school, but I know what he means. I'm white, the only white person on the crew and the only white person in the fields. "So I thought maybe you were a supervisor. But you don't know what you're doing with the lettuce." He laughs. "Candelario thinks you're with immigration." He makes a dismissive gesture with his right hand and turns around, waiting for me to catch up. "But why would you be working in the fields and not stopping people at the border?"

We've nearly reached the lettuce machine, where two dozen crewmembers are putting on gloves and sharpening knives. A radio is blasting a Spanish love song and a few men and women are laughing at something; it sounds like a party.

We're late, but Manuel remains stopped in his tracks. "You're an American. But you're not a supervisor and you're not with immigration. So what are you doing?"

I shrug my shoulders. "I don't know, I just—"

"Manuel! Gabriel! Let's go!" The foreman is impatient and the question is quickly forgotten. "*¡Vámonos!*" We hustle our butts to the machine, grab our knives from a box of chlorinated water, and set up in neighboring rows, just as the machine starts moving slowly down another endless field.

"WHAT ARE YOU doing here?" Over the course of the year I would hear Manuel's question dozens of times. I'd ask it myself when things weren't going well—which was often. But because I was undercover, I couldn't explain that I was writing a book. Instead I made up a variety of responses: I was traveling and needed money to continue my journey; I enjoyed learning new skills; or, later in the year, with the economy collapsing, I needed whatever work I could find. At other times, in the middle of a shift so draining that I didn't have the energy to make something up, I would simply say, "I don't know." At those moments the answer felt honest enough.

I do know what gave me the idea for this book. In the fall of 2007 the *New York Times* published an article entitled "Crackdown Upends Slaughterhouse's Workforce." Written by labor correspondent Steven Greenhouse, the piece documented the difficulty that Smithfield Foods was having in securing a stable workforce at its massive hog slaughterhouse in North Carolina after a series of raids by immigration agents. Although the crackdown resulted in the arrest of only twenty-one undocumented immigrants, more than 1,100 Latino workers subsequently quit, leaving the 5,200-employee plant severely short staffed. Some of the workers were no doubt working without proper papers, while others simply wanted to avoid a situation in which government agents could come barging into their trailers in the middle of the night.

In response to the exodus of immigrants, Smithfield stepped up efforts to recruit U.S. citizens. Based on wages alone, this shouldn't have been overly difficult: Most of the local jobs paid minimum wage and positions at the plant averaged $12 an hour. Still, as Greenhouse reported, "The turnover rate for new workers—many find the work grueling and the smell awful—is twice what it was when Hispanics dominated the workforce . . . At the end of the shifts, many workers complain that their muscles are sore and their minds are numb."[1]

As a teenager, I relished George Orwell's accounts of going into dangerous coal mines in *The Road to Wigan Pier* and washing dishes in *Down and Out in Paris and London,* and was likewise moved by Barbara Ehrenreich's adventures scrubbing floors and waiting tables in *Nickel and Dimed.* I've always been drawn to chronicles of immersion journalism; they have a unique ability to explore fascinating and sometimes brutal worlds that are usually kept out of sight. I thought it would be exciting to try this type of reporting myself, and immediately upon finishing the *Times* article, a project formed in my head. I would enter the low-wage immigrant workforce for a year and write about it.

In many ways, this project was a natural outgrowth of my previous work. I had reported on immigrants for the past three years—mostly Latino because I speak Spanish—and I have always been interested in documenting what life looks like through the eyes of my subjects, transforming them from statistics to real people. The notion of going undercover to work alongside immigrants in the factories and fields—assuming I could actually get hired—held an immense appeal. In 2008, the Pew Hispanic Center estimated that there were 8.3 million undocumented workers in the United States, making up 5.4 percent of the workforce. The role that these low-wage workers play in our economy is, of course, a matter of much debate. But whether one believes they are a threat or a boon to the economy, the fact remains that very few of us nonimmigrants know what it's like to do the jobs they do. I wanted to find out.

I ULTIMATELY DECIDED to seek employment in three industries that depend heavily on Latino immigrants: agriculture, poultry processing, and back-of-the-house restaurant work (this refers to the people who work in the kitchen and do not interact with customers). While I could just as easily have elected to slaughter cows, work in construction, do landscaping, or clean offices, I chose farmwork, chicken factories, and restaurants mostly out of sheer curiosity; they were industries I wanted to know more about. (I've been a vegetarian since grade school, so my curiosity was tinged with apprehension when it came to poultry.) Having decided on the three jobs, it quickly became clear that my year of work would also be a year of travel. The poultry industry is concentrated in the American South, and there are few fields in need of harvesting near my apartment in Brooklyn. I planned to go west for farmwork, south in search of a chicken plant, and return home to New York to find a restaurant job. Heading to the southern states where the Latino population is growing fastest would also grant me the opportunity to report on how the region is adapting to its newest arrivals.

The neat little itinerary that I drew up in my apartment left a critical question unanswered: How in God's name would I get hired? It seemed likely that I would face skeptical looks from hiring managers, perhaps even be laughed out of an office or two. I figured that the increase in immigration enforcement might make it easier to find work—and that the sorts of jobs I was looking for would have openings due to high turnover. But ultimately, from the moment I left Brooklyn, I was operating on little more than blind faith.

I SET SEVERAL parameters for the year. When discussing my project, I learned that a fair number of Americans had some experience with farmwork. Many were similar to my father's time spent hoeing beet fields in the Red River Valley of North Dakota. As a youth he had planned to spend a summer in the fields; after just a few days—perhaps a week—he had had enough. So I set myself a goal: No matter how unpleasant, I would stay with each job for two months.

The second guideline was that while I was away from New York, I would live among the immigrants that I worked alongside. This would be the most cost-effective arrangement and would allow me to get to know my coworkers better.

STRICTLY SPEAKING, THERE is no such a thing as an "immigrant" job. There are many industries that rely heavily on Latino immigrants, but many of these also employ at least a handful of U.S.-born citizens (though not in the lettuce fields, as I discovered). Often, when workplaces offer a variety of jobs—restaurants are a good example—immigrants tend to be assigned the most strenuous, dangerous, and worst-paid positions (e.g., washing dishes and delivering food). So a book about the world of immigrant work is also one about the very poor Americans who labor with them. As I would discover, these Americans had much in common with undocumented immigrants—for one thing, they are ignored equally in the stump speeches of politicians—and despite the lack of a shared language, the drudgery of the workplace can contribute to a sense of solidarity.

SOME FINAL WORDS on what this book is and is not. It is not my attempt to get by on the wages an immigrant earns or to "walk in their shoes." Wages figure into this story, but unlike Ehrenreich in *Nickel and Dimed*, it is not an experiment to see if I can survive financially. My challenge is to keep showing up for the next shift.

Nor will I be walking in anyone's shoes but my own. In Alabama, for instance, I worked the graveyard shift at a poultry plant, often next to a man named Jesús. Many nights we spent eight hours doing identical work, tearing thousands of frigid chicken breasts in half and tossing them onto a conveyor belt. Although we both suffered frozen hands, our identities did not blend together. I was still a middle-class American citizen who spoke English and graduated from college. Jesús had fled a civil war in Guatemala at the age of fifteen and spent the majority of his life picking tomatoes in Florida and processing chickens in Alabama. I eventually left the plant behind and fill my days with reading and writing; tonight, Jesús will probably spend another eight hours tearing up chicken parts. This book was an exhausting learning experience for me; for my coworkers, it is life.

The learning began in early 2008, when I traveled to my first stop, the state of Arizona. I packed several empty notebooks, a laptop, a bottle of painkillers, and a collection of books about immigrants and labor. By the time I left, I'd read them all, but my real education was just about to begin.

Part One

SALAD DAYS

January–March, Yuma, Arizona

GETTING THE JOB

Wedged into the corner of southwestern Arizona, the city of Yuma sits at a crossroads. Mexico is twenty miles to the south, California a stone's throw to the west, the cities of Phoenix and Tucson about a three-hour drive to the east. Yuma is a place to eat and perhaps spend an evening en route to somewhere more interesting, or at least less oppressively hot. One of the sunniest places on earth, the city receives less than four inches of rainfall a year and temperatures in July frequently exceed 107 degrees. A soldier back from Iraq—Yuma is home to a Marine Corps air base—observed that it wasn't so hard to adjust to the Arabian Desert after surviving a Yuma summer.

I relocate to Yuma on a balmy January day during the first week of 2008. Each winter Yuma's warmth attracts 90,000 retirees from Canada and the northern states, doubling the city's population and filling the local malls, restaurants, and movie theaters. Nearing

Yuma I pass a number of RV campgrounds—really just expansive slabs of black asphalt with water and electricity hookups—packed with some of the largest land vehicles I've ever seen. I pull over and take photos of what seems a distinctly American scene: the desert wilderness paved over, with folks sitting on lawn chairs under the shade created by their gas guzzlers, angled so that they can watch the cars zoom past on the highway.

By the time I enter the city limits, green fields of lettuce stretch from either side of the highway to the horizon, irrigated with water from the nearby Colorado River. Buses are parked among the fields, and I can see groups of farmworkers in the distance to my right. A California native, I've seen this scene many times while driving up and down the West Coast, a glimpse of a workforce that seems to belong to another universe entirely. This time I pull over to the shoulder and park. It's hard to see much detail—the workers are too far away—but I watch the figures for a few minutes, letting the idea sink in that in a few days, with some luck, I'll join them.

WHY BEGIN IN Yuma? It's mostly a question of timing: While doing research I learned that Yuma has been the "winter lettuce capital" of America since the early 1980s, when companies moved to the area from California's Imperial Valley. Today, there are about one hundred growers—individual contractors who are responsible for the crop until two weeks before harvest, overseeing aspects like irrigation and pest and weed management. These growers can be in charge of anywhere from 500 to 5,000 acres, and sign contracts with companies like Dole, Fresh Express, and Tamimura & Antle, who supply the laborers to harvest and pack the crop. At the height of the winter growing season, Yuma farmworkers are harvesting an astounding 12 million heads of lettuce a day.

Along with a ready supply of water from the Colorado River, Yuma's climate is a key reason the winter lettuce industry is centered in the area. When the weather turns cold in Salinas, California—

the heart of the nation's lettuce industry from the spring to the fall—temperatures in Yuma are still in the seventies and eighties. Each winter, Yuma produces virtually all of the iceberg lettuce and 90 percent of the leafy green vegetables consumed in the United States and Canada. Yuma lettuce is slapped between the buns of Big Macs, topped with anchovies in Caesar salads at posh Italian restaurants, and packed into ready-mixed bags that line grocery aisles from Monterey to Montreal. Still, the area's contribution goes unrecognized: it's a billion-dollar-a-year industry that most people outside of Arizona don't even know exists. "Companies think that customers associate quality lettuce with Salinas and California, so that is what you'll see on the labels," explains Kurt Nolte, an agriculture specialist at the University of Arizona Cooperative Extension in Yuma.

The second reason I chose Yuma is that the industry needs people like me. I've come across several articles documenting a shortage of farmworkers. They cite an aging workforce (the median age of Yuma farmworkers is forty-five); immigration crackdowns; and long delays at the border implemented after 9/11, all of which discourage many workers who have green cards and live in Mexico from commuting to the fields. American-born workers can help fill the shortage, and wages have been rising somewhat in response to the demand for laborers. But Doug Mellon, a grower interviewed by the *Arizona Republic*, scoffed at the notion that U.S. citizens would ever flock to the fields. "I don't care if you paid $40 [an hour], they'd do it about three hours and say, 'That's not for me.'"[1]

Senator John McCain, speaking to a group of union members in Washington, D.C., made the same controversial point. "I'll offer anybody here $50 an hour if you'll go pick lettuce in Yuma this season, and pick for the whole season," he said. Amid jeers, he didn't back down, telling the audience, "You can't do it, my friends." Although I don't plan on staying the entire season, if I manage to land a job I certainly hope I last longer than three hours.

AFTER MILES OF lettuce fields, the terrain turns more generic: Like any number of fast-growing cities, Yuma seems well on its way to becoming one long commercial strip. I pass several huge shopping centers and a Burger King, whose sign makes the odd boast that it has the largest indoor play area in the state. Checking into a nondescript motel, I tell the manager that I'm looking for work in the fields. She pulls out a photocopied map of the town and marks an intersection. "Mostly Mexicans in the fields, you know. But here's the Dole building—maybe you should go there. Sometimes people from Dole stay here, seem nice enough to me."

For weeks I've been digesting everything I could find on farmworkers, from documentaries and novels to investigative exposés and government reports, but I haven't given much thought to the particular company I want to work for. Dole sounds like as good a place to start as any: It's large and well known. I unload some of my possessions and head over.

Dole Fresh Vegetables, part of the company that is the largest producer of fresh fruits and vegetables in the world, is located several miles from the motel, across the street from the Marine Corps air station and down the block from a windowless Adult XXX superstore, both of which are surrounded by fences topped with concertina wire. It's an ugly area, but the narrow road leading into Dole's headquarters is grassy and lined with palm trees, like the entrance to a small college. A large sign sits next to a beige one-story building, which reads Headquarters Office—Agriculture and Harvest.

Inside, a young Latina woman is seated behind a desk. "May I help you?"

"Yes, could you tell me where I should go to apply for a job picking lettuce?"

She directs me back outside and around the corner to human resources. That she doesn't seem the least surprised by the request bolsters my confidence. I follow her directions, pushing open a door to find myself in a small office where a man is holding a telephone conversation in Spanish. When he hangs up, I repeat my request, and he switches to English.

"The fields? You want to work outside in the fields?" He smiles, like I've cracked a joke. A long moment of silence follows. "You know, maybe it would be better if you worked inside, in the plant. You could make more money and it wouldn't be so hard. That might be a better fit."

"No, I think I want to try working outside."

"Have you ever worked in the fields before?" I shake my head.

"Well, I can tell you one thing: It's not easy out there. Every year a few people come in who look like you. They last only two days, sometimes only a few hours. They get out there and realize it's not for them."

"Yeah, I know it's hard. But I'm looking for a job that I can start right away. I don't want to have to wait weeks for an interview—I just want to get started."

"You want to get started," he repeats. I fill the silence with vigorous nods. "You want to work in the fields."

"I want to work in the fields," I insist. "Are there any openings?"

He chuckles. "We can put you in the fields right away. That's not a problem." He tells me to stop by tomorrow—Friday—and fill out an application.

THE FOLLOWING AFTERNOON the skeptical man has been replaced by a middle-aged woman wearing heavy makeup and standing behind the front desk chatting in Spanish to several teenagers. I take a seat next to a cubicle wall that is covered with a poster reading We Use E-Verify. E-verify is a voluntary federal program that checks Social Security numbers against given names. Dole is using the program—which has been shown to be error prone—because three days earlier a new law went into effect. The state policy, known as the employer sanctions law, can permanently revoke

the business licenses of companies that knowingly hire undocumented workers, and was pushed by anti-immigrant forces and
signed into law in July 2007 by Democratic governor Janet Napoli-
tano (who is now the secretary of homeland security under President Obama). Using E-verify will protect Dole from legal action.
It will also protect lettuce-picking jobs for Americans like me.

After the teenagers leave she turns to me. "May I help you?"

"I hope so. I'd like a job picking lettuce." Her penciled eye-
brows rise.

"*Lettuce?*" She makes the word sound ridiculously out of place.

"Yes."

"You want to cut lettuce?"*

"Yes. Are you by any chance hiring?"

"This time of year, there is always work in lettuce. But have you
done this kind of work before? Do you know what it's like in the
fields?"

"No, but I've worked construction. I like learning new things."

She nods politely and hands me an application. I imagine she
has seen this before: eager (or, more likely, financially desperate)
gringos, not knowing what they're signing up for.

"Fill this out and come back Monday morning. We'll do an orientation and you can start Tuesday, if you really want to do this."

I quickly fill out my personal information but pause when asked
to give employer references. I've spent the last three years writing
about Mexican immigrants, but this isn't something I'd like Dole
to know. They also probably don't need to know that I've completed an internship with a union, or just published a book about
community organizing. Instead, I put down the Fifth Avenue
Committee, a nonprofit organization in Brooklyn where I have
done part-time work; more importantly, I am good friends with

---

* I'll soon learn that, contrary to common terminology, no one actually
"picks" lettuce; instead, it is cut at the stem with a knife.

Artemio Guerra, the director of organizing, and I list him as a reference. I note that I did translation.

"So you speak Spanish," she says when I hand over the application. "Do you happen to know how to drive a forklift?"

"No, no idea. But anyway, I think I want to try working in the fields."

"You could even get training," she insists. "I know they've been looking for a bilingual driver. The money is much better."

I've been in this office twice and both times have been offered promotions on the spot. I have a hard time picturing myself writing an entertaining book about driving a forklift. Trying to underscore my desire to harvest lettuce and nothing else, I say, "I'm just looking for something a little simpler."

On hearing these words her posture straightens. "Oh no, cutting lettuce is *not* simple. I worked in the fields all my life, since I was sixteen. That's all I did before moving here to the office. Let me tell you, there is nothing simple about it."

I immediately regret my choice of words, but she seems more amused than insulted by my ignorance. "We don't get many Americans around here. There was one guy who came earlier this year. He was from Colorado, I think."

"Is he still around?"

"No, but he lasted two weeks. I felt really bad for him because he didn't speak Spanish and he said he got lonely in the fields. It can be very hard work. You'll learn."

"Two weeks isn't very long, is it?"

She flashes a knowing smile. "To tell you the truth, it was longer than I expected."

I USE THE weekend to search for a place to stay. I have an idea of what I should be looking for in farmworker housing: ramshackle trailer parks, or long one-story complexes, filled with bunk beds and tucked away behind corners or down dusty roads. But during hours of searching—in Yuma and the nearby towns of Somerton and San Luis—the closest thing I find to migrant housing are RV parks filled with retirees. Out of curiosity I tail a bus carrying farmworkers from the field, but after twenty minutes it pulls into a large parking lot near the border and the workers file into Mexico.

On Sunday afternoon I move into a room I found on Craigslist. The owner of the house is a gregarious elementary school teacher named Janice who lives in the western section of Yuma, just blocks from a long series of lettuce and broccoli fields. She is initially skeptical about my source of income—"You are doing what, exactly?"—but after I explain the project she seems to get a kick out of it.

On Monday, I go through a short orientation with two other employees, both female.* They both live in the Mexican border city of San Luis Río Colorado. The older of the two worked in broccoli for Dole last year but had to stop midseason when she gave birth. The younger, Rosa, is in her twenties and has harvested lettuce for other companies; we will be placed on the same crew. We are all given a thick packet of papers, covering items such as the number to call if we're going to be absent, how to file sexual harassment claims, and general safety rules. There is also, to my surprise, a section of papers that includes a collective bargaining agreement and membership application for Teamsters Local 890, based out of Salinas. The only thing I know about the Teamsters in the fields is that they undercut a number of United Farm Worker union drives in the 1960s and '70s by signing sweetheart deals with growers, but I will later learn that it was another Team-

---

* A recent University of Arizona survey found that Yuma's agricultural workforce was 40 percent female, about four times greater than the national average. I surmise that this is because many migrant farmworkers are undocumented men who travel long distances to land jobs; in Yuma, the workforce is local—living on both sides of the border—so that families remain unified and can head to the fields together.

sters local (unions are divided into locals that can pursue different agendas) that fought with the UFW. I decide to pay a $50 initiation fee and have the $24 dues taken out of my paycheck. The two women decline this option. (Because Arizona is a "right to work" state, employees who work for a union company can elect to withhold their union dues, which makes building a powerful union difficult.)

Once we've finished signing papers, our last stop is with the company nurse, for what an overweight security guard calls the "whiz quiz." I'm not worried—I'll be clean—but I'm amused to think that the first time I take a pre-employment drug test is for a job cutting lettuce. A supervisor wearing yellow gaiters and a bib drives us to and from the nurse's office; as I'm waiting for the others to take the test, I read more carefully through the wages section of the packet.

On the short drive back to human resources, I say, "The packet says that lettuce cutters make $8.37 an hour, but broccoli cutters only get $7.69. Why is that?"

"Broccoli grows higher up," the supervisor tells me. "So you can cut it higher. For lettuce you have to cut it near the ground, so you bend over more." He rubs his back and grimaces. "That's why you get paid more."

"So lettuce is the hardest?" I ask, suddenly thinking that perhaps readers will find tales of cutting broccoli more interesting.

The driver considers the question. "Well, maybe a little harder. But *trabajo es trabajo.*" It's all just work. "You have to do it and see. For people like you who haven't worked in the fields, you never know if your body can take it or not until you try."

CHAPTER 1

At 6:45 a.m. the lot behind Dole's office is empty. As instructed, I'm parked in my car waiting for bus no. 158 to pick me up. Though it is still dark, I can make out a row of portable toilets stacked on trailers to my left, and when I roll down the window a sharp smell of disinfectant seeps in.

A white truck turns into the lot at seven o'clock. It backs up to one of the restroom trailers and a man steps out, attaches it to his truck, and drives off. Over the next thirty minutes a dozen more trucks pick up toilets, but there is no sight of a bus. By now the sun is rising over the foothills, illuminating the sky: another cloud-free day in Yuma.

Just when I'm convinced that I misheard my directions, a sedan pulls up parallel to my car, driven by a woman whose face is swathed in several bandanas to protect against sun and dust. We make eye contact—using the only part of her face that's exposed. I've seen photos of female farmworkers wearing bandanas, but in person it is an intimidating sight: I half expect her to pop her trunk and toss me a rifle, ready to expand the Zapatista rebellion to U.S. soil.

Instead, she gets out of her car and pulls a pair of rubber galoshes from the backseat. "*Hola, mi hijo*," she says in a high-pitched voice, erasing my insurrection imaginings. As she pulls on her boots we exchange good-mornings, after which she asks the inevitable question: "What are you doing here?"

I should have a stock answer prepared; instead, I give a rambling and incoherent explanation. I'm from New York. Some of my Mexican friends in New York have parents who worked in the fields. Right now I have a few free months, so I decided to try cutting lettuce. My parents live in San Jose. Most of the Mexicans in New York are from the state of Puebla. That's a long ways away. I'm thirty years old. It's hot in Yuma, isn't it?

The woman, Dalia, listens as she places various items in her backpack. "Well, this is hard work, but I enjoy it," she says when I finish my monologue. The first bus of the morning drives by and stops to pick her up; like the others I've seen around Yuma, the vehicle is an old American school bus that's received a fresh coat of white paint. After a brief phone conversation, the driver informs me that my bus, which has picked up workers at the border, will be arriving in ten minutes. "If you're here tomorrow," Dalia tells me as she boards her bus, "I'll have an extra taco for you."

Minutes later my bus roars into the lot. The driver dashes down the steps, nods at me, and jogs back to attach the portable toilets. I've been excited about this project for months, yet I am suddenly overwhelmed by a severe lack of confidence, that first-day-at-a-new-school sinking feeling. Inside the bus most of the people are asleep, their legs sprawled in the aisles and heads wedged against bundled sweatshirts. I don't see an open space but then notice Rosa from orientation seated to my right. She moves over and I sit down, scrunching my knees up against the back of the seat, which has clearly been designed for kids who have yet to hit their growth spurt.

As we drive west on the highway, I sneak glances at Rosa, who is assembling her face mask. She first pulls down a fabric that fits like a hood, followed by a bandana wrapped around the top part of her head. Another wrap—what I come to call the ninja bandana—is wound tightly above her nose and then knotted in the back. It looks like it must get awfully hot in there.

After twenty minutes we turn off the highway and head down a dirt path, parking in the middle of the same lettuce fields I stopped to observe on my initial drive into Yuma. A slender foreman greets us when we step off the bus, walking us to his truck for a field orientation. "Since you haven't worked in the fields before," he says to me, "I'll do your orientation last."

While he goes over safety issues with Rosa, I keep my eyes on the field. Men and women are rushing back and forth in front of a large contraption, which I will later learn is simply called *la maqina*—the machine. The machine has two waist-high wings jutting out to the left and the right—at least fifty feet long from one end to the other—connected to a number of extensions. Behind the wings is an eight-wheel flatbed. While the majority of the crew fiddles with the machine, two men stand on the flatbed, stacking wooden pallets and folding boxes. A third man is tying a yellow Dole flag to two poles above the wings.

"*¡Ejercicios!*" someone shouts. The crew gathers in a circle and begins doing coordinated stretches, swinging their arms and touching their toes. Who knew farmworkers have a formal warm-up routine?

The foreman is talking louder now, and it dawns on me that Rosa has departed. I turn away from the farmworkers, now doing a series of squats. "You're switching crews," he tells me. "A guy's on his way to get you."

I turn my attention back to the field. The calisthenics wind down and the crew divides into pairs, each pair taking a single row immediately behind the machine. A radio is switched on, flooding the field with the famous voice of Mexico's Vicente Fernandez, as the tires of the machine start to slowly turn. In each row, the person farthest from the machine bends down, quickly cuts a head of lettuce with a knife, stuffs the lettuce into a bag from a packet hanging from his waist, and drops the lettuce on an extension. The second person in the row snatches the bag from the extension and packs it into a cardboard box that is resting on the machine.

I spend fifteen minutes watching the crew, made up of eighteen men and twelve women. As they move away from the road, it becomes difficult to make out the details of their activities, but one thing is quite obvious: *They move fast.* A dozen knives are stabbing and slicing and slashing, sending hundreds of leaves flying in all directions. As they march across the field they are military in their efficiency, leaving nothing behind except glistening white stumps and the occasional discarded head of rotten lettuce. The flatbed quickly fills with completed boxes, which are stacked on pallets by two barrel-chested men wearing flannel shirts. A third man, perched on a ledge of the machine directly above the rows, frantically assembles empty cardboard boxes and shoves them to his right and left to replenish the supplies. During the fifteen minutes that I observe the workers, they harvest more than 1,600 heads of lettuce.

On most crews, each cutter harvests six heads of lettuce each minute, or 360 an hour. At this pace, a farmworker earning an hourly wage of $8.37 is paid just over two cents per head; these heads are then sold in stores for about $1 apiece. Although total farm labor costs are less than one-third of grower revenue, companies argue that low wages are necessary in an industry forced to deal with unpredictable weather and shifting market demands. But Philip L. Martin, professor of agricultural economics at the University of California–Davis, has shown that even a dramatic increase in labor costs—passed fully to the consumer—would have a very modest impact on the typical American household budget, which spent $322 on fresh fruits and vegetables in 2000. Martin's detailed analysis of the agricultural industry found that a 40 percent increase in farmworker wages would increase a household's annual spending on fruits and vegetables by only $8, to $330. A single head of iceberg lettuce, selling for $1, would increase by just two to three cents.[2]

"You sure you want to do this?" asks a deep voice. I turn around to find a bronze-faced man staring at me from beneath a cowboy hat, behind the wheel of a truck.

"I think so."

"So get in. You're going to be working in Somerton," he says, referring to a town ten miles south of Yuma. On the drive over, I learn that the man has been with Dole for fifteen years. "During all those years I never saw a single white person. But this year you're the second American we've had."

"Why is that, do you think?"

"I don't know. Maybe because people know we need workers." He eases off the accelerator as a Border Patrol truck passes us on the left. "Things have become very tough here for Mexicans without papers. They can't get jobs anymore in the fields, so they leave for California or Las Vegas. Too much Border Patrol, too many problems." He points at the truck disappearing in the distance. "And so we have a lot of jobs that people like you could do, if they wanted."

We drive through Somerton and make a left at Cesar Chavez Boulevard. (Chavez, the iconic founder of the United Farm Workers, was born in 1927 near his family's farm in Yuma; he died in

San Luis, Arizona—just ten miles away—in 1993.) Turning down a dirt path, the tract homes open up into a wide field. "There's your crew," the driver tells me. "This is the first year for most of them, but you'll see they learned quickly. They won't think you're going to last, I can tell you that right now. They had the other American, and he left right away. We put you both here because the *mayordomo* [foreman] speaks English." I step out and thank him for the ride.

A chubby man—Pedro—ambles over to greet me. But when I take his outstretched hand, the soft white flesh of my palm is crunched between cement-hard calluses. This is a man made thick not from eating but from labor. And though he may speak more English than the other foremen, it's still fairly basic, so he is relieved when I interrupt his halting introduction in Spanish.

"Don't worry about anything," Pedro tells me, assuming—correctly—that I'm nervous. "Right now you are beginning, but soon you'll be cutting like a pro. The first thing you need is your equipment." I follow him to his truck.

A lettuce cutter's uniform consists of a surprising number of items, which I struggle to put on as he runs down the basic rules (no running, safety above all else, paychecks every Friday). Pedro introduces me to his assistant, Diego, who hands me large black galoshes to put over my shoes. Next comes the *gancho* (hook), a metal S-shaped bar that slips over my belt. The gancho has two metal prongs, and the packets of plastic bags have two holes at the top, so that they slide onto the gancho just like paper slides into a two-ring binder. A gray glove goes on my left hand, a white glove on my right; the gray glove, according to Pedro, offers protection from cuts. (I'm skeptical—it looks like a normal glove.) Over the cloth gloves I pull on a pair of latex gloves, then put on a black hairnet under my baseball cap, slide on a pair of protective sunglasses, and slip a leather sheath onto my belt: I'm good to go. I feel ridiculous.

"When you're going to the machine, always walk along the *camino*," Pedro explains as we head toward the crew down a narrow dirt path. Rows to our right have just been harvested and are littered with thickets of lettuce leaves.

He stops when we reach the machine, which is identical to the one I observed earlier. "This is Manuel," he says, motioning to the nearest cutter, an attractive and wiry man with brown hair, a trimmed mustache, and fair skin. Manuel pauses from his work and waves, a knife in his hand. I notice, too, that every other member of the crew has turned to stare at me. "Manuel has been cutting for many years, so watch him to see how it's done." Pedro walks away, my field instruction apparently complete.

Manuel resumes cutting. Every several seconds he bends down with the knife in his right hand, grabs the head of iceberg lettuce with his left hand as if palming a basketball, and makes a quick cut, separating the lettuce from its roots. Next, he lifts the head of lettuce in front of his stomach and makes a second cut, trimming the trunk. He shakes the lettuce to the left and right, and the outer leaves fall to the ground; the lettuce has been reduced to half its original size. With the blade still in his right hand, he brings the clean, white-and-green head of lettuce toward his stomach and the bags hanging from his gancho, and with a flick of the wrist the lettuce is bagged and on the extension. A woman standing in front of him grabs the bag, tapes it shut, and packs it in a box that sits about waist high on the machine. When the box is full she shoves it forward onto a conveyor belt, which takes it to the middle of the machine, where a tall man stacks it on the flatbed.

Manuel does this over and over again, looking bored as he explains each movement. I watch and give my assessment. "You make it look easy, but I know it's not."

"It's not so hard," he argues, and takes me through the entire movement again. "That's all it is, right there."

I watch for five more minutes, walking forward with the crew to keep up with the machine. Pedro reappears. "Gabriel, now it's your turn—come get your knife." I follow him to the end of the machine, where a metal case of chlorinated water is affixed, and reach in and grab the handle of a knife and begin walking back to Manuel's row.

"No, Gabriel," Pedro says. "Anytime you are walking with the knife, it has to be put in its sheath." I do as told, putting the eighteen-inch knife away. Lesson number one.

"Try this one." Manuel points at a head of lettuce to my right. I bend over, noticing that most of the crew has turned to watch. I take my knife and make a tentative sawing motion where I assume the trunk to be, though I'm really just guessing, as the head is over-flowing with outer leaves. Next, I secure the head with my left hand and raise it up as I straighten my back, doing my best to im-itate Manuel. Only the head doesn't move; it's still securely con-nected to the soil—so now I'm standing up with nothing to bag.

Pedro steps in. "When you make the first cut, it is like you are stabbing the lettuce." He takes my knife and makes a quick jab-bing action, then lifts the large head and turns it upside down. "You want to aim for the center of the lettuce, where the trunk is, with the front section of the blade. Then, when it's cut, you turn it and with the side of the blade you make another cut on the trunk, higher up." I watch him do as he describes, and again it looks effortless. Someone calls for Pedro, and he hands me back the knife. Manuel points out another head.

This time the lettuce comes up. I cradle the head against my chest, as if hugging it, and look for a good place to make the sec-ond cut. I make a second slice through the trunk, trying to shake the lettuce, but I lose my grip and send it to the ground. When I pick it up, it's covered in dirt.

"Make another cut," Manuel says. "There are still too many leaves." I hold the lettuce upside down and make another trim, and the dirty leaves fall. Now it's starting to look like the iceberg lettuce in the produce section of grocery stores.

"That's good, right there. Now you bag it." Manuel does another slow demonstration of bagging, which I do my best to follow. His right hand holds the lettuce and the knife. He inserts his left hand into the outermost bag hanging from the gancho, spreading his fingers to open the bag as wide as possible, and lifts it from the packet. With the bag fully open, he passes the lettuce from his right to his left hand—thereby encircling the lettuce in the bag—and with both hands grabs the top corners of the bag and twists the head over, so that it swings around. The bag is then separated from the packet and is ready to be placed on the extension. It is a complicated process, but done correctly it takes less than a second and looks quite graceful.

I need about a minute to figure out how to get the damn lettuce in the bag. The first bag rips in half. The second bag somehow expels the lettuce, which flops to the ground. On the third attempt I am finally able to massage the lettuce into the bag, flip it over correctly, and tear the bag from the gancho. Only I have somehow managed to pull the entire packet of bags off the gancho, so I'm holding a head of properly cut and bagged lettuce that is attached to another hundred bags.

"I know what's wrong," Manuel says. He takes off a plastic glove and folds it twice, lengthwise, then pulls it taut in front of me. "Make a cut over here by the end." Confused, I do as told, slicing off a section. He takes the section I have cut and opens it; it's now a wrist-sized rubber band. He slides the bags back onto my gancho and winds the band around the prongs, and now I get it: This will prevent more than one bag from tearing off at a time. I look at Manuel's gancho and see that he too has this custom-made rubber band. Lesson number two.

Ten minutes later, Pedro comes over to see how I'm progressing. I've probably cut twenty heads of lettuce so far and feel pretty accomplished. With the first stab I sometimes cut the stem correctly, though when my back tightens up, I don't stoop far enough, and my stab—instead of landing an inch above the ground—goes right through the head of lettuce, ruining it entirely. The greatest difficulty, though, is in the trimming. I had no idea that a head of lettuce was so humongous. In order to get it into a shape that can be bagged, I trim and I trim and I trim, but it's taking me upwards of a minute to do what Manuel does in several seconds.

Pedro watches me cut several heads and go about my endless trimming routine. "Act like the lettuce is a bomb," he suggests. He goes through the motions of cutting and bagging with his hands, pretending to drop the lettuce on the machine's arm before it explodes. "Imagine you've only got five seconds to get rid of it."

Surprisingly, I find that I'm able to greatly increase my speed when I keep the phrase *like a bomb* in my head. I vigorously shove the lettuce into bags, then drop the bags on the extension before they can harm anyone. "Look at me!" I want to shout at Pedro, who is several rows over, talking on his cell phone. For a minute or two I feel euphoric; I'm in the zone.

The woman packing the lettuce swivels around to face me. "Look, this lettuce is no good." I study the contents of the bag I've just handed over. She's right: I've cut the trunk too high, breaking off dozens of good leaves, which will quickly turn brown. I've also jammed the lettuce in sideways—you're supposed to bag so that the trunk sticks up toward the bag's opening—and there are a bunch of outer leaves, connected to nothing and that don't belong. I look at the three other bags I've placed on the extension. None looks very appetizing.

"Okay, sorry," I say. With her left hand she holds the bag up, and with her right she smashes it violently, making a loud pop. She turns the bag over and the massacred lettuce falls to the ground. She does the same for the three other bags I've placed on the extension.

"It's his first day," Manuel tells her. Then to me: "It's okay. She's not feeling well. You shouldn't try to go too fast when you're beginning. Take it slow." Pedro passes by, catching Manuel's comments.

"That's right," he tells me, seconding Manuel. "Make sure the cuts are precise and that you don't rush." So I am to be very careful and precise, while also treating the lettuce like a bomb that must be tossed aside after five seconds.

An hour later, when I am just starting to notice the slightest signs of improvement, the female packer stands up and walks around the wing of the machine. As I continue to cut, I can see her through the slits in the metal. She is doubled over and looks on the verge of vomiting. Manuel walks around to join her and they talk briefly before returning.

"Are you feeling okay?" I ask.

"I have a stomachache," she says, pulling her gloves back on.

"Sorry about my lettuce." She doesn't respond. "I'm impressed you come to work when you're sick," I continue, wanting to make amends. "When I'm sick I become such a baby. Even when I just have a cold, I don't get out of bed."

She turns around to face me. "Some things you do out of necessity—you don't have a choice. You, are you here for the money, or just to see what it's like?" It's not exactly a hostile question, but her tone sounds more aggressive than merely curious.

I'm a terrible liar, and I decide to abandon any prior notions of passing myself off as a down-on-my-luck, possibly alcoholic guy doing whatever he can to earn some quick cash. "I can always use the money," I say, as any struggling freelance writer can attest. "But mostly, I want to know what the work is like."

She turns around and doesn't say anything else.

DURING THE THIRTY-MINUTE lunch break, a number of people ask me why I'm there, and I give them what will become my standard response: I had a few months off and thought it would be interesting to see what farmwork was like. They ask how long I'll be staying, and I tell them until March. They don't argue, but it's obvious they don't expect me to last.

After lunch I take up my spot next to Manuel. We have a new packer, a man people call Nacho, who looks like a Vietnamese rice farmer under his giant conical straw hat.

"What happened to the other woman?" I ask Manuel as we begin to cut.

"That's my wife, Maria. She went to see the nurse. She isn't feeling well."

The rest of the day goes smoothly. I continue to cut slowly but am picking up techniques, like how to bag the lettuce. Resisting the impulse to stuff the lettuce in forcefully, I learn from watching Manuel that it requires a gentle motion: the less effort, the better. He deftly places his left hand into the bag to open it wide, uses his right hand to push the lettuce into the opening, lets it go, and with a flick of his wrists uses the momentum of the head to do the work. I even succeed in emulating the motion several times before the day is over.

It's nearly six o'clock when we finish. Following Manuel's lead, I drop my knife in the box of chlorinated water and place my remaining packet of bags in a box. Pedro gives me a ride to the office, telling me that from now on I should drive my own car. We'll be working the same field tomorrow, starting at 8:00 a.m.

As I drive home I take an inventory of my body. The most noticeable pain is in my swollen feet, but it isn't too terrible: It reminds me, if anything, of how I feel when forced to spend a day wandering in a museum. My thighs are a bit rubbery and my hands have that early-morning weakness, though they don't feel sore. By far the most remarkable development is that after completing my first day in the fields, my back doesn't ache.

It's not until the following day, when Maria doesn't show up, that I learn she won't be returning for the rest of the season. I'm her replacement. I ask one of the workers, whose name I don't yet know, how he can be so sure she won't return.

"She didn't seem like the kind of person who would quit over a stomachache."

"A stomachache?" he says. "Who told you that? She's nearly eight months pregnant."

CHAPTER 2

A woman wearing bandanas over her face—for some reason, I've noticed that only women wear the bandanas—is already leading the calisthenics when I walk up to the crew the next morning. I see Manuel and say hello as he swings his arms with the group.

"You're back?" he asks, sounding surprised.

Nacho, standing next to Manuel, gets into the act as well. "Look who returned," he tells me. I reiterate my plan to stay for two months while struggling to get the gancho locked onto my belt (the first sign that my hands are beginning to weaken; it will get much worse).

"Gabby, exercises!" yells the calisthenics woman, whose name I later learn is Adriana. (How does she know my childhood name was Gabby?) For some reason—perhaps a vestige of my lack of enthusiasm for high school gym class—I half-heartedly swing my arms. "No, better!" she calls again. "Or else you'll lead the group!" I straighten up and begin to participate, squatting and stretching and doing whatever the boss-woman says I should with maximum enthusiasm.

Once the exercises are completed, Pedro calls us in for a group huddle, something we'll do every morning for the rest of my time in the field. He explains that we will be using bags with the Dole logo this morning but might shift to another brand after lunch. "The ground is dry, but that doesn't mean that we should stop being careful," he says. "Sometimes we can get careless when it's dry, and that's when injuries often occur." (Pedro, I will learn, gives one of two speechess every morning: Be careful because the ground is wet, or be careful because the ground is dry.)

During the morning session, which runs from 8:30 to 11:30 a.m., I cut next to Manuel. While everyone else cuts two rows, I am still responsible for only half of one row at the end—selecting every other head of lettuce from one of Manuel's rows. I gradually get the hang of it and am just able to keep up the pace—although I'm clearly working harder than anyone else. Thirty minutes into the day, I'm already stripped down to a long-sleeve T-shirt, blinking burning sweat out of my eyes while the others are bundled in sweatshirts and knit beanies, trying to stay warm.

About an hour into the day, just when I'm beginning to feel my back tighten up for the first time, a tall man wearing a cowboy hat, Wrangler jeans, and a large belt buckle swaggers over to me and introduces himself as one of the supervisors. He asks me the usual question—why are you here?—and then watches me struggle through a few especially poor cuts.

"Give me your knife and watch." A second later, somehow, he's got a fully trimmed head of lettuce in his hand. "Bag this." He does it again: lightning-quick bend and stab, another lightning-quick trim. "Bag this." He spends ten minutes showing me the correct technique, explaining as he goes along.

"The most important thing is to find the head of the lettuce and grab it hard before you make the first cut. If you need to, take extra time to reach down through the leaves and search for the head—that's the part that you need. If you do that, it won't be so hard to trim it, and you'll know right away if it's a twenty-four or thirty."

"What's a twenty-four?"

"Oh, you're very new, no? Twenty-four is what we normally do—they are the bigger ones. It means twenty-four heads of lettuce will fit in the box. The smaller ones are thirty. You see how your packer has two boxes in front of him?" I look at Nacho; indeed, on the machine's rack he has a box to his left and his right. "That one on the left is for smaller lettuce, for the thirties."

A few minutes after the supervisor leaves, I reach down and cut a head of lettuce, which feels spongy and has a stem that is partially purple. "Manuel, is this one okay?" I ask, holding it up. He shakes his head.

"That one is sick, just leave it." The next, too, is purple, and the next. "That's good," he explains. "It means you get to take a break for a second."

By now I'm in need of a break. I walk to the orange cooler, which is attached to the side of the machine, and gulp down several cups of water. When I resume my cutting, Adriana comes over with a suggestion.

"Gabby, I've been watching you. After you cut the lettuce you stand up straight to bag it. It's better if you stay bent over the whole time." She shows me this method, looking like a hunch-backed grandmother shuffling down the street.

"Hmm. That looks like it might not be so good," I say quietly. "For your back, I mean."

"No, it's much easier."

I try it. Instead of straightening up, I remain slightly stooped when bagging. By the third head of lettuce, my back, already tightening up, is screaming for relief. Adriana's gone by now, so I revert to my original style. Sweat is pouring down my face so fast that I have to keep taking my cap off to mop my forehead, which causes my pace to slow. The temperature must be in the eighties. Manuel, working next to me, is talking about something, but I can't understand: Fatigue has cut my Spanish comprehension level in half. I'm about to take another trip to the cooler when Pedro calls out to take our break, and the machine halts.

I follow Manuel's lead, taking my gancho and gloves off and placing my knife in the chlorinated water. We sit with a group of others—three men and a woman—on white plastic chairs that have materialized from somewhere. I open my backpack and drain a 32-ounce bottle of Gatorade.

"The first five days are the hardest," Manuel tells me. "That's when you feel the pain the most, but then it goes away." I nod, opening my second bottle. A skinny man with dark skin, seated to my left, introduces himself as Julio. He tells me that he still remembers his first week, but now, after three years, he's accustomed to it. I nod again. I'm sure I must have a lot of questions to ask—I'm a reporter, after all——but it's all I can do to just drink and nod.

"Let's go, guys!" Pedro calls. *That* was our break? I follow the group with my chair, stack it on the back of the machine, then grab my knife and slip on my sweaty gloves, as the work resumes. Pedro comes over at one point, looking cheerful. "Save your energy for tomorrow, Gabriel. That's when you'll have your own row to cut."

The rest of the day is a blur, and it ends with the gathering darkness. When I get home I eat dinner, take a shower, and type up some quick notes before falling into a sound sleep. In what will become my frequent first line, I write: *Today was a long day.*

THERE ARE SEVERAL problems with my body the following morning, starting with my hands. Both are swollen, and my right ring finger has doubled in size. I broke it several years ago and never went to a doctor, but assumed it had healed correctly. Evidently I was wrong: It now remains hooked no matter how hard I try to straighten it, and I can actually feel my pulse in the digit.

Ambling to the bathroom, I feel like someone must have crept into my bedroom overnight and beaten me on the back with a two-by-four, then continued pounding on the soles of my feet. I swallow several painkillers and put in my contact lenses, noticing that my eyes are bright red. My neck is also crimson; I'm lathering myself with sunscreen twice a day, but it doesn't stand a chance against my overactive sweat glands. There's also a tennis-ball-size bruise on my right thigh, where the gancho jabs each time I bend. It seems impossible—simply impossible—that I can spend another day cutting lettuce.

After coffee and breakfast I feel a bit better, and less melodramatic. I tell myself that there are more than a million farmworkers in America, doing this every day, some for years. Plus, I remind myself that Manuel said the first week is the toughest.

We're back at the same field today, and as promised, Pedro has found me a special row to do all by myself, next to Julio. The first few minutes aren't promising—my hands are so weak I have a hard time holding on to the lettuce—but once the blood starts pumping through my system, I feel better. I'm starting to get a sense of the lettuce, learning more about its various shapes with each new cut. The easiest are the ones whose outer leaves are already spread away from the head, so you can immediately see what you need to cut. The hardest are the massive heads with the outer leaves wound tight; for these, I lose time peeling off each individual leaf, using what Pedro calls the "she loves me, she loves me not" method. With a single cut, more skilled cutters are able to trim these large monsters down to size, but when I attempt this I invariably cut too deep—into the good leaves that make up the head—and have to discard the lettuce.

I eat lunch with two middle-aged men, Angel and Tomás. Though they live in the same small Mexican village, Mezquital, they have different interests: The first question Angel asks is whether I am a Christian; Tomás wants to know my favorite beer. Both have worked at Dole for three years and spent many years before that in the fields. They were part of the same broccoli crew for the previous two years but were switched to lettuce this season. "Broccoli was definitely easier than lettuce," Tomás says. "But anything is better than doing farmwork in Mexico," where, he explains, he earned only one hundred pesos a day. It's a big pay increase to harvest crops on this side of the border—from about $10 a day to $8.37 an hour.

In the afternoon we switch from using Dole bags to harvesting lettuce *desnudo*, or naked. When cutting *desnudo*, we don't trim or bag the lettuce, instead placing the heads flowing with extra leaves directly on the extensions before they are crammed tightly into boxes for Sysco. It's an easier job, especially since we can dispense with the heavy packets of bags hanging from our belts, but to make sure we don't get too comfortable, Pedro speeds up the machine's pace. Before we reach the afternoon break, Pedro stops the machine and tells me to help load materials. I sheath my knife and follow the crowd to a spot in the field where a truck has dumped hundreds of flattened cardboard boxes and a dozen wooden pallets.

Crewmembers begin carrying the cargo to the machine, tossing the packets of flattened boxes to one of the three men who work as loaders. It wouldn't be too difficult a task on flat ground, but the uneven terrain—we are walking across several rows of uncut lettuce—causes one person to stumble. I grab a bundle of twenty-five boxes and lift them over my head, as I've seen others do, crossing two rows without incident before my front foot slips and I nearly plant my face into an iron bar of the machine.

"Careful!" someone shouts, too late to be of any use. I mercifully regain my balance, which leads to a series of hoots, and toss my boxes. I smile at the crew as I return for another load, too tired to be embarrassed.

During the break I join the group sitting on the ground next to an irrigation canal. I've been feeling stronger today, but as soon as I get off my feet I realize how swollen they've become. I rest them on a row that has been harvested and feel the blood draining back to my legs. People are having animated conversations, but I don't care. I close my eyes, the sun beats down, and I drift off.

I'm awakened by Diego, who is talking to Manuel. "How much more time do we have?" I ask.

"It's already been sixteen minutes."

"So what are we waiting for?" Diego doesn't know. Others are wondering as well. From this vantage point I can see that there remains only a small section of the field to cut, less than an hour's worth of work. Once we finish, we'll be done, as Pedro will have to relocate the machine to our next field. I wouldn't mind getting started so we can get out of here.

We sit for another few minutes. Pedro isn't calling us back, and the machine isn't moving—the two signals that the break is over. Eventually we begin to meander back. As we're putting on our gear, Pedro pops up from somewhere and calls for us to gather around.

"How long has it been?" he asks. "Has it been more than fifteen minutes?"

Most of the crew nods, but my head stays steady: I don't like the tone of voice Pedro has adopted.

"I just did an experiment," he continues, looking extremely pleased with himself. "I waited to see and observe how long it would take for you to finish your break and come back if I didn't say anything. You all know that the break is fifteen minutes long.

And my experiment showed that it took you more than twenty minutes to return. From now on, I want everyone to make sure that they keep an eye on time." He goes on about his experiment for another five minutes, enjoying playing the role of management genius, but I stop trying to follow. I look at Manuel as we head back to our rows, and he gives me a shrug. I roll my eyes and make that talk-talk-talk motion with my right hand, then take my knife and stab a lettuce, with a little more force than necessary.

WITH SOME EXCEPTIONS, the schedule of my first several days will be repeated throughout my time in Yuma. We arrive thirty minutes before the machine starts—me in my car, most of the others in the white agricultural bus that picks them up each morning on the U.S. side of the border. Our early arrival allows us to put on our equipment, sharpen our knives, do calisthenics, and listen to Pedro's instructions. Work begins either at 8:00 or 8:30 a.m., and we put in two or three hours before the first fifteen-minute break. After another two hours of work, we get a thirty-minute lunch. Another two hours or so, and another fifteen-minute break. Then we work until the day is over. When demand is low, we may leave the field before the afternoon break. When demand is high, we'll work until dusk. (One year, Julio told me, they frequently worked until 10:00 p.m., under bright lights connected to the machine.) Because demand fluctuates and lettuce begins to wilt the moment it's cut, there is very little planning ahead: Most mornings even Pedro doesn't know how long we'll be in the field.

We use four different types of bags: Dole, Dole Canada, King Size, and UPC (no brand with only a barcode on the bag). At times, as during my first few days, we use only one type of bag, but typically we're instructed to have two ganchos hanging from each side of our belt, one that holds bags for medium to large heads of lettuce (24s) and the other for the small (30s). There is no rule as to what goes where: In the morning, Pedro could instruct us to bag all 24s with Dole Canada and 30s with UPC; in the afternoon, Dole Canada for the 24s and regular Dole with 30s; the next morning, UPC for 24s and King Size for the 30s. (We often put the small heads of lettuce in the King Size bags, which made little sense to me.) It was a constant struggle to keep this straight in my mind as I rushed to keep pace with the machine as it moved down the field.

While cutting, one has to constantly check the quality of the lettuce. Crops like onions grow in a uniform manner and can therefore be harvested by machine; but about 20 percent of a lettuce field will be unusable, a key reason why lettuce is still harvested by hand. Some lettuce is too small (I see heads less than two inches tall); some too big (twice the size of a human head); some too light; and many get hit with infections that turn the trunks red or purple. Others have yellow leaves from sun exposure or have suffered damage from cold nights, creating unappetizing rivets in the leaves. What we do with the rejects depends on the preferences of the supervisor wandering the fields on any given day. Sometimes Pedro will tell us to turn all rejects upside down on the row; other days, we are instructed to slice up the head thoroughly and dump it in the furrow.

Several times a day a truck drives into the field to dump boxes and pallets and to pick up the lettuce we have cut, generally while we are taking a break. Each morning we complete 10 pallets of lettuce. Each pallet has 40 boxes, and each box about 25 heads of lettuce—which means that our crew cuts and packs 10,000 heads of lettuce before the first break, or nearly 800 heads a person. In a typical day we cut 30,000 heads of lettuce, enough to fill 1,200 boxes. On the longer days—the ones beginning just after sunrise and ending at dusk—we can harvest in excess of 40,000 heads.

For a cutter, that means 3,000 heads in a single shift; put two of those long days in a row, and getting out of bed at 5:30 the next morning becomes a true test of willpower.

Once the lettuce is on the truck, it heads straight to Dole's cooling plant, located next to the office where I first applied for the job. The pallets are transferred into a large vacuum tube, and within seconds the warm air is sucked out and replaced with air that is precisely 33 degrees, a temperature that extends the shelf life of lettuce to four weeks. Once the lettuce is cooled, the pallets are transferred to a refrigerated truck. A head of lettuce cut on Monday will arrive in San Francisco by Tuesday, most parts of Canada by Wednesday or Thursday, and New York City by Thursday or Friday.

In the field, it can be hard to remember that the lettuce I harvest will end up in someone's salad—perhaps tossed with walnuts and dried cranberries in a wooden bowl on a large dining room table, with family members gathered around chatting about their days. Harder still for the recipients to imagine our crew out here, with swollen hands and sweaty shirts. But as Daniel Rothenberg writes in *With These Hands: The Hidden World of Migrant Farmworkers Today*, the connection—whether acknowledged or not— is an intimate one:

> When we reach into a bin to choose an apple, orange, or plum, our hands stretch out in much the same way as a farmworker's hands—harvesting our nation's fruits and vegetables, piece by piece. While the produce may have been mechanically sorted and packed, supercooled, chemically treated, waxed, and shipped hundreds, if not thousands, of miles, often the last hand to touch the fruits and vegetables we buy was that of a migrant farmworker. Through the simple act of purchasing an orange or a head of lettuce, we are con-

nected with a hidden world of laborers, a web of intercon-
nected lives, with hands on both ends.[3]

It is an arresting image—that the next person to touch the lettuce I personally harvest will be the person who puts it in their
mouth. It's also a connection that, without coming across this passage, I would never have made. Rothenberg wants us to remember
that each time we eat food that has been harvested by hand, we
do so in the presence of strangers. I see them—my crewmembers—
knives in hands, wiping sweat off their brows, taking a break as
they hover over our plates and bowls to proudly whisper: "Enjoy.
I cut that, you know."

THE THIRTY-ONE members of my crew are divided into three
categories. Three men, the loaders, are on the flatbed of the machine, stapling and stacking the completed boxes; thirteen men,
like myself, are cutters; another thirteen—including three women,
after Maria's departure—are packers. The remaining two members
are Pedro and his assistant, Diego.

Crews at Dole work together for the entire season, but unlike an
office setting—where personalities frequently clash over an e-mail
or a comment taken the wrong way—there doesn't seem to be
much conflict in the fields. For one thing, we're not maneuvering
for advancement: Our roles and wage of $8.37 an hour will remain
the same. Equally important, we lack the extra energy needed to
gossip or hold grudges for long; our exhaustion ensures that
there's simply no time to develop the dysfunction that plagues
many work environments.

During my first week, most people remain strangers, although
a few names and personalities start to emerge. I come to think of
Tomás as the heart and soul of our crew. He is one of the older
cutters, probably in his fifties, whom others affectionately call *tío*,

or uncle. Decades of farmwork have left him with strong hands and skinny limbs, and decades of beer drinking have left him with a medicine ball under his sweatshirt. His distinguishing feature is an unruly handlebar mustache, which is always on the verge of swallowing his entire chin (one of the packers, a young man named Andrés, threatens to pull a hairnet over Tomás's entire face if he doesn't trim the growth).

Tomás speaks fast and enthusiastically. He's missing many of his teeth, so although others can understand him, I hear a lot of mumbling and only occasionally a decipherable word. Despite our inability to communicate, I enjoy hanging out with him and listening to him ramble. As I gulp down Gatorade and Clif Bars, he smokes as many cigarettes as possible. Tomás is given to belting out an enigmatic line several dozen times a day: "*Si a tu ventana llega un burro flaco,*" which translates to: "If a skinny donkey arrives at your window." I have no idea what the lyric means, and Tomás never finishes singing the song. No matter, the line gets stuck in my head whenever I hear it.

If Tomás is the crew's heart and soul, then the lithe thirty-year-old Julio is its driver, the fastest cutter who is also in charge of managing the machine's speed. He always cuts at one of the end rows, and keeps a remote control near him with buttons that he presses to speed or slow the pace (when I'm near him, I badger him to take it down a notch). Julio, like a handful of others, is originally from the state of Sinaloa, more than 500 miles from the border. He came north in search of work and found a job in a *maquiladora* (factory) before signing up with Dole three years ago. His wife, Norma, also from Sinaloa, packs the lettuce that he cuts. (I encounter a number of married couples in the field; they always work together, with the man cutting and the woman packing. During my months in the fields, I never see a female cutter. I'm not sure why this is, just as it is never adequately explained to me why men never cover their faces in bandanas. "That's just how it's always been," is how one worker explains the arrangement.)

Besides his speed, Julio attracts my attention because he never seems to tire. In the morning he is bouncing around, and in the early evening he's still chatting up a storm and laughing: Someone has clearly forgotten to tell him that this is hard work. He, like Manuel, is a good guy to cut next to because he'll always swoop in and snag a couple of my heads of lettuce when I fall behind. He can actually cut three rows without falling behind the pace of the machine.

Manuel, thirty-seven, has a workmanlike attitude. He comes, he cuts, he goes home. He's the senior cutter on our crew, with five years' experience in lettuce, and he has spent most of the past two decades in the fields, many in California. Along with lettuce he has labored in the strawberry fields of Watsonville, cut broccoli in Salinas, and picked apples and pears in the San Joaquin Valley. He even worked at a slaughterhouse in Texas. (He lasted only a month: His job was to shoot the cows in the head with an air gun all day. "That was no good.")

I was initially leery of Diego, the stocky assistant, until I learned that he earns the same pay as everyone else and does not serve as the eyes and ears of Pedro. Early on, Pedro often had me helping Diego with odd jobs, like placing plastic sheets on lettuce to prevent ice from forming overnight, and I was surprised to find that Diego spoke the best English of the group. Unfortunately, I learned this while suffering through his rendition of "Ice, Ice, Baby," followed immediately by "Hammertime." Surprisingly, Diego had not been to the United States before beginning the season (it wasn't just songs he knew; he could speak and understand enough to roughly communicate). I persisted in querying him about his English—it just seemed so odd—and he finally offered a clue toward the end of the season, when he said that he had worked for many years as a bodyguard to a Mexicali-based *narcotraficante* (drug dealer). At first I thought he was kidding, but he insisted he was telling the truth, describing the weapons he had at his disposal. He left the job after the birth of his first child, choosing to move his family to San Luis Río Colorado to get away from the scene. I came to believe his account as he wasn't given to boasting, and I gather that he picked up his English through the job.

Adriana, the strong female voice of the group, is a packer and responsible for driving the bus from the border to the fields and back. Second in command to Pedro, she is a U.S. citizen and lives in San Luis, Arizona, just across the border from Mexico. A Dole employee for decades and now in her forties, she declined an offer to become forewoman, saying she "didn't want the responsibility."* Early on she adopted me as her project—she was going to teach this gringo to work—and while I was struggling to trim a particularly annoying head of lettuce, I'd frequently hear, "Gabby, no!" directed my way. She'd grab my knife and correct my technique, all the while insisting that I was "so close" to getting it right.

It was harder to make up my mind about the foreman, Pedro. He was not abusive—I'd asked around, and everyone said that they were paid on time and never shorted wages. He stressed safety and made sure we had our proper gear, replacing it if it ripped (as the plastic gloves seemed to do daily). But he also had an aggravating tendency to come over when I was falling behind and stand really close to me. I wanted to turn around and say, "Hey, this really isn't helping," but instead I'd just keep plodding along, cursing him silently.

---

* In Yuma I came across one Dole crew that was headed by a woman. When I asked a man from the crew how he felt about his forewoman, his answer was much as I felt about Pedro: "She's *tough*."

What was most striking about the crew, after several days in the field, was how quickly they welcomed me as one of their own. I expected, and encountered, some skepticism and suspicion, but neither lasted long. Simply showing up for a second day seemed to be proof enough that I was there to work. If I took a seat on the ground alone during a break, someone would call me over to join their group, usually offering me the plastic chair they were sitting on along with a homemade taco or two. People whose names I didn't yet know would ask how I was holding up, reminding me that it would get easier as time went by. When I faltered and fell behind, hands would come across from adjacent rows to grab a head or two of my lettuce so I could catch up. On Thursday, we worked a field with another crew, and I could hear them talking about me during lunch. Tomás, sitting beside me and smoking furiously, stood up. "The white guy can work!" he shouted. I felt like I had passed some sort of test.

ON FRIDAY WE move to a new field, south of Somerton and ten miles from the Mexican border. We begin cutting in silence, until Cesar, a jolly man who has gladly shared his sharpening stone with me, calls out *"Música, maestro!"* Within seconds our workplace is filled with song.

Nearly every crew has their radio set to the same station: 104.9 FM, *Radio Campesina*. The Spanish-language station is run by the UFW, broadcasting in Arizona, California, and Washington State. It's probably the only station where a listener can hear DJs regularly say things like: "Greetings to all the farmworkers in the different crews of the many companies out in the fields today."

Much of the time, though, you wouldn't be able to distinguish the station from other commercial Spanish radio; the most popular songs—which I'll hear repeated until I want to stab myself with a fork—have titles like "I Cried" and "I Love You a Lot." But each morning we also listen to *Punto De Vista*, a call-in show hosted by Mary Martinez, who is often joined in the studio by a doctor or immigration specialist. This particular morning, a woman from Bakersfield, California, calls in worried about a growth near her stomach. She's been to a white doctor, who said they were fatty deposits and not to worry. Though she doesn't say it outright, it's clear she doesn't trust the gringo.

"That's very common, the fatty deposits," the doctor tells her in Spanish. He goes on to explain the differences between these deposits and a dangerous, cancerous growth. The relief in the woman's voice is palpable; she's been worrying herself sick.

Another caller speaks to an immigration attorney. He's been caught three times while crossing in the Yuma area (the crew hoots when they hear this), and once spent fifteen days in jail (the crew quiets down). Each time he's signed a voluntary deportation document. His girlfriend is a U.S. citizen and lives in Yuma, and they're planning on getting married. He wants to know whether his previous crossing activities will keep him from eventually gaining legal residency.

"No, not if you signed voluntary deportation papers," the attorney says.

He's happy to hear this but has another pressing question. "Is it better to get married in Mexico or in the U.S.? It would be easier for her to come here, but if I need to go there, I have to save some money for the smuggler." He has heard that even more Border Patrol agents have been massing, and he's nervous about his chances of crossing without incident.

The immigration attorney can't help chuckling. "Don't cross," he says. "You want to start following all the laws so you won't have any problems, so have her come to Mexico. And then, just so you know, be prepared to wait some time for the process to go through."

"You're gonna have to wait a long time for the fucking process," I hear someone to my left say. "A long fucking time."

While listening to the radio, I'm still doing half as much work as everyone else—one row to their two—but I'm finding that I can keep pace with the machine and that my endurance is increasing. I fall behind twice early on, before my muscles have warmed up, and have to place my bagged lettuce on the ground, to be picked up later. But after that I'm able to stay even with Manuel and the others, and when lunchtime comes I'm starting to feel less like a fraud. I'm just about done with my first week of farmwork (albeit a four-day week as I spent Monday in orientation), and although my body is aching and my face is a sunburned mess, I've survived.

Today is the hottest day of the week, probably reaching the low eighties, and as there isn't any shade in the field, the crew heads to the bus to eat their lunch. I hesitate, wondering if I'm welcome, when Adriana yells out, "Come, Gabby! You're a member of the crew!" I smile; I suppose she's right.

I sit next to a tall twenty-one-year-old named Andrés, who has even more trouble than I do in figuring out where to put his legs. I noticed Andrés early on because he was one of five people in the crew who didn't look like a "typical" farmworker: He wore brand-name sweatshirts, chatted on his cell phone during breaks, and didn't have the weathered face of someone who had spent years outdoors. Tomás, Angel, and Julio were *campesinos* through and through—one look and you knew they had grown up in the country. Andrés, on the other hand, I took for a city guy, someone who used computers and went out to clubs on the weekend.

My instinct is correct: While I'm opening my backpack, Andrés is busy sending a text message to a friend. This is his first year doing farmwork, he tells me, and he's not sure he'll do it again. He graduated from high school and previously worked, like many, in a maquiladora in San Luis Río Colorado. He's got a girlfriend in Phoenix who is a U.S. citizen; they met while she was visiting her Mexican grandmother, who lives next door to Andrés. He plans to join his girlfriend in Phoenix once he "gets his immigration papers taken care of."

I am extremely out of place out here—I never see another white person, supervisor, or other crewmember—but Andrés isn't exactly at home either. Most of the workers, besides their lack of schooling and previous farmwork experience, are members of an older generation. Andrés recently used his cell phone to take video of Tomás and another man, Humberto, singing. When he played it back they were astounded: How did Andrés's phone do *that*?

Still, Andrés tells me, *la lechuga*—the lettuce—is the best option at the moment. "You work in a factory and you make one hundred, maybe one hundred and fifty pesos in a day [about $10 to $15]. That's it. You could go to college but that won't enable you to get a better job. If you keep going and become a professor, even, you still won't earn that much. We're making more than anyone."

Andrés's comments point to the ironic situation of my crewmembers. Farmworkers, after all, are among the poorest of the poor. In the United States, the average farmworker is an undocumented Mexican immigrant who earns about $11,000 a year. Most have only a grade school education, and 80 percent don't have health insurance. Generally young—the average age is thirty-three—four out of ten are defined as migrants, forced to travel throughout the year in search of work. And though workplace conditions have improved since the 1960s, one out of five farmworkers still isn't provided water on the job, and 7 percent don't have access to a bathroom. It's hardly a dream job, especially when the average wage is $7.25 an hour.[4]

Farmworkers like Andrés earn only one dollar an hour more than the national average, but they have a critical advantage: They are commuters. Each night they return home to Mexico, where they can stretch their dollars. This in part explains the huge challenge Mexico faces in building an indigenous middle class: Who is going to stay and study, knowing that they could take a bottom-rung job in the United States for a higher wage?

At the end of the day, Pedro hands out the paychecks. Mine won't arrive until next Friday. "I'll see you all Monday morning, right here," Pedro says. That's good—I was worried that we might be working Saturday (I'm lucky in that we'll never end up working a weekend). As I'm putting away my knife, he asks me how I'm doing.

I smile. "*Estoy sobreviviendo.*" I'm surviving.

"Now you've got a long time to rest and relax."

"Not so long."

"Oh, yes, two days is a long time. You can relax and drink your little coffee and come back Monday like new."

"Two days is normal," I say. "It's called a weekend." He laughs loudly at this "joke," and walks away.

CHAPTER 3

One morning the crew is less than half its normal size. In an apparent attempt to make up for the missing members, Pedro tells me that I'm now ready to cut two rows. I look at him and nod: He's the boss. Sharpening my knife, I wonder if he has seen a blossoming potential that I have missed. It's not a simple matter to take stock of my development as a *lechugero*, or lettuce worker, when I'm in the trenches, waging mighty battles without pause. Yes, there have been moments when a certain cut and trim felt right, or times when I got into a groove with the bagging. But those were brief moments in very long days; what I brought home each night was a growing sense of impotence and frustration.

When all is going well—when I'm not struggling with the sweat in my eyes or inadvertently launching my knife into the air—my maximum speed when cutting one row is still equal to everyone else's relaxed pace for cutting two. This is beginning to chip away at my initial confidence, the confidence of a rookie who acknowledges his ignorance but is also, due to ignorance, certain of progression.

The first week of the job was one thing. I was learning the basic techniques: bend, cut, bag, place. Midway into week two, though, it isn't clear to me what more I can do. I know the techniques and am moving as fast as my body will permit. All of my mental and physical energy is focused on the task, and yet I need to somehow *double* my current output to hold my own.

Dealing with one row—up to now, usually the row to my left—allows me to turn my entire body in that direction. When cutting, my feet are both pointing to the left, and I am looking sideways, across the rows, while everyone else is facing forward. I slowly shuffle along the furrow in the manner of a basketball defender, swiveling my upper body to the right in order to place the bagged lettuce on the extension, and then returning to my sideways position. Though it's not terribly comfortable to have my feet going across the furrow, and my outer thigh muscles are sore, the position is stable, akin to a horse stance in martial arts. My weight is evenly distributed, and I have no need to teeter along the furrow, worrying about falling to the left or right. Shuffle-shuffle-cut-cut, shuffle-shuffle-cut-cut.

That approach—that of the shuffling defender—doesn't work with two rows. Now responsible for the lettuce to my left *and* right, my body has to face forward, with both feet jammed into the narrow furrow, one in front of the other, as if walking along a tightrope. What makes it especially awkward is the need to twist and bend to the right and left—cranking my neck and upper body around while my feet remain pointed straight ahead—all the while cutting lettuce and moving forward to keep pace with the machine.

I cut perhaps fifteen heads of lettuce before the machine is out of reach. Manuel begins to snatch every second or third lettuce of my left row, allowing me to remain within striking range; I can't quite place the lettuce on the machine, but I can toss it. The workday isn't yet ten minutes old, and already sweat is pouring down my face. My "unusually strong" back, as I have begun to proudly think of it, is throbbing.

"That's it, that's all there is to it," Manuel says, snatching up two heads of lettuce that should be my responsibility. "Do you think you're getting it?" I grunt. This will become a regular communication tactic of mine in the coming weeks. Farmworkers want to talk while cutting and packing lettuce: weather, politics, music, the many cultural differences between a guy like me and guys like them. That's great, of course. I'm here to learn. Unfortunately, I can't cut and talk at the same time and have to make a conscious effort just to listen. So, until my lettuce cutting starts to shape up, questions launched my way will get one of three replies: grunt (I hear you); smile (I hear you and that was funny); or occasionally a verbal "yes" (which often means I am really tired, didn't hear or understand you, and assume the question was rhetorical). This last answer, the ignorant yes, leads to some confusing interactions:

"Gabriel, are you going to get yourself a nice prostitute in Mexico this weekend?"

"Yes."

Or:

"Gabriel, do you have any sisters living in Yuma that you could introduce me to?"

"Yes." I'm an only child, in fact.

Invariably, a long and convoluted discussion would ensue after my yes—no matter how much I tried to retract it—further distracting me from the lettuce and involving half the crew. (How many sisters? Cousins?) So for the first few weeks I usually grunted, smiled, or grunted and smiled.

I last a total of maybe twenty minutes this morning, eventually falling so far behind that even Manuel's help isn't enough. Pedro, noticing that I'm placing lettuce on the ground and that my pace has slowed dramatically, moves me to the front of the machine, where I can cut at my own speed. If Pedro hadn't relieved me, I would soon have been moving at half-speed. How someone could cut two rows for an hour—much less an entire day—is beyond me.

"Oh, you will get it," Pedro tells me when I share this thought. "You will most definitely get it." Maybe he's trying to be hopeful or inspiring, but it comes across as a threat.

DURING THE MORNING break, the bus pulls up and the rest of the crew joins us. Julio bounds over to where I'm seated, shouting good morning.

"Where have you been?" I ask.

He pulls out his passport and shows me a piece of paper that is attached to it. It's a temporary work permit—a flimsy thing, really. "We had to fill out some more papers, for our H-2A visa," he explains, referring to what's otherwise known as a guestworker visa.

This is a surprise. I never considered the possibility that I would be working on a crew with guestworkers. Of the approximately 1.2 million farmworkers in the United States, only about 6 percent have H-2A visas. I had guessed that about half my crew was working with fake papers, roughly in line with the national average for the industry (which might actually be closer to two-thirds, according to the Department of Labor).[5] But it turns out that nearly the entire crew is made up of guestworkers. (Pedro and Adriana are both dual citizens, while Manuel and Roberto, who steers the machine and loads boxes, are permanent residents.)

A number of people on my crew worked in the Yuma fields without papers, but that was years ago. One such individual is Juan, a middle-aged man with a skeletal frame and nearly black skin, whose grave face belies a fantastically dry sense of humor. "Before, sure, I worked as an illegal, in melons," he tells me. Melons in Yuma are a summer crop; this is not an advisable position for anyone wanting to avoid sunstroke. "Now, forget about it. There is too much attention." This is his first year as a guestworker.

In the past, undocumented workers could move between Salinas and Yuma, harvesting lettuce year-round. Now, with numerous immigration checkpoints around Yuma and a beefed-up Border Patrol—whose helicopters frequently fly over us when we work within sight of the border—those without papers stayed in California. The immigrants who had gained permanent residency or citizenship through the 1986 amnesty had been the backbone of the Yuma workforce, but that period was now coming to an end. "There is a severe labor shortage brought on by an aging workforce," explains grower C. R. Waters, the past president of the Yuma Fresh Vegetable Association. "We are not able to bring in many new workers, since not too many of them want their kids to grow up to be farmworkers."

One strategy to attract new workers to the fields is to increase the pay, and wages have begun to climb. According to Waters, the average pay is now between $10 and $12 an hour. "The best crews, paid piece rate [according to how fast they harvest] will be making up to $16 an hour," he says. I shudder to imagine what sort of pace they are working at.

Along with offering a slight increase in wages to address the looming labor shortages, several years ago companies like Dole began recruiting guestworkers, who are paid $8.37 an hour, which is Arizona's Adverse Effect Wage Rate (AEWR). The idea behind the policy, which originated with the original bracero program, is to ensure that the wages paid to guestworkers don't depress the local wages paid to citizens or legal residents. Advocacy groups like Farmworker Justice, based in Washington, D.C., have criticized the AEWR as being too low. When I told Waters that we were earning $8.37, he said that it "was definitely at the lower end of the wage scale."

I had read a few short articles about the potential use of guest-workers in Yuma to fill the predicted labor shortage, but companies were said to shun the program because it required that they provide temporary housing in the United States, a nonsensical clause for a workforce that would be making the daily commute to the fields from San Luis Río Colorado. Workers crossed the border each morning to work and returned at night—to their families, to their homes, to a much lower cost of living.

Dole began using guestworkers in 2005. In order to qualify, they had to prove that there was not a sufficient number of American workers willing to do the work, and to show the government that they have the ability to house their workers—regardless of whether or not anyone would take them up on the offer. As a result, the town of Dateland, about seventy-five miles east of Yuma, has enough housing for the 293 guestworkers the company employs during the year.

Nobody in my crew—or any other Dole crews that had guest-workers—lived in the employer-owned housing in Dateland. In fact, the reason there weren't any migrant farmworker camps spread across Yuma is because there aren't many migrants (except Mexicans from the interior who moved to the border for work). Roughly half of the workforce comes from the Yuma area, and the other half from Mexico, principally from San Luis Río Colorado, but also Mexicali.[6]

GUESTWORKER PROGRAMS HAVE been controversial since their inception, when between 1 and 2 million Mexican *braceros* (literally, strong arms) were brought into the United States to do farmwork between 1942 and 1962.[7] In the 1950s, a young Cesar Chavez criticized growers for refusing to hire Mexican Americans in Oxnard, California, and instead filling their fields with braceros to drive down wages. Although growers were required by law to give priority to U.S. citizens, Chavez and others filled out employment applications and were repeatedly told that no work was available—which they could easily refute by noting the foreign laborers in the fields. "The whole system was rotten," argued Chavez. "The Farm Placement Service was in cahoots with the federal government, which was in cahoots with the growers to keep the local workers out of jobs, get all of the braceros in, and then exploit the braceros."[8]

The critique of guestworkers hasn't changed much over the past sixty years. Unions see guestworkers as making the already difficult job of organizing virtually impossible. (Chavez would later say that had the bracero program not been terminated in 1964, the first grape strike by farmworkers in 1965 would have been easily broken.) Companies in the United States hire private agents in foreign countries, which are in charge of recruiting workers. Guestworkers usually come to the country unfamiliar with U.S. labor laws and are in an exceedingly delicate position: Because their ability to stay and work in the country is tied to their employer, they must please their bosses or face deportation. A boss isn't going to be pleased with a worker that complains about workplace dangers or not being paid for overtime.

Before they even arrive in the United States, many guestworkers find the system stacked against them. Since they are poor, they often need to raise money to apply for visas, arrange transportation from their home country, and pay a fee to the recruiters, an amount that can sometimes exceed $10,000. Guatemalan guestworker Alvaro Hernandez-Lopez, for example, was one of many who signed over the deed to his home to a subagent of his forestry employer because he was told it was a condition of getting work. As the Southern Poverty Law Center (SPLC), which represented Hernandez-Lopez in a lawsuit, points out: "It is almost inconceivable that a worker would complain in any substantial way while a company agent holds the deed to the home where his wife and children reside."[9]

When guestworkers do come forward and complain, they open a window into abuses that led New York congressman Charles Rangel to call the program "the closest thing I've ever seen to slavery." Human Rights Watch and SPLC have both documented many systemic violations of the law, including nonpayment of wages, unsafe working conditions, unsanitary housing, and the seizure of passports and work visas—which in effect controls the movement of the worker and renders them unable to prove who they are or that they have a right to be in the country. One doesn't need to be a labor relations expert to understand the abuses that will inevitably be committed when employers—holding what the SPLC calls the "deportation card" over the heads of their workers—aren't closely monitored by the government.

Some of the themes of disempowerment played out in my time in Yuma. Workers in my crew all understood their relative impotence. "For you it is different," a cutter named Candelario told me during an extended lunch break, as the crew watched in glee as a supervisor tried to get our machine out of a deep rut in the field. "Our parents can't pay for school, so we go right into the fields. When we come here, we make $300 a week. For you that is nothing, maybe like three hundred pesos. But for us, it's more than we ever made before. That's why people here won't complain about anything. You can complain or change jobs, but we're just going to keep our heads down and work."

I heard versions of this statement from a number of guestworkers who considered themselves lucky to be cutting lettuce and didn't want to jeopardize the job. Julio, for example, worked in a maquiladora making car seats during the off-season. He earned 700 pesos a week, the equivalent of a day of farmwork. Manuel's wife, Maria, washed dishes in a restaurant in Mexico before the harvesting season began, earning 120 pesos (about $12) a day. "The restaurant paid higher wages than any other," Maria told me on the day I visited her and Manuel in Mexico. But even with this higher-paying job, after ninety minutes in the field she earned what she would make in a nine-hour day at the restaurant.

But while people were grateful for their jobs, they weren't as powerless as might be expected. One day Pedro was pushing us to finish a section of the field before our afternoon break. We had already been working for three hours since lunch and the crew was tired. While Pedro maneuvered the machine to line up the last section, we stood around at the edge of the field. No one made a move; I heard several people say a break was long overdue. What followed didn't look like a confrontation, but it was. Pedro, slowly understanding that we weren't coming back, pretended to work on the machine. The crewmembers sharpened their knives and looked busy, but stayed put. Eventually Pedro called out, "Take your break!" It was a subtle victory, but a victory nonetheless. Pedro never pushed us again to work such a long shift between breaks.

I wouldn't find any glaring abuses in Yuma. Instead, Dole, from my limited perspective, seemed to run a pretty fair program. No one was being shorted on wages, and health and safety procedures were explained and enforced relatively effectively. Perhaps this was due to our being represented by the Teamsters, but I doubt it: I saw a union representative only twice, and it was unclear what he actually did in Yuma for guestworkers. (The guestworkers, likewise, felt little connection to the union, and no one—aside from myself—paid union dues.)

When I spoke with workers from other companies, they didn't report any abuses either, except for the general complaint that they weren't being paid for the time it took to travel to the fields. This could amount to more than four hours a day and was a serious injustice.

I eventually concluded that the key to the lack of abuse was simple: Yuma's close proximity to Mexico. It's easy to understand the vulnerability of workers who mortgage everything to company agents in order to pay for transportation, and then spend entire months under the watchful eye of intimidating goons thousands of miles from home. But Yuma's guestworkers are commuters who cross the border to work and cross it again to return home. Many have relatives in Yuma; the United States isn't a mysterious country where they have to check their rights at the door. People need work, yes, but they also know that the companies need workers, and since nearly everyone is coming from the same city, if one company is known to be abusive, word spreads quickly.

ON A FRIDAY evening toward the end of January after working for three weeks, I ask Pedro where I should show up on Monday morning. "Avenue G and County 19," he tells me, which sounds simple enough. But in the spacious fields that begin just south of Yuma and run clear to the border, the roads are laid out in mile increments—so the distance between County 19 and 20 streets is one mile, as is the distance between Avenues F and G. It can be quite an adventure to track down the crew; knowing the nearest intersection only means you know where to begin the search.

Early Monday morning I drive through Somerton and head south, making a right on County 19. As I approach Avenue G, I pass a half-dozen machines and buses on my right-hand side. The first few are from a different company, Foothill Packing, but then I spot the familiar red-and-white Dole buses, and I pull over and park, just east of Avenue G. I'm a bit early, and as I sit with the engine idling and heat blasting, I keep craning my neck around, looking for my bus. A woman with her face covered in a bandana walks up and motions for me to roll down the window.

"What company are you with?" she asks.

"Dole."

"You're down at the end," she says, pointing in the direction I just came from.

"Okay, thanks," I tell her, grateful that she's just made my day a little less stressful: It's not easy to pull on my galoshes, smear sunscreen on my face and neck, and get my gear together while maintaining a watchful eye for the bus. I make a U-turn and park in the area she suggested. At 7:20 a.m., ten minutes before I'm supposed to be at the machine, I still haven't spotted our bus and decide to start walking down a path in the middle of the field, following a line of workers. Several machines are in the distance; one must be ours.

But as I head down the path, I notice that these machines have a different design, slightly bulkier and quite a bit wider. I also realize that I'm in the middle of fields of romaine lettuce, not iceberg. I call Pedro on my cell phone, who tells me that the crew is set up on the west side of Avenue G. I turn to my left. There is a collection of buses in the field across the road, perhaps a quarter mile away. Pedro gives me detailed directions, which I don't entirely understand, and I hang up and walk quickly in what I take to be their direction. I check my watch as I near Avenue G. Ten more minutes have passed (these fields are big). I'm late.

To complicate matters, I stumble upon a new barrier when I reach the end of the field: A cement irrigation canal, previously hidden, runs along the field's boundaries, preventing me from reaching the road. I look up and down the canal; often, every several hundred feet or so, little cement footbridges allow safe crossing. But there are none here. I peer across. The water seems about seven feet wide, maybe four feet at its deepest point, with the cement sides sloping downward toward the water at 45-degree angles. A fifteen-minute walk or a quick leap? I'm young and strong: easy answer.

I take a few steps back and make a running leap, pushing off as hard as I can with my left foot and swinging my arms to gain momentum. Here are a few things I fail to consider: I'm wearing a pretty heavy backpack, with three 32-ounce bottles of Gatorade and lunch; galoshes worn over shoes aren't especially conducive to athletic feats; it's early in the morning and my muscles are stiff; I've gained a decent amount of weight during the journey from twenty-five to thirty years old.

Any combination of these explains why, a moment later, my hands are clawing at the top ledge on the other side of the canal, both my elbows are scraping the cement, while everything below my waist is submerged in murky water. After a second or two of all-out exertion, I'm able to scramble to my feet on the other side, completely soaked. As I stride across Avenue G—too embarrassed even to glance around to determine if anyone witnessed my little physics experiment—I tell myself that what transpired will hopefully remain a shared secret between the canal and me.

The first crew isn't mine. A man, who I figure must be a foreman, is sorting through equipment in the back of a pickup.

"Do you know where Pedro's crew is?" I ask.

"Pedro?" he says, tossing aside a folded black tarp. "He's all the way at the end. Just keep—" He looks up. "What . . . " He stares at my pants, and then behind me. I turn around to find a long trail of water in my wake. "What, ah, happened to you?"

Well, I guess I won't be fooling anybody. I say the only sentence that comes into my head. "*Yo anduve por el agua.*" I walked in the water. Simple enough, though idiotic. He looks at me, perplexed, but I have no desire to elaborate, and so continue walking.

When I arrive the crew is already doing calisthenics, swirling their arms and flexing their hands. I go to the truck and ask Pedro for a new white glove and hairnet, hoping that we'll just pass over the obvious. "And you? What happened?" he asks, staring at my pants and then into my eyes.

I again explain the unfortunate occurrence, adding comments about the importance I place on punctuality. He tells me that next time I should walk around the canal and be a little late. In retrospect, I say, that makes plenty of sense. As he opens the storage bin to retrieve my requests, I hear a sloshing sound coming from my feet. I shake my right foot, and yes—there's a lot of water moving around in there. I bend over and pull off the right galosh and dump it upside down. Several cups of water come gushing out.

Pedro, who has been watching, looks concerned. I flash a wide grin at him, trying to look like everything's fine, but realizing mid-smile that the gesture doesn't feel entirely appropriate.

"Are you okay?" he asks. It sounds like an expansive question, as if he's inquiring about my physical state, yes, but would also appreciate knowing whether I happen to be, you know, deranged. He's got a white guy on his crew who shows up wet, smiling enthusiastically, with tales of walking in the water at dawn.

I'm grateful when the machine finally starts moving. I'm cutting two rows between Julio and Candelario, both of whom inquire about my soggy state. I quickly fall behind, and it soon becomes clear that today isn't going to be a good day. Although my face is dripping with sweat, my feet and thighs are freezing, and my left hand—essential for holding the lettuce and shaking off the leaves—is throbbing. (I will later learn during the morning break, when I take off my gloves, that in the scramble to pull myself out of the canal I've cut my pinkie and ring fingers, and the top knuckle of my pinkie has become an enormous wart of swollen flesh.) Julio and Carlos help me out, popping over and snatching up heads of lettuce to allow me to briefly catch up, but I simply can't sustain the pace, and minutes later I've fallen behind again.

Two hours into the day, Pedro calls me away from the machine. He is standing next to a man who I later learn is Dole's director of safety. "What happened?" the man asks. I repeat my stupid story. "Do you want to go home and change?" I shake my head, and offer an attempt at humor.

"Well, today you know that you have one *mojado* working in your group." It's a play on the Spanish slang for undocumented worker, or wetback. This draws grins from Pedro and the supervisor, and during the rest of the day, I use the line whenever someone asks what happened. This injection of humor, as it often does, distances me somewhat from the pain of the present.

I somehow make it to lunch, requiring substantial assistance from Carlos and Julio. Normally I would feel bad about my inability to keep up with the machine, but I'm too miserable and weak to really pay it much mind. People are clearly aware that I'm having a rough day, and Manuel and a young man named Miguel both ask me how I'm doing and offer bags of chips in condolence.

Lunch passes as it always does, quickly, and once the machine is moving again I immediately fall behind. I start placing the lettuce on the ground—the telltale sign of a cutter that isn't keeping up—and Pedro comes over a number of times to borrow my knife and cut for me while I bag. As a team we quickly catch up with the machine, and while he cuts, Pedro tries to instruct me on proper cutting techniques.

"Look, before you cut, you should grab the lettuce tight with your left hand and find the head," he says. My left hand isn't going to be grabbing anything tight, but I stay quiet and nod. "Then, make the cut quickly." Pedro stabs the lettuce and lifts up the head, makes another cut to trim the stem, shakes it once, and hands it to me, ready to be bagged. I nod again. Yes. Nice cut, Pedro.

"You see, *fácilisimo* [so easy]," he says, making another perfect one-two cut combination. "Gabriel, I can't think of an easier job than cutting lettuce." I don't even bother to respond.

During the afternoon break, I apologize to Candelario and Julio for cutting so slowly, which has forced them to cut more than their fair share. "Oh, don't worry, Gabby," Candelario says.

"You are doing very, very good. Not a problem at all." Julio echoes Candelario in his own odd way—"I like cutting extra lettuce!" he earnestly exclaims—and my spirits lift. Above all, I don't want to be a burden to my new coworkers. I finish out the last hour after the break strong, needing assistance only a few times.

At the end of the day, Pedro calls the crew over to his truck. We gather in a circle, and he explains that Dole is giving every member of our crew a gift since we have gone without an injury thus far. He hands out black Dole duffle bags, which are of much higher quality than I would have expected, with wheels on one end and a pull-out handle—the sort that I'm always bumping into while navigating crowded airports. As I collect my bag, someone mentions that the crew working alongside us isn't receiving anything because one of their workers fell off the machine several weeks ago and broke his ribs.

I begin the long trek back to my car, this time content to walk around the irrigation canal. Now that I'm able to consider it from a less hurried perspective, it does seem forbiddingly wide. I plod slowly along its rim. My feet are still wet and my left hand is bloodied and swollen, but the sky above is turning brilliant shades of pink and purple, a cool breeze is blowing at my back, and I've got twelve hours to recuperate. I've survived the hardest day thus far in the fields—the hardest workday of my life—but I have a new bag to show for it, and driving home, admiring the gashes on my hand as it rests on the steering wheel, I feel oddly triumphant.

CHAPTER 4

I begin what Pedro calls my "championship training" during week four. By now I'm cutting one row without a problem and can handle two rows for short stretches, until my back starts to tighten and my general enthusiasm for the task drops. It's like the wall marathoners hit, I suppose: One minute I'm chugging along and the next I'm depleted and scarcely able to move.

Like most effective torture tactics, Pedro's championship training is simple and repetitive. The one-step process involves saving the lettuce that the machine would normally roll over and destroy. Although the tires of the machine run along two furrows, they are wide enough to damage the lettuce in the four adjacent rows. Normally, before the machine rolls through a field, the crew cuts these four rows, shoving the heads of lettuce to the side; they will later be trimmed and bagged by the two cutters walking the furrows of the tires. It's a group effort, with each cutter covering a small stretch, and takes less than half an hour.

Pedro tells me at the beginning of the day that my sole task will be to cut the four rows of lettuce in the path of the machine. He points to the end of the especially large field we're harvesting this morning, which must be at least a quarter mile away. "This will be fun for you," Pedro promises, a smile on his face. "You're going to be saving the lettuce today—all four rows. Start with one row and do it to the end, then walk back and start the next." I peer across the field again; this looks like an all-day activity.

Since I won't be using them, I hang my two ganchos and six packets of bags on the machine, and at first the task feels fine. It's a relief not to have the metal ends jabbing into my thighs or the weight of the plastic bags dragging me down. My only responsibility is to bend over, stab the trunk, and shove the head into the next row. Because there isn't any need to stand and bag, I remain hunched over the entire time. I'm cutting far more quickly than normal, already well in front of the machine, and when I finally straighten up, my back cracks. I look toward my destination; it's still a long ways off.

It takes me nearly an hour to get to the end of the field. I've cut 907 heads of lettuce and the throbbing in my back has forced me to stand up and stretch after every twenty-five heads or so. I now realize why Pedro has given me this task: I've already cut the equivalent of a half-day's worth of lettuce, and it's not even 9:00 a.m. Of course, I don't have to trim the lettuce or bag it, but this leaves me more time to engage in the hardest part—the part that requires stooping—without relief.

Turning around, I see that I'm so far from the machine that I can't even make out individual figures, so I figure it's safe to take an unauthorized break. I sit on the ground, wipe the sweat from my face, and lay down, thinking this will give my back the chance to realign itself. Instead my back starts tying itself in knots—intense, charley-horse knots—and I fling myself back into a sitting position. I take a few deep breaths, toss a dirt clod against the ground, and figure I might as well head back. I finish up the last row just before lunch, losing track of the number of heads cut somewhere after 2,500.

THIS BECOMES MY morning routine for the week. Through sheer repetition, I'm starting to make the initial stab quickly and cleanly, instead of searching around for the trunk and making multiple attempts. By day three I'm also able to increase the number of heads cut from twenty-five to fifty without needing to straighten my back. It might be silly, but I find that it helps to think of this as "training" rather than "work."

I grew up on a steady diet of martial arts movies, many of which follow a tried-and-true storyline: A weak young man is beaten up by a group of bad men; said young man finds mysterious martial arts master; receives special training; beats up group of bad men. The details may vary (young man's brother has been killed and must be avenged), but the timeless arc of each movie remained. Through sheer determination an unlikely figure overcomes great adversity to become tougher, harder, a champion.

Working away from the crew, my mind is free to roam as I develop my movie's plot. The odds are stacked against the white kid from the city. No one knows he's saved all his money to enter the upcoming "National Lettuce Cutting Championship," a riveting program broadcast on ESPN. Each day finds him sweating in the fields, having been taken under the wing of veteran lettuce-master Pedro, perfecting his form and learning to be one with the dirt. At night he hits the books, studying the various types of lettuce, and when he goes to bed he places his knife under his pillow for good luck. Little do his competitors know that on the day of the competition . . .

After lunch, Pedro has me back at the machine, which, compared with my training, comes as a relief. I'm still fumbling with the lettuce, but a huge distraction—the pain in my back—is gone. Or if not gone, muted: Several days of cutting thousands of heads of lettuce before lunch can do wonders for redefining pain. Instead of a debilitating pinch, my lower back now gives off a low-level throb.

With my back no longer so large a distraction, my work-time responses expand beyond the monosyllabic. Manuel is the first to sense the shift, and he's been waiting with a growing collection of words he wants to learn in English. At a Yuma car dealership recently, someone came up to him and a sales representative and said, "Hey guys." Since then, he's been dying to know what it meant.

"It's just a greeting," I say. "Like, 'How are you doing?'"

Manuel nods. "*Ay guz. Ay guz.*"

"Hey guys," I repeat.

"Ay guys," he says.

"Very good," I tell him.

After I've translated a number of words and phrases, I ask Manuel how he came to harvest lettuce in Yuma.

"That's a long story, probably as long as your own," he replies. His childhood was like that of many Mexicans: He grew up in a very large family—one of twelve siblings—in a very small town. When he was fourteen, his father and an older brother left their village in the interior state of Michoacan for the fields of Salinas, where they quickly found work cutting broccoli. The passage of the Immigration Reform and Control Act in 1986 allowed them—along with 1.2 million other farmworkers—to become permanent residents. Manuel's father soon petitioned for his son to join him. "I knew that I wanted to leave," Manuel says, "but I also knew that I would someday want to return, where life is quiet and simple."

Like many legal immigrants, Manuel's path to permanent residency was anything but simple. In 1990, he decided that he was done waiting, and he and his brother hatched a plan: They would share a green card. His brother sent the identification back to Manuel, which he used to cross at a checkpoint in California. "You could never do that now," he says, "but at the time they just glanced at the photo and let me through."

He spent much of the next decade in the fields of California, away from his family. ("I refuse to cross as an illegal," his wife, Maria, later tells me. "I don't want to have to worry about being caught, about what might happen to the children.") He traveled throughout the state, harvesting a wide range of fruits and vegetables, and crossed the border several times with his brother's green card without incident. In 2000, still waiting on his case, he was apprehended at a checkpoint in El Paso, Texas. This time, luckily, he was using a fake green card—not his brother's—but was detained for a month before being deported. He was somehow able to petition for a pardon, so as not to undermine his ongoing immigration case, and finally became a resident in 2002.

In 2003, Manuel, Maria, and their four children moved to San Luis Río Colorado. It was a compromise measure: Manuel could work in the United States during the day and return home to Mexico each night. He's worked at Dole ever since, and when he heard that the company was looking to hire guestworkers, Maria applied. Although her season was cut short by pregnancy, she plans on being back next year. "After this I think we're done having kids," Manuel says.

Dole, like the other growers, follows a strict harvesting schedule. From May to September the company has crews in Salinas; the work shifts to the town of Huron in California's San Joaquin Valley during October; then to Yuma from November to March; and back to Huron for April before returning to Salinas. Mexican guestworkers are allowed to commute only to Yuma, but as a permanent resident Manuel begins and ends each season in Huron—working about seven months of the year. While in Huron he lives with other workers in company housing, "right in the middle of nowhere." At the end of the season he collects unemployment for four months, a privilege not granted to guestworkers, and in the early fall, before the lettuce season begins, he harvests dates in Yuma for several weeks.

He knows he could make more money for a company paying piece rate, but he prefers the steady pace of the Dole machines. "Other contractors I've worked for have always tried to make you go faster and faster, but that gets tiring." Some employers docked him for refusing to work on both Saturday and Sunday; that kind of life doesn't allow any time with the family. His pay has remained almost flat—he started at $8.10 an hour in 2003—but he's satisfied, especially because Dole provides good health-care benefits for his family. "They take $40 a month out of my check, but we're able to go to the hospital right by our house whenever we want." Julio and Norma, too, will state that the health care they receive is a big reason they've stayed with Dole.

Manuel tells me about the other white person who briefly joined the crew earlier in the year. "Ronnie made me sad," is how he begins, describing Ronnie as a rough-looking, often frustrated man in his forties. "His hands were always shaking, like he was really nervous or angry, and no one knew what to do." Ronnie would leave many good heads of lettuce untouched, and the ones he did harvest were often unusable, but no one stepped in to criticize— not Pedro, not even the field supervisors. "Everyone just watched and wondered what to do. I think people were afraid of him."

By the time he departed, Ronnie hadn't come close to being able to harvest a single row. Manuel remembered one instance when, falling behind, Ronnie lit into the lettuce, slicing several heads to shreds as they sat rooted in the ground. He stuck around for two weeks, long enough to collect his first paycheck, and the rumor that circulated throughout the crew is that he was imprisoned; apparently he told Pedro that he had a court date and might not be able to return.

I learn many details of Manuel's life while visiting him and Maria at their spacious four-bedroom house in Mexico on a Saturday afternoon. After a lunch of eggs and beans, I'm given a driving tour of San Luis Río Colorado, which strikes me as an unremarkable border city: We pass a few *maquiladoras*, a handful of strip clubs ("Table Dance All Day!"), and many dusty streets lined with modest but sturdy homes. The following day I return to the city to visit Norma and Julio, who have recently purchased a modern townhouse through an affordable housing program; like Manuel and Maria, they have achieved a level of economic stability through harvesting lettuce.

Ironically, the one thing that is lacking in San Luis Río Colorado is edible lettuce. With Julio and Norma I stop in at two large grocery stores. Each is filled with the most rotten heads of iceberg lettuce I've even seen. The leaves are purple, brown, or black; when I lift a head, it squishes like a sponge and drips some sort of rancid liquid. "It's like this everywhere," says Julio. "That's why we all take lettuce home from the field."

ON AN 80-DEGREE day in early February we're short a crewmember. Arturo is a fair-skinned thirty-five-year-old who is always the first person to alert Pedro when we hit the two-and-a-half-hour point in the morning by shouting, in English, "I'm hungry!" He learned the phrase from his wife, a U.S. citizen; they're meeting with an immigration attorney this morning, part of Arturo's process to become a legal resident. With his H-2A visa, the couple can live together in San Luis, Arizona, and once he can settle permanently in the United States, he plans on starting a family. "Now is the perfect time," he told me. "Mexicans like to have kids when they're young, but I don't think you're really ready until you get to your thirties."

Arturo is one of the crew's fastest packers, which presents a problem for Pedro: Without his presence, some unlucky packer will be burdened with doing twice the work, and lettuce will stack up on the extensions, slowing down the entire machine. Pedro's solution is to give me a shot at packing, setting me up next to Gloria. As with cutting, there's not much of an orientation. "Just watch Gloria and do what she does."

I've gotten to know Gloria during breaks. She's a heavy-set thirty-two-year-old who usually spends her free time with Andrés and is always passing me tacos during lunch. She's demonstrated extreme concern that all I seem to eat are "my little bars," and she also lets me know—repeatedly—that she has a cousin hoping to move to the United States who wouldn't mind "getting to know me." Like Andrés, this is her first year in the fields, and she tells me that she has a tourist visa that is good for ten years that allows her to cross the border whenever she wants. Still, she tells me, she hasn't spent much time in Yuma—her primary trips north have been to the hospital to give birth to her three children. "I'm smart like that," she says, and though her face is shrouded in bandanas, I can tell from her creased eyes that she is smiling.

I had imagined that the division of labor between cutters and packers would engender some animosity. Now, after a month in the fields, the fact that it did not seemed especially curious. Cutters are stooped over all day under the blazing sun. Packers stand right next to the machine, in the shade provided by a sun visor that extends above their heads. While I ended every day covered in dirt and sweat, a packer could wear a white sweatshirt—as Arturo often did—and go home stain free. It seemed particularly unfair that we all earned the same wage. I bent down in the sun, trimmed a head of lettuce, placed it in a bag, and placed that bag on the extension. A packer's only job was to grab that bag, tape it shut, and stuff it in a box. I've stuffed things in boxes before: It's called moving.

Those were my prejudices going in. I watch Gloria for a few minutes: She takes the bag from the extension, cinches it shut, and twirls it around. She takes the twisted end and places it against the bag, and slaps the end against a tape dispenser in front of her with a quick motion. The bag of lettuce is now taped shut. She stuffs the bag into a box, and when she has twenty-four heads, she closes the edges of the box and shoves it forward onto the conveyor belt, which brings the box to the center of the machine where it will be stapled and stacked on pallets by the loaders. She grabs an empty box, writes her identifying number on the edge with a red crayon, and starts the process over again. (As a means of quality control, supervisors regularly choose a box at random and check its contents; they therefore need to know who's packing what.)

After watching her pack three boxes, I'm confident that this, at last, is a test I can pass with flying colors. "Let me help you out there," I tell her. I grab an empty box from above and place it in front of me. Pedro hasn't given me a number, so I don't bother with the red crayon. With Gloria watching, I grab a bag of lettuce and twirl it. As I do, the tips of the fingers of my left glove get caught in the mix. I try again; it happens again. On the third try I'm able to successfully extract my left hand from the twirl. Now I'm ready to tape.

From what I've been able to gather, there is nothing special about taping. The tape is mounted vertically on the machine, sticky end out. I press the bag against the tape, which affixes as planned, and move my bag to the left. This is supposed to cut the tape. Instead, I pull out two feet of tape, still connected to the dispenser. I pull harder to the left, and now I've got three feet of tape, which has wrapped itself around my right hand and is still connected to the damn dispenser.

Gloria, watching with glee, rips the tape from the dispenser. By now the tape is everywhere except where it's supposed to be. I spend ten seconds getting it off and try again, but the same thing happens. I decide to resume my apprenticeship by watching Gloria.

I study the moment she cuts the tape and don't see anything special. She simply affixes the tape by banging the bag against it, and then pulls to the left. I've already tried that. "How are you getting the tape to rip?" I ask. A smarter, less cocky person might not have waited this long to ask a single question.

Now she's really enjoying herself. "It's easy, like you said!" She cackles and makes the motion with a flourish, not slowing down at all to aid in my development.

I never figure out what I'm doing wrong. Over the course of thirty minutes, I'm able to pack three boxes, but my technique is ridiculously slow. Whenever I try to separate the tape from the dispenser in one motion, I end up yanking out a yard's worth of tape and securing it against my chest, then grab at it with my hands, which secures it to my gloves. Others in the crew start to notice. "Stop playing with the tape," calls Candelario, who is cutting nearby. It's not long before I've emptied the dispenser, and I have to ask Diego to bring me another roll of tape. With the new roll installed, I decide to take a different approach. Instead of attempting to mimic Gloria and the others, I slowly pull an inch's worth of tape from the dispenser, and then take my right hand and carefully pull down on the tape, which works. It also takes three times as long, but at least I'm not burning through the crew's tape supply.

"*What* are you doing?" Pedro asks when he checks on my progress. I explain that this is the only way I can get it to work. "Haven't you been watching Gloria?"

So I try again—maybe I'll get lucky?—and pull hard to the left, but the result is the same: The tape doesn't tear. "Go get your knife," he tells me. He takes over my position, packing as fast as Gloria with the same dispenser that has been giving me fits. He won't suggest again that I help out with packing.

AFTER TWO CONSECUTIVE ten-hour days, we are dismissed at 4:00 p.m. On the drive home I am excited about this turn of events because I've been thinking about making my first real grocery run. During working hours—that is, during most of my waking hours—I've been consuming virtually nothing but Gatorade and Clif Bars. I have cereal and coffee each morning, and pick up a veggie sandwich from Subway each night on the way home. The middle of my day is powered by three to four calorie-rich nutritional bars and four 32-ounce bottles of Gatorade, which I dump into my backpack as I head, bleary-eyed, out the door. I have been thinking utility when sliding the bulk purchases into my shopping cart each weekend. At work, I couldn't care less about the food I eat—I just want to make sure it will provide the necessary energy so that I don't end up light-headed. Another advantage of bars is they can be eaten very quickly: I can consume my "lunch" in three minutes and have twenty-seven minutes to lay back and relax. I've watched Julio and Norma unpack an elaborate salad, fiddle with salad dressing, and toss it in a plastic bag. By the time the food was ready to eat, the lunch break was nearly over.

Now, however, after weeks of this monotonous diet, I'm craving real food during the day: pasta, burritos, even something as simple as a peanut butter and jelly sandwich is beginning to sound exotic. On the drive home I compile a list of purchases in my head: Romaine lettuce, black bean veggie burgers, roasted garlic pasta sauce, pepper jack cheese. Pickles, apples. Ice cream, Guinness beer. I'm going to fill the fridge with food.

I get home and shower. By the time I towel off and have clean clothes on, I'm starting to get hungry, so I eat a bowl of cereal. It's nearly six o'clock. My face is overheated from a combination of sun and a hot shower, and my eyes are stinging. With my shoes on, I lie down on the bed, lacing my hands behind my head and closing my eyes. This is beautiful: Early dismissal means there is time for a five-minute rejuvenation nap. The moment I shut my eyes they begin to cool, finally allowed to protect themselves after hours of exposure to sun and wind and dust.

Sometime later, I'm aware that a bird has climbed inside my head. It chirps steadily, and the chirps turn to beeps. I journey slowly through the various layers of semiconsciousness and eventually, on the cusp of awakening, the noise finally becomes clear: Outside my window a car is honking, over and over again. I sit up, groggy, and wait for the world to seep back into focus. The overhead light is on, illuminating the room, but it doesn't look like *my* room. Someone turns off the car alarm, creating an eerie silence. Where the hell am I? I look around, and notice that my sheath is on the floor next to my bed. Oh, yes, that's right: I'm in Yuma. I got off work early. I'm going to buy groceries. I should do that now.

I stand up in the bright room and pull back the curtain. It's pitch-black outside. I check the clock: 1:37 a.m. I've slept for nearly eight hours. I turn off the lights and close my eyes, feeling drugged, and am awakened four hours later by my alarm.

I learn an important lesson from this episode: If I want to accomplish something after work, I have to do it on the way home. Once I've taken a shower and eaten, the life force rushes out of me—and no matter what time it is, I'm ready for bed.

Farmwork leaves a person with precious little energy. Luckily for me, I don't have a life in Yuma. Anything that people normally do aside from work—raising a family, having dinner with friends, seeing a weeknight movie—is, for me, completely out of the question.

But for many of my crewmembers, farmwork is something that must be juggled along with raising families, caring for elderly parents, running errands, and cooking meals. Much of the parenting must be squeezed into the weekends, as people leave their houses by 4:30 a.m. and don't return until well after dark. When both parents work in the fields, they rely on relatives to watch their children. When Julio and Norma get home, Julio's sister has already fed the kids dinner, but Norma must still go over her daughter's homework and make lunch for the following day. Where does she find the energy? I ask her, but of course there's no good answer: "I just do it."

If being exhausted at the end of the day is the drawback to this kind of work, there is also an advantage. I find that my typical, more existential worries fade away. What am I doing? Is it worth doing? Is someone doing something more important? Should I be doing that? These questions no longer seem so pressing—I simply don't have the surplus energy to give them any space. I work, I eat, I sleep.

The outside world fades quickly too. In the early spring of 2008, there is a hotly contested presidential primary under way, an historic campaign pitting a woman against an African American. I know this because I tune in to NPR on the way home from the fields each day. For fifteen minutes I hear dispatches from excited journalists, listen to pundits expound on voting trends, catch excerpts from the candidates as they crisscross the country and respond to their opponent's latest gaffe. Politics animates me; politics is a factor that motivated my current project. But now I find that I just can't muster the energy to care.

I MEET MATEO the day after my drugged slumber. There aren't many farmworkers who are still in the fields by the time they reach their fifties; the ones I see usually don't look like they'll last through the season. It's simply not possible to do this work for decades and not suffer noticeable body modifications, such as a permanently hunched back, crooked fingers, and hands so swollen that they look as if someone has attached a valve to a finger and pumped vigorously. The punishing nature of the work, along with exposure to pesticides and poor access to medical care, help explain why farmworkers don't live very long; the National Migrant Resources Program puts their life expectancy at forty-nine years.[10]

Mateo is the one exception to the rule, looking fresh and fit despite having spent more than twenty years in the fields. His face is broad and friendly, with a graying mustache and slightly mischievous eyes, and he has a trim body that, when walking, shows no noticeable signs of ailments. Each day in the field looks like it could be his first. He and his wife, Veronica, belong to a different Dole crew, but on many days we harvest the same field, and I usually end up parking my car behind his large blue truck. But it's not until Mateo and I are both chosen by our foremen to "clean" a nearby field that we start talking. "Hello, how are you?" he asks in English. "My name Mateo."

"My granddaughter speaks English, but she won't talk to me," he continues, shifting to Spanish. "And my daughter-in-law knows some English, but she's too embarrassed." After we've finished cleaning the field—a very easy task in which we walk through a recently harvested field looking for trash—he writes his phone number and address on a piece of paper and hands it to me. "Come. My house. So we speak English," he tells me.

I visit Mateo that Sunday. He lives less than a mile from where I'm staying, in a one-story house that he and his wife purchased in 1990 in a predominantly Mexican American neighborhood. During my time in Yuma, Mateo seems to be the only person I'm not fooling. "You are here to make a report," he says matter-of-factly when I sit down at a table in the living room. "That is good. Americans should know the hard work that Mexicans do in this country." I don't agree or disagree, allowing the comment to pass as I say hello to Veronica, who is preparing a meal in the adjoining kitchen.

"I knew lettuce would be hard, but not this hard," I say in response.

"That is for a very simple reason that everyone knows: Americans have become lazy," he says. "They are not used to work like this. They have jobs where they sit in a chair all day and play with computers. There was a *gabacho* [American] in your crew earlier, but he couldn't do the work so he left. Are you cutting two rows yet?"

"Yes, more or less."

"That's good." Mateo leaves the table and returns with coffee. "I was watching you on Friday. You looked pretty good. But remember, the main thing is that you show up, that you keep coming back."

"Yeah, but I thought I'd be better by now."

Mateo takes a sip of coffee and gently shakes his head. "You don't understand how this works. One month is nothing. It takes a long time to learn how to really cut lettuce. It's not something that you learn after only one season. Three, maybe four seasons—then you start understanding how to really work with lettuce."

Mateo begins to tell me about his lettuce career in English but soon grows frustrated and reverts to Spanish. He arrived in California in the early 1980s, harvesting Brussels sprouts near Watsonville before moving on to lettuce in Salinas. He and his wife gained permanent residency through the 1986 federal immigration reform bill, and together they spent a decade following the lettuce seasons, bouncing between Salinas and Yuma. From his veteran perspective, Mateo sees guestworkers as less about filling a labor shortage than eroding the rights of workers. "They want to get rid of the old guys like me, people with residency or citizenship. Instead they can get young people who live in Mexico and who won't complain, because if they complain they won't be allowed to work next year."

In an ironic twist that has echoes within American manufacturing, Mateo was asked at the beginning of the year to teach members of my crew how to cut lettuce—in effect, training the people who he believes will be taking his job. But if he harbors any resentment, it is muted: Mateo is nearing the end of his career as a farmworker. His son, who is in his late twenties, tried cutting lettuce a few years ago, but like most folks with other work prospects, decided to move on. "*La maqina . . . ,*" his son tells me when I ask why he quit, and I don't need to hear another word: I know his pain. He survived one season of lettuce before finding work at a construction company, where he is still employed. While he may occasionally come home tired after a day of pouring cement, it's nothing compared to the fatigue of farmwork. When it's slow, his son marvels, "We get to stand around a lot and talk." Once you've worked in the fields, you notice these sorts of luxuries.

Over a lunch of tortillas, eggs, rice, and beans, Mateo and Veronica talk about their newest jobs. Last April, instead of heading to Salinas to continue on the lettuce circuit, they traveled to St. Joseph, Missouri, where they had heard from a friend that they could find work at a pork processing plant. "You should go there sometime," Mateo says. "Just to hear the way they speak. Normally English doesn't sound good to me, but in Missouri they speak very beautifully, almost like singing."

He and Veronica earned a couple dollars more an hour than in the fields, and they might return once the lettuce season concludes. Their task was to slice away excess fat from the torsos of pigs that zoomed past on a belt, using an electric knife. The temperature of the plant was just above freezing, but the pace of the work kept them from getting cold.

I ask them to contrast cutting lettuce to cutting pigs. Since my next job will be poultry processing—which I imagine must be similar to pork processing—I'm interested to see how the two stack up. To my mind, no matter how nauseating a poultry plant might be, it *has* be less strenuous than cutting lettuce.

That's not what Mateo is telling me, however. "First, it's easier to learn how to cut pigs. But I would say that it is a more difficult job overall. With the pigs, they make you work so rapidly that there's never any time for rest." Despite wearing five gloves on one hand and two on the other, his hands ached terribly. "But you can't ever stop, you just keep cutting and cutting or the boss will get angry."

"The breaks are so short," adds Veronica. "They begin when the line stops moving, so you have to use five minutes of your break just to take off the gloves and equipment." Fifteen minutes after the line stops, it begins again—so almost two-thirds of the "break" is spent taking the gear off and putting it back on. "It's also depressing because you are stuck inside all day, doing the same thing," she adds.

"That's right," Mateo says. "In the field you can look at the sky, but in the plant . . ." I had wanted to hear about the plant, but as the husband and wife continue to describe the job in a manner that paints lettuce in a favorable light, I stop paying close attention.

IN MID-FEBRUARY, A new week brings a "breakthrough." Mateo casually mentions that his feet sometimes hurt more when he wears the boots over his shoes. I am reminded of this comment as I rub lotion on my aching soles one evening. Breakthrough: Of course my feet are sore—I've been wearing the boots! I leave them off for two days; at the end of the experiment, my feet are still killing me, and now my shoes are coated in mud. The pain, it turns out, is caused not by the boots but by walking along uneven ground all day and jamming my feet into the furrows. I don't waste time reflecting on these setbacks, however, because doing so would get in the way of my search for the *real* breakthroughs. The possible solutions are endless. My knife isn't sharp enough; my knife is too sharp. I should cut walking backwards, as a young man in our crew named Abel does. Why should this make anything easier? I'm not sure, but do it anyway, learning that it's difficult to see what's in front of you when you walk backwards. It's much easier, though, to fall.

A new insight hits me on a Tuesday, when for some reason Pedro has me cutting a single row for the entire day. Since my week of training I've been cutting two rows, and I now use the extra time to watch the others. Julio, as usual, seems to have ingested a fair amount of methamphetamines. He chats with Pedro and darts to his left and right, snapping up the lettuce and trimming it at a frenetic pace. When he catches me watching, he shouts out "Gabriel!" and waves, hopping up and down as if he's been stung by a wasp, and rejoins his conversation with Pedro. I like his athleticism—I *want* his athleticism—but by now I know he isn't a good model for me. Not everyone can be the star.

The temperature is in the mid-80s, but when I look over at Manuel I see that he has kept his sweatshirt on and his face is bone dry. Although he is able to cut nearly as quickly as Julio, his guiding principle is energy conservation. While Julio expends an enormous amount of effort as he careens around the field, Manuel proceeds in a daze, apparently on the verge of falling asleep. There is no anxiety on his face: He can keep up with the machine and he knows it. I watch him make the same simple motions again and again, as he stares off into space.

At one point I notice that Alfonso has lost ground to the machine and is placing bags of lettuce on the ground. A tall man with a deep voice and trimmed goatee, Alfonso is the most likely person to fall behind the machine's pace (after me, of course). I leave my row to help out, knowing that, cutting only one row, I can easily catch up. By now he is huffing and puffing, making violent thrusts at the lettuce and slamming the heads into his bag. Perspiration is streaming down his face into the lettuce—I'm glad to see another person in the crew has functional sweat glands—and his eyes have a frenzied look. I glance back at Manuel, who is stifling a yawn.

When I return to my row it hits me: I've been my own worst enemy. When I attempt to cut fast, my muscles tighten, my anxiety rises, my heart beats faster . . . but I actually cut slower. In the rush to keep up, I expend more energy and make more mistakes, which causes me to fall behind, which causes me to rush, which causes me to fall further behind. At the end of the day, I'm exhausted not only because the work is hard, but also because I've been unwittingly generating tension.

I begin to mimic Manuel, taking deep breaths and moving smoothly, and find that the precision of my cuts increases. Of course, I'm cutting only one row—so remaining relaxed isn't nearly as difficult—but I'm convinced the lesson will be equally relevant when applied to two rows. When I share this insight with Manuel at the end of the day, he nods. "You have to put your mind somewhere else," he explains. "Like the Chinese. If you concentrate right, you feel no pain." Zen and the art of lettuce cutting.

I am actually excited to come to work the following morning, so eager to show off my new knowledge. At 8:30 a.m. the machine roars to life, and I take my place between Julio and Manuel. Normally there's a knot in my stomach as I cut my first few heads of lettuce, worried that I'll fall behind. But not today. I notice that within five minutes I am being forced to reach farther to place my bags on the extension, but this doesn't rattle me. Instead of trying to increase my pace, I continue in a steady rhythm. Take it easy.

Five minutes later I'm beginning to wonder what's wrong: The machine is leaving me behind. Pedro notices and comes over. "Let's go, Gabriel!" he yells. I'm a foot away and he's yelling. I hate it when he does that.

"Pedro, I'm working like Manuel today," I say, trying to regain my equilibrium. "Very calm, so that I cut the lettuce better."

Pedro doesn't look impressed. "Let's go, Gabriel!" he shouts again. "Let's go! Let's go!"

While speaking to Pedro I've lost even more ground, and while I try to stay relaxed, I realize that this determination to stay relaxed is starting to stress me out. The machine has inched out of reach, so I put a head of lettuce on the ground, then another. The morning's first drop of sweat flies off my nose. Goddamn. I bend over quickly and stab the lettuce too high, rendering it worthless. I toss it into the furrow and vigorously stomp on it, obliterating my mistake. I take another head of lettuce and cut. I'm about to bag it when I see that there's a yellow leaf wrapped around the head. I try to grab it but can't get a hold of it. I finally peel off the leaf and bag the lettuce, dropping it on the ground, and sloppily grab for another. My left hand is wrapped around the bottom of the head, and as my blade cuts through the stem it connects with my middle finger. The pain is intense, but I'm relieved to see that when I take off my glove, though my finger is already turning purple, I didn't break the skin. I put my glove back on, now a good ten feet behind the machine, and start cutting in my typical, maximum-intensity style. Another once-cherished insight, quickly discarded.

I TAKE MY lunch sitting on the ground in a group that includes Candelario, Cesar, and Manuel. "I am dying today," I tell them as I rip open the package of my thousandth energy bar. "People said that the soreness would go away. But I don't think the soreness goes away. You just get used to it. You forget what it's like to not be sore."

Manuel considers the comment. "That's true, that's true. It always takes a few weeks at the end of the year to get back to normal, to recover. But the first week is the hardest. The first week is the week you'll always remember."

Candelario takes a long drag on his cigarette and exhales the smoke, which is taken away by a light breeze. He straightens his back and clears his throat, a professor of agriculture preparing to deliver an address. "I will tell you how it is. This is one of the hardest jobs you can do. Why? Okay, I'll tell you. You come in Monday and you're okay; Tuesday you're a little tired; Wednesday you're very tired; Thursday you can hardly walk; and Friday you're crawling. Friday, you *just want to get it over with*." Cesar, Manuel, and I are nodding: This is a very accurate description. Except that I'm crawling and it's only Wednesday.

After Candelario's comments, the lunch break shifts from a time of conversation to recuperation, as people lay back with their eyes closed or gaze without focus across the field. I finish another bar and then take inventory of my hands, which are swollen and lopsided. The middle finger of my left hand, which I banged with the knife, has ballooned at the end, and the nail has turned purple. When I touch the tip it throbs, which is inconvenient, since this is the hand that must grab each lettuce. The ring finger of my left hand is also looking more swollen than I've seen it before. I clench my right hand into a fist and open it, but my ring finger remains at a 90-degree angle—halfway open—and I have to take my left hand and manually move the finger so that it opens all the way. When I do, I hear a little pop, but no pain. I clench my fist again, and it happens again. I should really start icing it at night. I take two painkillers to get through the day.

I GO TO bed that night at 8:30 p.m. I'm exhausted, but it's a familiar exhaustion: I'm accustomed to my head hitting the pillow and my world going immediately black. If nothing else, farmwork is a medication-free solution to insomnia. What's different tonight is that lettuce invades my time of rest as well, no longer content with just dominating my waking hours.

In the first dream I am cutting lettuce as fast as I can, tossing the bags quickly onto the arms of the machine. People are working to my left and right, but their faces are nothing but blurs. The speed of the machine keeps increasing, as does my mental stress. I want to ask someone why the machine is going so fast, but when I look around I find that I'm alone. No matter how fast I cut, the machine stays just out of reach. I feel my entire body overheating, like I'm going to explode, and I come to the sensible conclusion that it's time to stop—this is just a job, after all. But in the dream I'm physically unable to stop, no matter how convinced I am that the pace is unsustainable. When I try to freeze my arms in place, they keep moving, as if I'm the puppet of a sadistic god. For whatever reason, I have to pursue the machine, I have to keep cutting, I have to catch up, I have . . .

That's how I wake up, in a state of frenzy. It takes me a few seconds to shift from dream to reality, and as the basic facts come to the surface, I feel a huge sense of relief. I'm in bed. I'm not working. It's okay to rest. I write up the dream quickly—it's not often that I dream, and I want to remember this one—and fall back asleep.

Only to have another dream, less vivid in its details but with the same frenzied quality: I'm cutting, but not fast enough. I awake from this dream in pain, with my right hand extended against the night table next to my bed. My ring finger is throbbing—I've apparently flicked my arm out, mimicking whatever motion I was making in the dream, and banged it against the drawer. I check the clock. It's 1:30 a.m.

I have two more of these dreams during the night. They also lack the details of the first, but they carry the same sense of dread that I can't keep up with the machine. The initial novelty of a lettuce dream has by now grown frustrating, and after the last two dreams I admonish my brain: Relax! Show some creativity! Take me someplace else, sitting on a beach or soaking in a hot tub. But just as I can't stop my body in the dreams, I can't stop my subconscious from returning me to the fields. The last dream wakes me up at 5:30 in the morning, again in pain: I've extended my left arm and slapped my hand against the wall—the hand with the injured middle finger. I'm mentally exhausted, both my hands are throbbing, and it's time to get up.

And that's when an idea comes to me, nursing my sore finger and staring at the ceiling: *I don't have to go to work today.* I can call in sick. This is obvious but it feels like an earth-shattering revelation. For whatever reason, until this moment, the thought never crossed my mind. I break into a grin, my schedule suddenly rearranging itself in my mind. Instead of sweating and lettuce and Pedro shouting at me, I can sleep late and drink too much coffee and read the paper. I can see a matinee! I get out of bed and go through the orientation packet, which has the number employees should call to report an absence. I leave a message on the machine, telling them my name and crew number, and fall back asleep.

This proves too easy. I finish a novel on Thursday and watch an afternoon movie, and when I wake up Friday, I'm still sore and tired. Most illnesses last at least two days, don't they? Sure they do. I call the number and leave another message, making sure to cough loudly into the receiver. With two quick calls I've created a four-day weekend.

LIKE ANY HUMAN being, after getting what I want I'm still not satisfied. Friday is filled with more reading, a trip to a museum of the old Yuma Territorial Prison, and another movie. But on Saturday I wake up and am immediately hit with a deep sense of loneliness. I've got two more days off and nothing to do; even if I thought of something, I don't know anyone to do it with.

Like many immigrants, I've settled in a new place with few connections. As is the case with many sprawling suburbs, Yuma proves to be a very difficult place to meet people, as folks emerge from their cars for only short periods—usually when walking from a parking lot to the store. If I had relatives in the area, or friends, or even friends of friends, I'd definitely call them. I leave the house, hoping to stumble across someone to hang out with. I visit a bar that's full of marines one night. I try out the local Starbucks, full of high school students. I go see movies, and I'm the only person under sixty-five. My alienation from Yuma feels complete.

On Sunday night, I receive a call from Pedro. He says that we'll be working away from Yuma tomorrow, so that I need to show up at Dole's office at 5:30 a.m. to catch the bus. This news might have caused me to groan before, but I'm eager to get back to work. That's what I'm here for, after all.

CHAPTER 5

Today should be easy. I'm rested, my fingers are opening properly, and I can walk without the soles of my feet hurting. I'm at Dole's office, waiting for the bus to come and the sun to rise, with two strong cups of coffee already in my system. I feel strong, healthy, recuperated—but no matter. It turns out to be the hardest day of my brief career in lettuce.

We're working a field near the town of Tacna, ninety minutes east of Yuma. After my two-day absence, a number of people are surprised to see me again. "I thought the lettuce killed you," Angel says, patting me on the back. "It almost killed me on Friday." It turns out I chose my vacation wisely, as the crew worked well into the evening on the days I missed.

The first notable difference in Tacna is that, for the first time, I'm actually seeing bugs in the field. When I had asked Pedro about the complete absence of insects, he responded by praising the "very good fumigation." I suppose this was true, if by good one meant effective in killing all life except that which is necessary to grow lettuce. But I was glad to finally see little black critters clinging to the heads of lettuce and wandering in the dirt. It was unnerving to be in a field with zero bug life, and for farmworkers the "very good fumigation" can be very dangerous: The EPA estimates that each year between 10,000 to 20,000 farmworkers are diagnosed with pesticide poisoning, while also admitting that the true figure is likely much higher, as many workers never visit physicians.[11]

Along with being buggy, the field in Tacna is wet, so instead of firm dirt I'm sliding around in mud. I can handle this, but there's a new challenge: The lettuce is soaked. Each time I raise a head of lettuce and trim off the leaves, I get a face full of cold water. Within the first hour my hands—the hands I believed were completely recovered—feel weaker than ever. I'm soon placing lettuce on the ground, and starting to wonder what's wrong with me. I've been doing this almost two months, I just had four days off, and I *still* can't keep up? Exhausted but aware that the morning break is still thirty minutes away, I make a drastic decision. After checking to make sure Pedro isn't looking, I forget about trimming or bagging the lettuce. Instead I cut each stem, slice through the head three of four times, drop the remnants between two rows, and nonchalantly crush them with my feet as I move forward. It's quicker and takes much less energy. Julio, working to my right, sees my new trick and dubs me the "lettuce assassin."

During the break I'm a wreck. I make no attempt to socialize, instead finding a patch of dirt to lie in away from the group. By the end of the day—a day filled with Pedro cajoling me and often taking my knife and helping me—I'm not even attempting to do two rows. Luckily, Julio is still to my right, and he doesn't seem to be having any problem handling three rows. There is something seriously wrong with this man. "Don't worry, Gabriel, I'm helping you! Three rows, *no problema!*" In between his manic encouragement, he says he and Norma left the house at 3:00 a.m. "We got up at two! To get ready! It was completely dark outside!"

I feel like I'm going to vomit from exhaustion. It's a very passive, nearly out-of-body experience; I don't feel sick but it seems that every ounce of energy is being sucked from my body, and the logical last step of this process is to release whatever is in my stomach. I keel over a few times but nothing comes out.

"*¡Ya!*" Pedro calls, signaling we're done for the day. If I could muster the energy I'd feel relieved. We track back to the bus and hop in. For a few minutes the crew is lively, but as we near the highway the bus goes quiet. I am sharing a seat with a sleeping Gloria, and I turn around to see that everyone—minus Adriana, who is driving and has a Christian rock CD cranking on the stereo—is unconscious, as if someone flipped the switch on the crew's power. Even Julio is out, collapsed against Norma with his beanie pulled down over his eyes.

When we get to the Dole office, Adriana drops me off at my car and continues on to the border. I get home after 7:00 p.m., having been away fourteen hours. Making dinner, I realize that the day I just survived was exactly what my coworkers have been going through all season. Only now, their workdays are even longer: Today they left their homes at 3:00 a.m. and will return sometime after 8:00 p.m.

The next day, also in Tacna, we work just as long. I feel good the entire day. Even my hands have a much better grip on the knife and the lettuce.

It's counterintuitive, but after talking with several coworkers who have had similar experiences, I come up with a theory. Early in the season—say, after the first week—a farmworker's body is thoroughly broken down. Legs and arms are sore, hands and feet swell up. Eventually, a tolerance for the pain is developed; the sharp aches dull but don't disappear. The weekend is just enough time for the body to recover from the trauma, but not so much that it actually starts to mend. My four-day break was actually too long; my body began to recuperate, and it wanted more time to continue. Instead, it was thrown right back in the mix, and rebelled. But the next day, I'm back to normal. (My belief in this theory will grow stronger once I quit the job and finally under-stand just how much time my body needs to fully recover. It takes two weeks until I feel comfortable shaking someone's hand, and an entire month before the numbness in my right foot disappears.)

We have four visitors today from the government, and they check that we are following the proper food safety procedures. It's a good thing we get a heads-up about their visit two hours before they arrive, or Dole would have been slapped with a number of violations. During every break, for example, we stuff our gloves in the packet of bags hanging from our belts. "You can't do that anymore," Pedro says, explaining that we must now lay our gloves on the machine. He's definitely nervous about the inspection. He checks to make sure everyone is wearing their hairnet (several people aren't), and tells us to make sure to eat our lunch away from the lettuce that hasn't been harvested.

After reminding us about the gloves for a third time, Pedro goes behind the machine to talk with the loaders. As I'm cutting I look over at a coworker who is chomping on a piece of iceberg lettuce as he works. Pieces of the lettuce are falling from his mouth. During breaks, we're not supposed to eat near lettuce that hasn't yet been cut, and we're definitely not supposed to eat *over* the lettuce and dribble remnants on produce that will soon be purchased by customers. "*No debes comer mientras cortas*," I say—

don't eat—quietly enough so that Pedro won't hear. "The government is coming, remember?"

We pass our inspection with flying colors.

AFTER A WEEK of long days away from Yuma, on Monday we're back at a field outside Somerton. As I'm grabbing my knife I let Pedro know that Friday will be my last day. Manuel and Julio overhear, and the people who didn't think I'd last a week are now telling me I need to stick around until the end of the season—in two weeks—if I want to say I've actually cut lettuce. Plus, there's a bonus for people who stay till the end.

The next several days I take out my camera and snap photos, and during a lunch break convince the crew to get together for a group photo. On Tuesday I run into Dalia in the field; I haven't seen her since the first morning when I was waiting at Dole's parking lot. Her crew is working the same field, and she learned from Adriana that I'd be leaving soon. She reaches into her backpack. "Here's the taco I said I'd give you."

Later that day we learn why Roberto, who normally steers the machine and helps load boxes, is absent: His mother has passed away. Several times men from other crews have walked along our line as we worked and asked for money. "My sister died in Salinas and we need to get the body home for the burial," one man said, wearing a tattered straw hat. The wife of another died of cancer. Sometimes a few details are given. Other times there is just the simple statement that someone died and money is needed, for a flight or a funeral or even, in one case, for a headstone. Once our crew hears news about Roberto's mother, we dig into our pockets for pesos and dollars, and someone is selected to solicit funds from nearby crews.

On Wednesday something new happens. Humberto and Alfonso fall behind the machine and are forced to put their lettuce on the ground. For whatever reason, at the moment I'm cutting pretty well. Pedro, of course, makes a note of this, loudly informing the men that I'm winning the race. For a moment I take a certain joy in the experience, but it's fleeting. I've been in their shoes for the last two months, and both men—like everyone in the crew—have helped me cover my rows at various times. I hop a few rows over and cut several heads for both, until they catch up. Of course, by doing so I fall behind, so Manuel helps me catch back up: from each according to his ability, to each according to his need.

On Thursday Manuel is absent—Pedro tells us that his wife gave birth to a healthy baby girl. This is wonderful news. It also means we're short a cutter, and Pedro informs us that we've got a big order today. As the week has progressed and my impending departure nears, I've actually felt waves of nostalgia. During the last two months I've enjoyed getting to know the members of the crew, and I realize that—barring some unforeseen development—I'll never find myself in the fields again.

That sense of nostalgia is easily crushed. It's the hottest day of the year, with temperatures reaching 90 degrees, and by 10:00 a.m. I'm drenched in sweat. For the first time, so is everyone else. We work more than ten hours, with the machine going faster than usual. Diego stirs powdered Gatorade into the water to make sure no one passes out, and I gulp down four painkillers to deal with the swelling in my right foot.

By the time the sun sets we've had our most productive day of the year. Each cutter has harvested about 3,300 heads. Altogether, our crew has cut, bagged, and packed 43,222 heads of lettuce (Pedro lets me look over the day's statistics). Our harvest has filled up more than 1,700 boxes of lettuce, for a combined weight of thirty-two tons. It's dark by the time I walk through my front door. I eat a bowl of cereal, peel off my clothes, and fall asleep without showering.

The next morning I wake up before the alarm clock, buzzing with energy since it's my last day. I arrive at the field early and while parking see Manuel walking to the machine. By the time I've suited up most of the crew has surrounded him, asking questions while he passes out celebratory chocolates. His daughter was born yesterday at 10:30 a.m. with no complications, and he's already back at work, while Maria recuperates at home with friends. During an extended morning huddle, Pedro congratulates Manuel and tells us to give ourselves a round of applause for the previous day's efforts.

The morning passes quickly, and for lunch Adriana has prepared a special meal in honor of my departure. Laid out on the ground in the shade of the bus are plates full of beans and rice, chicken and tuna salads, tostadas, and tortillas. I've been a vegetarian for twenty years, but I eat everything with gusto. People with cell phone cameras snap photos, while others, leaning against the bus, share their initial impressions of me. There's a moment of confusion when Carlos tells me that at one point he believed I was a *silla*—which means "chair" in Spanish.

"No, CIA," he clarifies. "Like some secret agent."

Pedro lets us take a longer than normal lunch, and while we relax in high spirits I'm tempted to tell them about my book. I know they will like the idea of Americans learning about the grueling work of *campesinos*. Since all of them are legally authorized to work, there is no concern that my writing could result in their being deported. But I hesitate; in the end, I suppose I keep my secret because as we're sitting, eating, and reminiscing, I enjoy feeling like a member of the crew.

By the time the sun begins to set, there is still a small section of lettuce to cut. As some begin to pack up the trash, I join a group to finish harvesting. I have two rows to cut, perhaps twenty feet long. As I cut and bag each head of lettuce, I am aware that the experience is coming to an end, and so slow down. The last remaining head of lettuce is to my right, and I don't bend down quite far enough to cut it correctly, so when I lift it up I see that it's not usable. Well, that's that. I hold the lettuce in my left hand, and bring the blade down several times, chopping it to pieces. I dump the remnants of the last lettuce I'll ever kill on the ground, and step on it.

"That's it, Gabriel!" Julio, who evidently has been watching me, yells. "You are finished, finally free from lettuce!"

I turn to him and break into a goofy grin. "I killed my last lettuce!" I call out, and he laughs. Then I raise my right arm and point the knife toward the sky. The moment passes and I feel slightly silly. I put my knife back in its sheath, help break down the machine, and grab my backpack.

I turn around and see that many members of the crew are lined up waiting to say good-bye, and a sense of sadness unexpectedly overcomes me. As we shake hands, many tell me to drive safely back to San Jose, and not to forget about the *lechugeros* in Yuma. They head to the bus. Pedro is standing by the side of the machine, holding a stack of papers, calculating the number of boxes we've completed.

"Pedro, it's been a real pleasure. Thanks for taking me on and teaching me how to cut lettuce."

"No problem, no problem," he replies, extending his hand. "Now you're set for life. If you ever need a job, you know you can always cut lettuce."

I laugh and say that I'll keep that in mind, then turn and walk back to my car, waving good-bye to the bus as it pulls out of the field.

Part Two

SPEAKING QUICHÉ IN THE HEART OF DIXIE

June–August, Russellville, Alabama

GETTING THE JOB

An hour after pulling off the highway and entering Russellville, a 10,000-person town in rural Alabama, I start to think about leaving. I've checked into a motel—I'm the sole occupant—and I am wandering the streets of downtown. I know it's downtown only because a sign tells me so. I walk along the main strip, in what can fairly be called the heart of the city, which resembles a movie set for small-town America, circa 1950. There are furniture stores, bargain shops, and a local insurance company and bank. I can see two church steeples in the distance, along with a classic movie theater, the Roxy, which is shuttered. I stumble upon a coffee shop and try to enter, but the door is locked. A Spanish-language bookstore is next door, also locked. Although it's a Wednesday afternoon, most of the establishments are closed and the few that are open don't appear to have any customers. I spend fifteen minutes exploring downtown on foot without seeing another living creature. It's unbelievably hot. This could be a long summer.

I get back in my car and find a desolate Mexican restaurant on the outskirts of town. The Spanish-speaking waitress doesn't know of anyone with a room for rent, or whether the chicken plant is hiring. I eat my enchiladas, consult the map, pay the bill, and drive to the plant, located several miles outside Russellville's city limits. I'm the only car on a two-lane road, littered with chicken feathers, that winds through fields of corn and grazing cattle. A few ranch houses dot the countryside, but the main sign of human habitation is tumbledown trailer parks.

I already know from online research that the plant, owned by Pilgrim's Pride, can kill and process nearly 1.5 million chickens a week, but I'm still surprised by its size. The white and mostly windowless structure is as long as a city block and about thirty feet tall, with all the charm of a large cement box. On one side of the plant is a large parking lot filled with hundreds of cars, whose windshields shimmer in the heat; on the other, three trucks loaded with crates of live chickens are waiting at a checkpoint. I take the middle entrance and drive up to a security booth. An obese man with pale skin steps out.

"I'm looking for work—is there someone I can speak to?"

"Nope." He walks back into the booth and returns with an application. "Just bring it back to me when you're ready."

"You happen to know if they're hiring?" I ask.

"Nope."

This is not a promising beginning. I was hoping it would be like Dole: Show up and get hired on the spot. My anxiety grows as I look over the application. Pilgrim's Pride wants to know every job I've had in the last ten years, and promises to check my employer references. They also want three personal references, along with the jobs my references currently hold. For the first time, I begin to worry about whether they'll actually hire me. My driver's license is from New York, and Russellville isn't the kind of place that draws a lot of outsiders—except migrants from countries south of the border. If the company is suspicious about potential "salts"—covert union organizers who get a job to organize from within—I'm probably a likely candidate.

About the only thing I have in my defense is my work at Dole, a reference that clearly suggests dire financial straits. Again I put down Artemio, this time identifying him as the owner of a construction firm where I worked for many years.

The process of filling out two work references helps me come up with a cover story, which I hope I won't need. Unless I'm questioned in detail, I plan on keeping it vague: something along the lines of "I'm traveling for awhile," or the less plausible "I've always wanted to visit Alabama." If that's not enough, I'll offer what to me seems like the most believable story from my limited options: I left my construction job in New York over the winter eager to leave the cold behind and see the country. I started in the Southwest, harvesting lettuce in Yuma until I saved enough money to continue. While visiting a friend in Montgomery and low on funds, I learned that there were chicken plants in this part of the state, and figured I could find work and live cheaply. That night I actually practice in front of a mirror, preparing for an interview.

Early the next morning I drop off my application with the guard and head into the city of Decatur, fifty miles east, to check out another poultry plant, this one owned by Wayne Farms. I'm less interested in this plant as I would prefer a completely rural experience, but since I'll be giving up my rental car soon—I have enough funds to cover only a week's use, after which I'll be relying on my bike for transportation—I want to make certain I explore every option.

The Wayne Farms plant is in an industrial area crowded with big rigs. The plant is surrounded by a high fence, and next to the security booth is a large sign that reads: Our Team Has Worked 934,380 Hours Without a Lost Time Accident. This is meant to be a statement of pride and integrity, but to me it raises questions about creative record keeping. Nearly one million hours of repetitive work with sharp knives, and not a single employee has suffered an accident causing them to miss a shift?

Inside the office my luck doesn't improve. "We don't have any jobs right now," a woman in human resources tells me. "But we'll keep your application on file." I walk out the door increasingly convinced this experiment is destined for failure. The only other poultry plant I know of is more than a hundred miles away.

Heading back to my car I pass three African American men seated at a picnic table wearing blue hairnets. "The woman in the office told me the plant is full," I say. "If I come back in a few days, do you think I'll get hired? Do people quit a lot?"

The man sitting nearest to me takes a long drag on his cigarette. "Sheeyiit," he says in a five-second exhalation of smoke. "Two people just quit. They're laying down over there right now." He points across the parking lot. Two men are stretched out on the ground next to an old sedan in the shade provided by a row of trees. "They had the easiest job in the plant, not doing nothing but mopping up the damn floor. They walked out an hour ago, rather be taking a nap enjoying the day." He flicks his cigarette. "You come on back, you'll get yourself a job."

I look again at the two figures. One is lying on his back with his arms and legs spread out, as if frozen in the act of making a snow angel. The other is facedown, with his right cheek pressed hard against the gravel. They don't look like they're taking a nap—they look like someone dropped a bowling ball on their heads. I thank the men and head out.

Not yet ready to stare at the walls of my motel room, I decide to swing by the Russellville plant again. This time, coming from a different direction, I notice a small white building at a quiet intersection not far from the highway. A faded sign reads: Mama's Kitchen Country Cookin. Painted in yellow across the window are various specials, including *huevos rancheros* and *ricos tacos de tripe y lengua* (tasty tripe and tongue tacos). Looks like Mama's been changing up her country cookin'.

I step into a bazaar of Latino products ranging from Mexican soccer jerseys and Lucha Libre masks to Guatemalan flags and international calling cards. As I sit down an attractive woman with fair skin steps out, smiling politely. I explain in Spanish that I'm looking for a place to stay for a few months. She looks at me with undisguised curiosity and takes a seat across the table. For twenty minutes I answer her skeptical questions—What am I doing here? Where did I learn Spanish? Why do I want to work in the plant?—but we finally find common ground when I learn that Sabrina is from the Mexican state of Guerrero, which I've visited.

"Before I opened this restaurant I worked in *la pollera* for two years," she says, referring to the plant. "I don't know why you would want to work there."

"Just for awhile, so I can save some money and practice my Spanish. But right now what I'm looking for is a place to stay."

She begins to say something, pauses, then starts again. "Well, I have a trailer that is empty since my sister moved out. It's close, near the plant. But I don't want to rent it to a single person for only two months."

"How much did she pay?"

"$300 a month."

"If I get the job, how about I pay you $600 up front?" Sabrina considers the proposition. I can see that she is conflicted. On the one hand: Who the hell am I? On the other: I'm familiar with parts of Mexico and she's impressed that I speak Spanish. She eventually concludes that while I may be odd, I also seem harmless, and nods her assent.

I CALL PILGRIM'S PRIDE the next morning, a Friday, and leave a message. Next I check in with Wayne Farms, and am told to call back on Monday. By now it's 11:00 a.m. and I'm sitting in a motel with nothing to do. Bored, I go on the Internet, searching for items related to immigrants and Russellville and find an article about a Ku Klux Klan march that was held in the town in 2006. This links to a white supremacist site called Stormfront.com, and a group called the Council of Conservative Citizens (CCC), which is the reincarnation of the White Citizens' Council, formed in the 1950s to fight desegregation. Not surprisingly, they have added the threat of a "Mexican invasion" to their list of concerns. But I really start paying attention when I read a posting about their annual conference, which is being held *right now* in Sheffield, Alabama, only twenty miles away. Though the CCC doesn't disclose where the meeting will take place— only that it will be in a hotel—I figure I can drive around town and find it without a problem. If nothing else, it'll give me something to do.

It takes me twenty minutes of driving around Sheffield before I come across a large hotel and conference center off the highway with a scrolling electronic sign that reads: Welcome to the Council of Conservative Citizens. I park my car next to a row of large trucks with confederate flag bumper stickers and walk inside, following the posted flyers for the CCC straight past the welcome desk. I'm hoping to project an image of confidence.

Down the corridor burly white men with shaved heads are standing in front of two doors that open into a conference room. They are wearing camouflage pants, with handguns strapped to their belts. Not what I was expecting. I seek refuge in a nearby men's room. While I'm doing my business a man steps up to my left. I can't help but notice the large handgun hanging on his right hip, just inches from my left thigh. I turn and walk right out of the hotel, get in my car, and drive away.

Which is when I start feeling stupid. If there is a day in which I can fairly say I have nothing to do, this is it. What are they going to do, shoot me? (A quiet voice in my head, which I try to suffocate, answers: "Perhaps.") I turn around, drive back to the hotel, and park. Now there are a dozen men standing outside the door, all armed, athletic, and (to my mind) angry. I take a deep breath and ask one of the men—trying hard to keep my voice from cracking—if he's here for the CCC meeting.

"Nah, they're next door. We're the NRA." I let out a deep sigh of relief—the National Rifle Association, how moderate!—and push through the double doors into a room whose occupants are focused on an older speaker behind the podium. A young white man wearing a suit dashes across the room, apparently quite excited about my presence. I play it straight, introducing myself as a journalist who writes about immigrants, and ask if I can sit in.

"Immigrants, of course!" He ushers me to an open seat near the back. There are about seventy-five white people in the audience, a larger turnout than I expected.

The first speaker I hear is an elderly man named Drue Lackey, whose head of soft white hair resembles two cumulus clouds. His lecture is called "Civil Rights in Alabama," which ought to be interesting. Lackey begins with a caveat: "There are some things I can't talk about because the statute of limitations hasn't run out yet." It turns out that Lackey was the police officer who fingerprinted Rosa Parks in Montgomery after her arrest, an iconic image of the civil rights movement. He spent twenty-two years in law enforcement, retiring as the chief of police for Montgomery in 1970, and recently self-published a book on the era. In his first anecdote, Lackey speaks about the firebombing of four churches and the homes of Martin Luther King Jr. and Ralph Abernathy. While investigating one of the incidents, Lackey noticed a car slowly driving by. "This is something that for some reason criminals like to do, to revisit the scene of the crime," he comments. His police instincts turned out to be correct: He pulled the car over and won a confession from the men, who led him to a stash of explosives that they were planning to use in the future.

"We had an all-white jury on that case," he continues. "They deliberated for forty-five minutes, and they returned a 'not guilty' verdict on all counts." The people sitting at my table start to clap. Others join in, some standing, until the room fills with applause. Lackey looks heartened by the response. He explains that one of the reasons he wrote his book was to tell the "other side" of the Montgomery Bus Boycott. In his rendering, "The communist Rosa Parks refused to give up her seat to an elderly, feeble man," and "Martin 'Lootin' King was a traitor to his country." Presumably the only journalist in the room, I take notes nervously, expecting someone to chase me out of this movement-building meeting.

I needn't have worried. Over the two-day conference, I hear a number of wildly racist claims, and no one seems to mind that I'm writing them all down. "We're witnessing the demise of the greatest race in the history of the world," thunders Paul Fromm, who I later learn is Canada's leading white supremacist. A speaker named Joel LeFever argues that the recent "pro-sodomite marriage" ruling in California can be traced back to the disastrous legalization of mixed-race marriages. Roan Garcia Quintana, a Cuban American who is quick to point out that his ancestors are from Spain, laments the "invasion of aliens" from Mexico, who "bring diseases and don't know how to use the toilet."

What's shocking to me, as the day goes on, isn't just that this white power group has granted me entrance even after I've identified myself as a journalist, but that a politician is proudly participating. Alabama state senator Charles Bishop, who represents a district near Russellville, speaks during a buffet luncheon (catered by African American women who are in and out of the room too quickly to glean what the conference is about). Bishop's rant about the critical need to reject "Mohammed" Obama is followed by a presentation that delivers a biblical defense of slavery. As speakers compete to see who can make the most incendiary remarks, I keep waiting for someone to take offense. No one does.

Judging from the presenters, the group's mission has evolved as the demographics of the South have changed, and the influx of Latino immigrants has drawn at least some of the members to the conference. A man from Russellville pulls me aside when he hears where I'm staying. "We've now got more Mexicans than niggers," he spits. The implication is clear enough: There's a new target in town. Nearly everyone I talk to mentions the imaginary *Reconquista* plot whereby immigrating Mexicans are motivated by a desire to recapture the Southwest. "They're not coming to be good little immigrants; they're coming to take over!" thunders Fromm.

The rhetoric about immigrants is offensive, with frequent complaints about "Mexicans bringing leprosy" and an "illegal alien crime wave," but what leaves the biggest impression on me is the still-raging hatred of blacks. No one expresses that hatred more vehemently than Fromm, in a talk entitled "Immigration." A more accurate title would be something like "Let the Blacks Die."

I hang in as long as possible—writing notes, trying to keep my face expressionless, adopting the posture of a passive sponge— but by Saturday afternoon I quietly make my exit. Driving back to Russellville, I feel like the rental car has become my personal time-traveling machine. I step into the car, the year is 2008; I drive twenty miles north and emerge in a year that could be 1950, or 1900, or even 1860 (minus the electric lights and air-conditioning). Liberal Yankee goes south and is taken aback by racist rednecks: I realize this is a trope. And the CCC is very low-hanging fruit: This is a cuckoo group consisting of mainly very old white men who were on the wrong side of history fifty years ago and have been nurturing their sense of victimhood ever since. I also acknowledge that what I've seen does not represent "the South."

But there are two things that stay with me. The first, which reflects very poorly on the political culture of Alabama, is that a state senator addressed the group and spoke highly of their work. It's not everywhere that an elected official feels comfortable speaking to an openly white supremacist organization. The second—and this is due to my own agenda—are the words of the Russellville man: "We've now got more Mexicans than niggers." I wonder how much more of that sort of talk I'll come across.

ON MONDAY AFTERNOON I receive a call from Pilgrim's Pride. A perky woman tells me they have an opening in the debone department. It'd be from 11:00 p.m. to 8:00 a.m. Am I still interested? "Of course!" I tell her, doing my best to contain my excitement so as to not come off as too eager. She's glad to hear that I want the job, and tells me to come by the office the following afternoon.

At Mama's Kitchen I hand over a check and Sabrina writes up a crude lease and gives me the keys to the trailer. I head into town and have the city turn on the electricity and water, then drive to my new home. It sits about a mile south of Mama's Kitchen on Highway 75, which is really just a two-lane street. I pass dozens of trailers and a few houses before the grasslands open into a large field; my trailer is the last one on the right, sitting alone down a long gravel path. One of the windows to a small shed attached to the trailer is broken, and a spare tire rests against the front wall. It looks abandoned.

I push the door open and find a kitchen table with three wooden chairs; a washer and dryer; a flimsy child's desk; a broken refrigerator; and two air conditioners. Small bedrooms, each with a tiny bathroom, are at either end; the space between them is taken up by the living room and kitchen. Every drawer is crawling with spiders, which is okay because I like spiders. I also like the kitchen floor, which consists of a sheet of plastic faux tiles. The rest of the trailer's floor is covered in blue carpet and littered with spider webs, dead insects, and nails. It will take me a few days to sweep all the debris into the trash.

The trailer has two quirky touches. There are ten mirrors in the living room. Every time I walk into the living room from the kitchen, I see ten different versions of myself.

The second oddity is a circular bar that is in one corner of the living room. There are two cabinets below the bar—also claimed by spiders—and the exterior is covered in padded purple vinyl. A bar situated in a county where alcohol hasn't been sold since Prohibition might not be the most practical piece of built-in furniture, but it pleases me nonetheless.

The trailer's major drawback is that it resembles "living in a hot tin can," as one of my neighbors pointedly observes. After taking a quick tour of my new home, every inch of my skin is coated in sweat. I open the windows in the living room, but as they are north and south facing, and the wind seem to be flowing east, it's hard to notice any difference. The trailer's only west-facing window is in the bathroom and a foot wide. Still, despite the small size of the window, the bathroom quickly becomes the coolest area (and the place I go to watch afternoon storms march toward me across the grasslands). But it's not large enough to comfortably hang out in, and there's also a large swatch of black mold climbing up one wall.

To combat the humidity, I try leaving the trailer's two doors open, which leads me to an important discovery: a nearby wasp's nest. The space quickly fills with the large black beasts, so I shut the doors—neither has a screen—and go about smashing them with my shoe. With both doors shut, the trailer soon feels like a parked car sitting in the sun. It doesn't take long to realize that, with wasps as neighbors, I'm going to keep the air conditioners running pretty much all the time. I drive into Russellville and spend $30 on a fan, which, along with the two AC window units, keeps the place livable. As I turn into the driveway with the fan in the backseat, I look across the field and realize that I can clearly see the chicken plant to my left. I've lucked into the perfect location. If I want, I can even walk to work.

PILGRIM'S PRIDE HIRES me the next day. "Your app looks great," a blond-haired woman in human resources tells me, struggling to hide a yawn. "It shows that you are very patient and don't mind doing hard work." I assume the hard work comment relates to my lettuce cutting. I'm not sure how she determines I'm patient, but I'm glad she thinks so. During the thirty-minute interview she never asks me how I ended up in Russellville, even when I hand over my New York driver's license. They need workers, I can work: end of story.

There are three different shifts at the plant. The first shift is from 8:00 a.m. to 5:00 p.m.; second shift, which follows immediately after, is sanitation. "During sanitation we have workers come in and take everything apart and hose it down with bleach and chemicals," she says. After sanitation is the third shift, which begins at 11:00 p.m. and concludes at 8:00 a.m. the next morning. "All we have right now are jobs in the third shift."

She has several positions that she thinks I would enjoy. All of them pay $8.05 an hour, but if I arrive on time every day, I'll earn $8.80 an hour for the week. After sixty days the base rate will increase to $8.80, with the perfect attendance bonus reaching $9.45. If an employee makes it to the year mark, he will earn $8.95 an hour with a bonus of $9.70. The various numbers can make it seem complicated, but the basic truth is this: You could work at the plant for ten years, without missing a minute of a single shift, and never see your wage reach $10 an hour. (The one exception is a job in "live hang and killing," where workers are paid extra because they are in a department that is called *live hang and killing.* Their pay scale maxes out at $10.75 an hour. "We don't have any openings in that," she tells me. Not a problem, I assure her.)

There are jobs available in packing chicken into boxes, loading boxes onto trucks, or adding marinades to chicken in the "further-processing" department. What I want, though, is a line job in debone. Artemio, originally from Mexico, briefly worked in a Georgia poultry plant, and told me that all of the debone workers were immigrants, while the few American citizens were supervisors or performed less strenuous jobs.

"You said something about debone, right?"

"Yes, we have that too. Now, deboning is just what it sounds like. Each person has a place on the line and makes a certain cut. The chicken just sits there, stuck on a cone, passing by like this." She sticks out her tongue and smiles, apparently doing her dead-chicken-on-a-cone impression.

"After cutting lettuce, my back could really use a break, so I'd rather not be loading anything. If it's open, I think I'll go with debone."

"Because your application is so strong, I'm going to offer you the job right now," she says, handing me papers to sign while explaining the attendance policy. Pilgrim's Pride doesn't have sick days or personal days. Instead, employees accumulate points based on days missed: Every time we are absent for an entire shift, we are given one point; if we leave early or arrive late, we earn half a point. A point is erased six months from the date it is issued, and if we accumulate more than seven points we're fired. Seems simple enough.

"You'll be working Sunday through Thursday nights, but you first have to take an orientation class. You should show up Thursday for orientation, and then you'll begin Sunday night. Just one more thing before we're all set. It looks like your Social Security card was issued in Oregon. Can you tell me why you don't have a work history there?"

"We moved when I was in preschool."

She smiles and writes something down. "Sorry, we just have to ask. Homeland Security is really cracking down. They want to know about things like that."

At the nurse's station I pee into a cup and blow into a Breathalyzer. Since I don't do drugs and managed to come to the interview sober, I've cleared the last hurdle. I've got a new job.

CHAPTER 6

Pilgrim's Pride gets its name not from the group that came over on the *Mayflower*, and whose image serves as the company logo, but from its founder and chairman Lonnie "Bo" Pilgrim. During an eight-hour orientation that largely consists of receiving many handouts and then signing papers to acknowledge we received many handouts, that fact is one of the nuggets of data I retain. In fact, our ability to remain awake during the onslaught of papers and extended PowerPoint presentations actually seems to be part of a test. "You won't remember all of what we go over today," promises the African American woman who conducts the training. "But whatever you do, don't fall asleep." That's rule number one at Pilgrim's Pride.

Our trainer tries to project an aura of corporate cheeriness with a series of awkwardly timed smiles, but it's plain to see that she is tired and bored. Although she buries us with an amazing amount of eminently forgettable material—"We are a customer-focused organization committed to continuous improvement"—she's managed to memorize nearly everything. "This one here has one hundred and three slides," she warns us before dimming the lights and rattling off information so quickly it becomes one long word. High turnover makes it a challenge to keep the plant sufficiently staffed, forcing the people in human resources to give four of these orientations every week. A former employee who spent many years at the plant told me that over the course of a single week, 150 new people were hired. That's about one-tenth of the plant's entire workforce. It wasn't quite enough: During the week, 175 people quit.

The nine others in my orientation are mostly recent high school graduates or dropouts, though several people are in their thirties. Orientations are conducted in either Spanish or English; my English-speaking group consists of eight whites and two blacks. We'll all be working the third shift. Several in the group have worked at the plant before, and the black woman seated to my right has another job caring for people with dementia from 2:00 to 10:00 p.m. I've been wondering how I'll adapt to sleeping during the day; I wonder how she'll adapt to not sleeping. "I'll get along fine," she tells me. "You get used to it." She will arrive home from the plant just as her daughter is leaving for school, enjoy her four hours of "down time" until 1:00 p.m., take a shower, and head back out the door.

Christianity plays a big role in the company. A friendly, portly man tells us about the "Pilgrim's Cares" program, which is provided through a group called Marketplace Chaplains USA. "We have white, black, and Hispanic chaplains who can listen to you and pray with you," he says. Now that I'm an employee, I have the option of calling upon any one of the six plant chaplains, who will make hospital visits, plan weddings, even offer premarital counseling. The speaker worked for thirteen years in the live hang and killing department—"People told me I sure do kill a lot for a chaplain," he chuckles—and believes that our arrival at Pilgrim's Pride is sure to prove a blessing. He offers us free Bibles, which several people accept, and passes out a daily devotional. (Today's theme: "To be anxious about nothing, pray about everything.") After he leaves we're handed a brochure about the "Pride Line," which is a confidential number we can call to report any unethical behavior in the workplace. The front of the brochure features a photograph of a white-haired Bo Pilgrim with a Bible in his hands.*

Safety is discussed by a man who I am convinced has his bottom lip stuffed with chewing tobacco. He lays out his vision for the plant: that we "leave with the same number of fingers and toes as when we arrived." I'm new to Russellville but know that not everyone is so lucky: I've already bumped into one woman in town whose son lost part of his foot when it was crushed by plant machinery.

After the safety director leaves, our trainer explains that we will be in pain even if we follow every safety precaution. "You'll be using muscles and nerves and tendons all the time that you normally don't use. Remember, thirty-eight birds are going by every minute on the debone line. It's fast and it's hard and your hands are gonna swell and ache. That's why the nurses say it's best to take ibuprofen every four hours." I'll soon discover that alongside the vending machines selling candy and soda in the break room is an entire section stocked with various brands of painkillers.

We are offered other advice to make the job less painful. One PowerPoint slide argues that in order to prevent repetitive damage,

---

* In 2008, Bo Pilgrim received an award from the American Bible Society for "25 Years of Workplace Evangelism," and he has been called a "crusader for Christ." For Pilgrim, being a titan in the poultry industry isn't just a job—it's his calling. "There's no doubt that God wanted me to exemplify being a Christian businessman," he told one reporter, and his religiosity seeps into many areas that appear quite secular. "I want to thank Jesus Christ for our new Hawker 800 XP airplane," he wrote in the company newsletter after purchasing a second corporate jet for $12 million in 1999. "Another Bible has been added to the new airplane, thanking Jesus," he continued. "We are now operating both airplanes for our company which always praises Jesus."

it is necessary to "organize your daily activities," suggesting that a supervisor will present us with a variety of work options at the beginning of each shift. (They won't: Work at a chicken plant consists of doing one thing over and over again.) Another tip, "Take micro breaks," sounds more helpful, but I never hear anyone mention it on the processing floor, and several attempts to implement the strategy do not go over well with my supervisors.

One notable omission from the orientation curriculum is the topic of animal welfare. This is especially surprising in light of video footage released in 2004 by the People for the Ethical Treatment of Animals (PETA) that was taken inside a Pilgrim's Pride plant in Moorefield, West Virginia. The video shows workers stomping on live chickens and smashing them against the wall. Eyewitness testimony also included accounts of workers "ripping birds' beaks off, spray-painting their faces, twisting their heads off, spitting tobacco into their mouths and eyes and breaking them in half—all while the birds are still alive."

Pilgrim's Pride and one of its major partners, KFC, were hit with a firestorm of negative publicity following the video's release. One op-ed in the *Los Angeles Times*, written by animal rights activists Peter Singer and Karen Dawn, was entitled "Echoes of Abu Ghraib in Chicken Slaughterhouse." They argued that in any environment in which "humans have unchecked power over those they see as inferior, they may abuse it."[1] In fact, there was a very loud echo that the authors didn't yet realize: Lynddie England, the female soldier giving the thumbs-up in many of the Abu Ghraib photos, had worked at the Moorefield plant for seven months. She left, she says, after her complaints to a supervisor about "discolored and diseased-looking" chicken meat getting through were ignored. "People were doing bad things," she said about the plant. "Management didn't care."[2] But while Pilgrim's Pride fired eleven people after the video surfaced and pledged to "re-educate" their employees about animal welfare, I don't recall those words even being spoken during orientation.

The final segment of the orientation deals with the company's belief that "remaining union-free" is a key to making sure workers are "proud to be identified with the company." The trainer turns on the television and slips in a tape. "The union has tried to organize here three times before," she says. "Here is the company's view on that."

We are greeted by an attractive black man with a mustache, while a curious message is pasted across the top half of the screen: Not for Employee Viewing or Training.

"There are some things that we sign that can be very valuable," he begins. "Credit card charges, checks, loan applications—it's your signature that makes them valuable. Here's another example: union authorization cards, or multi-signature petitions." Be careful, the man advises, because "your autograph may mean you just agreed to become"—his voice deepens, forecasting doom—"a *union member.*"

Surprisingly, he praises earlier unions. "Back in the forties, unions weren't short of members—one out of three workers were union. And back then, unions did have good laws passed. Laws that put a stop to child labor, set up a minimum wage, improved workplace safety."

After these achievements, however, "The union's job was done. Over with. Nobody needed them!" The man celebrates, as should we all. Everyone in the room, it bears remembering, has been blessed: We're about to become members of a low-wage poultry plant, where employees make thousands of cuts a day with sharp knives. What could be less relevant than notions like workplace safety and higher wages? We turned that corner after the Depression.

The screen cuts to a series of painfully acted mini-dramas. In one scene, union organizers circle around a reluctant worker and tell her to sign the card because "everyone else is doing it." (Remember how well that argument worked in junior high?) Nearly all of the actors are white, and judging by their attire they apparently spend their days pushing papers around an office. When organizers aren't attempting to crush workers under the weight of peer pressure, the narrator continues, they might "put up notices about union meetings" or even "give out handbills!" We watch as a man stands next to a truck, speaking to a worker through the window. "Hey, brother, you've heard about our union, haven't you?" Cars are honking in the distance; the organizer is keeping honest workers from going home. "Listen, here's my card. Gimme a call sometime and I'll let you know all that the union can do for you."

"Yeah, I'll call you," the worker says, as the drama reaches a fevered pitch. Two young guys seated to my left are flicking a piece of paper back and forth.

The video concludes with more rousing advice from the narrator. "Keep the union out—do it! Don't get hustled into something that could hurt you. So think about it. Give a rip about being treated as an individual, and not a number." I've kept a straight face up until now, but at the "give a rip" line—which company executive wrote this script?—the audio recorder I'm holding under the table captures my giggle.

The video concludes our orientation. Since we're getting paid, I've just completed my first day of work.

I RETURN MY rental car to Huntsville Airport the next day. Unable to find any safe roads for cycling—the highways here don't have consistent shoulders—I'm forced to pay a taxi driver $100 to drop me off at my trailer. The driver is an older black man who's never heard of Russellville; when we pull up to my trailer he says, "Um . . . huh. Must be nice and quiet out here at least, right?"

I wake up early Sunday morning and bike over to Mama's Kitchen for breakfast. Sabrina is in the kitchen, and I call out a greeting and order *huevos a la mexicana*. Since I'm the only customer, she brings out the food and joins me at a table. Pouring salsa over the eggs, I ask how she ended up in Alabama.

"It started with a visit from my aunt," she says. When Sabrina was a young girl, her aunt returned home with an American husband. They were in a brand-new truck, towing a brand-new boat; the truck was full of toys for Sabrina and her eight siblings. "In my mind, the United States became a place where everything was good, where you could have anything you wanted." By comparison, the village of San Tomás offered nothing; it was so insignificant that it didn't even show up on maps.

Sabrina didn't begin school until the age of ten; because she was older, the other students called her a *burra*. Although she laughs now at being called a donkey, it wasn't funny at the time, and she dropped out of third grade at thirteen. Three years later her family moved to Mexico City to live with an uncle, and she started cleaning houses. "Mexico City is beautiful," she says, staring out the window. "That is where I opened my eyes for the first time. It is a place that will either smash you down or that will make you stand up and wake up."

In Mexico City she met her future husband, Cruz, and in 1992 gave birth to her daughter, Malena. Two years later Sabrina and Cruz crossed into the United States, leaving Malena with Sabrina's mother. It was a painful crossing. "The same day I crossed I also nursed Malena," she says, looking near tears. "I felt like I was losing my life, my daughter, but I also felt like I had to do it. During the entire crossing I was sick with a fever and a chest full of milk." At first they lived with a cousin in Washington State and picked apples, and a year later moved to Russellville, where another cousin had found work at the plant.

Sabrina's parents and daughter arrived in Russellville the following year. Cruz was hired at a nearby mobile home factory, and she took a job working nights at the chicken plant, then owned by Gold Kist. She was in the evisceration department, accompanying inspectors from the United States Department of Agriculture (USDA). "It was a good job for the plant," she admits. On the weekends, she began cooking batches of Mexican specialties like *pan dulce*, which she delivered to the homes of coworkers who yearned for familiar food. The two income streams from the plant and the weekend food business eventually netted her enough money to purchase the land where my trailer sits. She quit her job at the plant and began cooking full-time, hoping she could build a restaurant on the land one day.

In 2003, coming back from church, she saw that Mama's Kitchen had a closed sign. A neighbor told her that the owner was sick and hoping to sell. Sabrina toured the restaurant that evening. It seemed perfect. The only problem was money: The owner was selling for $37,000 and wanted a down payment of $5,000. Sabrina stands up and pulls out her empty pockets. "That's how much money I had. But my head was going crazy—I wanted that restaurant!"

On Monday morning she raced over to Franklin Community Bank, where she'd been a member for five years. At first they didn't want to give her a loan. "I almost started crying right there in the office," she says, but she returned later that day and obtained a $2,500 loan. She spent the rest of the day borrowing money from everyone she knew, mostly in $100 increments. By nightfall, she had another $2,500. The next day she paid the owner and signed papers in the courthouse; on Wednesday she was cooking in the kitchen of her new business. She didn't know anything about running a restaurant, but she printed up flyers announcing the change of ownership and spread word among her existing customers.

"Some days I didn't even make a hundred dollars, and lots of people told me that it was going to fail. I even started to doubt myself sometimes. But I never thought I was a loser, because the people that lose are cowards. Why do they lose?" she asks. "Because, Gabriel, they pass their lives lamenting what they might have done. What you *might* do doesn't exist." She brings her right fist down on the table three times, seeming to say *I might have started from nothing, but I will bend the world until it's in a shape I can use.*

The restaurant gamble eventually paid off. Business picked up, she added a small store, and she and Cruz purchased a mobile home equipped for cooking—dubbed Mama's Kitchen II—that he staffed in town. (They have recently separated, and he owns the truck, which he operates at a downtown intersection.) She has an employee to help with the cooking and was able to buy the house across the street.

"Enough about me," she says. "How is work?" I tell her that I survived orientation and start this evening. The look on her face is easy to read: She finds me perplexing. She's living proof that the American dream, if you're lucky and willing to take risks, can be attained. A third-grade dropout from Mexico who refused to be smashed down owns her own restaurant. So why would I be heading backwards, into the plant that she left?

I TRY TO sleep that afternoon but eventually give up after hours of staring at the ceiling. Thirty minutes before my shift is to begin I'm standing at the end of the driveway with my bike and backpack. It seemed a lucky break to find a trailer so near the plant—just a five-minute bike ride away—but I hadn't considered how dark the journey would be. With neither streetlights nor moonlight, I find myself pedaling slowly along the two-lane road, my small headlight pointed at the ground so I can dodge any rocks or roadkill.

All is quiet except for the thwacking of large insects against my chest until I near a bend in the road and hear a growing rumble from behind. I turn my head to stare directly into the headlights of a honking semi truck. I turn back around and veer to my right, tugging on the brakes as my tires hit gravel. I'm able to keep from falling and feel a large whoosh of air slam into me as the big rig careens past. Several seconds later, the truck a good fifty feet away, the smell hits. To say I smelled live chickens and their waste would be accurate, but incomplete. The sensation was more akin, I imagine, to soaking a rug in chicken urine and smearing it with feces, and tightly wrapping that rug around my face. In the future, whenever a chicken truck passes me I'll remember to breathe through my mouth, or not at all.

I make it to the plant without further incident, swipe my photo ID to pass through a revolving gate, and sit in the orientation room with the rest of the new hires. Various supervisors come in and collect their workers, but it seems that the three of us set for debone aren't needed (a fourth from orientation hasn't shown up—the first in what will be a long line of casualties among my orientation class). After thirty minutes of confusion, the nighttime head of human resources, a man named Bill, tells us that we're being transferred to a department called DSI. "No one really wants to go to debone," he says. Middle-aged with a round face and balding head, Bill smiles. "Y'all just got really lucky."

The others don't seem to care one way or another, but I've actually been looking forward to the debone line, primarily because I figured—correctly, as it turns out—that the department would be made up primarily of immigrants.

"If it's possible, I'd still like to do debone," I say. "I just finished a job cutting lettuce, and my back is sore. I was told in the interview that in debone I wouldn't have to lift anything." Bill doesn't seem to be listening, though he finally nods before leaving the room.

When he returns, he repeats that we're being transferred to DSI, and I decide to drop the issue for the moment. "How many of you worked nights before?" Bill asks. None of us. "Nights are great 'cause you can get stuff done during the day." He mentions that the schedule has allowed him to attend minister school in the afternoons. "And of course I have time to go to church on Sundays. It's not for me to say, but I hope all of you go to church." I agree: It's not for him to say. The three other workers are nodding, though, so I stay silent.

During the next twenty minutes of aimless waiting I strike up a conversation with my two new coworkers. Seated next to me is an eighteen-year-old named Ben. He keeps his blond hair military-short and must weigh at least 250 pounds, but Big Ben turns out to be a gentle giant, answering my questions in a soft voice that is barely audible. With a baby face, red cheeks, and small circular-framed glasses, he strikes me as a cross between an overstuffed teddy bear and Harry Potter's giant brother. He lives near Haleyville, about twenty-five miles south of Russellville, and graduated from high school two months ago. He pulls from his wallet a shrunken copy of his diploma, displaying it proudly. "This is gonna be my first job, but my mom worked in debone and so she told me some stuff about it."

"What are the other people from school up to?" I ask.

"I only keep in touch with three people. One guy is here at the plant. Another is at Wal-Mart, and one is at Jack's." Jack's is a fast-food chain that began in Alabama.

Sitting next to Ben is a twenty-three-year-old woman named Diane, who graduated from Russellville High School and is the mother of a two-year-old. She hasn't worked since giving birth and is anxious to earn a paycheck. With cartoonishly large blue eyes, long blond hair, and a waiflike build, she looks more like a southern belle than chicken worker. "The only reason I'm here is because I couldn't find any other job," she explains. "I put in applications all over, but no one is hiring right now. My ma says I won't last two weeks, but I know I can do it."

A new man enters the room, wearing a white overcoat and blue hard hat. He introduces himself as Lonnie, the plant's night manager, and tells us to follow him. We shuffle clumsily through the break room as if across a frozen lake, sliding over a floor made slick with chicken fat. Lockers line the walls, two of which have UNION NO stickers slapped on them. A corridor opens up into a smock room, where we are given a week's supply of white hairnets, a pair of white cotton gloves, earplugs, and rubber overshoes, which provide much better traction. "Okay, let's go," Lonnie says once we're suited up. We follow him dutifully in a single-file formation.

SUPERHERO COMICS AREN'T complete without an evil genius. Often he seeks to construct the ultimate weapon to hold the world hostage; if he's really deranged he simply wants to use it to end human civilization. Since the construction of the weapon must be clandestine, work goes on belowground or behind hidden doors. Walk through the door and an immense world of nameless and undoubtedly evil scientists are at work, tinkering with mysterious equipment while wearing smocks and continuously checking devices.

That's the image that immediately comes to mind when I push through the double doors that separate the break room from the plant floor. This isn't a workplace: This is an underground lair. In the first room, workers scurry around in plastic blue smocks akin to a surgeon's, carrying buckets of chicken pieces. Others lean over a long conveyor belt that moves a continuous stream of meat, their feet planted as they arrange the pieces in a line. We weave our way around large metal machinery and step through a frothy puddle of foam that spews from a thick hose on the cement floor. The smell is a mixture of strong industrial cleaner and fresh meat. To my left is a chest-high cylinder filled to the brim with chicken bits; while it captures my attention, I step on what feels like a sponge and lift my foot to find a piece of pink meat, now flattened. Up ahead, I can see from the puffs of condensation coming from his mouth that Lonnie is saying something to our group—the temperature is frigid, probably in the low forties—but I can't hear anything. I remove my earplugs and am greeted by the roar of machinery. It's not a piercing noise, more of a loud, all-encompassing rumble: Think of the sound you hear when putting your ear to a seashell and multiply by a hundred. I put my earplugs back in.

We walk beneath a doorway and the full scale of the processing floor is revealed. I see no walls in front of me, just open space filled with workers standing in various areas without moving their feet. Hundreds of dead and featherless chickens are hanging upside down from stainless steel hooks, moving rapidly across my field of vision. I hear a beeping sound and step aside for a man driving a scooter-like contraption, which is carrying a container of steaming chicken meat (the contraption turns out to be a pallet truck, and the steam is actually from dry ice). As we cross the plant floor we pass beneath a line of chickens, whirling along more steel hooks; liquid falls from their carcasses and lands with chilly plops on my scalp. Hopefully water. In front of us dozens of workers are slicing up chickens—the debone department—but we proceed further, until we're standing aside a blond-haired woman in her forties who, like Lonnie, is wearing a hard hat.

"This is your supervisor, Barbara," Lonnie tells us, "but she won't be needing you tonight." He tells Ben and Diane to follow him and motions for me to stay put. When he returns he leads me through another doorway. "You're going to work in a different department today, but check in with DSI tomorrow," he says. Lonnie deposits me at the end of a line where boxes are being stacked.

The nearest person is a skinny white man with the hood of his Alabama football sweatshirt pulled tight over his head. I stay quiet, feeling slightly intimidated by my new coworker, who has deep lines cutting across his gaunt face and is missing a few front teeth. But when he turns to me he flashes a friendly smile. "How long you been here?" he asks.

"About five minutes."

He lets loose a squeaking chuckle, his shoulders bouncing up and down. "I've only been here two weeks." Kyle, it turns out, is my neighbor. He lives in a trailer with his wife and two kids about half a mile from where I'm staying. "Been right at that trailer for eighteen years, on land that was my granddaddy's. I worked in the plant four years, then quit. Now I'm back . . . don't know exactly why."*

Kyle normally works in DSI, but he says that today they're short people in the IQF department, another mysterious trio of initials. In IQF, bags of chicken wings are stuffed into boxes, taped, and shoved down on rollers to us. Our task is to stack the forty-pound

---

* A note here on accents. Kyle, like many native Alabamans at the plant, speaks in a very heavy and melodic drawl. It was beautiful to hear, but that beauty soon becomes distracting when I attempt to render it accurately on the page. For example, when he told me had been at the trailer for eighteen years, it sounded to my ears like: "Been rahht at tha-yat trawla' for eightee-yin years." For the sake of readability, I will not try to capture every nuance of the local dialect. One final point to illustrate the strength of the country accent: It took me a week of hanging out with Kyle before I finally realized that his name wasn't, in fact, Kyle. It was Gil. Later, when I listened repeatedly to a message he left on my cell phone, I realized that it wasn't Gil, but another name entirely. Here, he will remain Kyle.

boxes onto pallets. Once a pallet is stacked with forty-nine boxes—seven boxes to a row, seven rows high—a pallet driver whisks it away and we start loading up another. This is almost identical to the stacking of lettuce boxes completed by loaders on the machine, except that the pace here is much slower. I help Kyle do this for twenty minutes, until the machine at the front of the line breaks. A black woman with short blond hair, who has been taping the boxes shut, lets out a good-natured curse. It takes several minutes for a group of men to fix the machine; several minutes later it breaks down again. Over the coming month, I'll occasionally be asked to help out in IQF, and during almost every shift the machine breaks down—hourly. For this reason alone, it's considered a good place to work (as one of the "good" jobs, it also doesn't have a single immigrant working in the department).

With nothing to do, Kyle and I take a seat on the rollers. "You ever work in debone?" I ask him.

"Way back when I started, they tried to get me on there. Stayed a month. They told me I couldn't work fast enough so they shifted me out. I made sure I wasn't working fast enough too. Run you like slaves over there. I already knew how they did, though, 'cause my old lady was on the debone line for years." Now, he tells me, she's working at Wal-Mart.

"It looked like they mostly got Mexicans working in debone," I say.

"That's good, that's where they should be. Most of them are illegal anyways. Didn't have no Mexicans around before the plant opened. Now, I look out my front window I could throw a rock in any direction and hit one of them."

The machine is finally fixed and we return to stacking boxes. After thirty minutes the black woman who was cursing the contraption asks me to come up and tape boxes. I'm happy for the change in scenery, but this task soon becomes tedious. My job is to shake the box so that the bags lie flat, then pull the two top flaps together and shove it through a machine that tapes it shut. Cutting lettuce confirmed in my mind that much of what we call "low-skilled labor" is in fact quite difficult. But at the chicken plant, I'm already learning, many of the jobs are designed so that a person off the street, with minimal instruction, can do them correctly the very first time. I'm sure this is considered a "breakthrough" by the managerial class, but all it does is leave me bored within fifteen minutes.

SOMETIME AFTER 2:00 a.m., I'm told to take a break. I hang up my gloves and white smock on a hook and walk away from IQF. A minute later I've pushed through one swinging door and walked beneath two other doorways, and I'm watching an endless line of carved-up carcasses fall into a large container. I have no idea where I am. To my left, dozens of immigrant men and women are cutting up chickens with knives and scissors. I approach one woman, who can't be much taller than four feet, and ask her in Spanish if she can tell me how to get to the break room. She looks at me and shakes her head.

"She doesn't speak Spanish," another woman says, in Spanish. "You go straight down that row and make a left." I hear the two speak in what sounds like an Indian dialect, thank them both, and follow her directions.

The break room is mostly empty, but I notice Ben sitting alone in a corner booth. We're both struck by how disorganized everything seems to be. Like me, Ben has been hired for one department (debone), transferred to another (DSI), and then relocated once more, with unclear instructions along the way. He doesn't even know the name of the department that he's in. "Whatever it is, they have me standing and watching chickens go by."

"That's it?" I ask. "Are you supposed to *do* anything?"

"Uh, I think like maybe they said to look for mold."

"Mold? The chickens have mold?"

"Not yet anyway. I haven't seen any. I'm looking for green stuff."

"And if they have mold, what do you do?"

"I dunno." Ben pushes his sliding glasses up, beginning to look concerned. "I hope that's what I heard. I'm pretty sure somebody said something about mold." He looks at his watch and stands up. "I gotta go."

By now there are perhaps fifty people sitting in nearby booths, with about an equal number of whites, blacks, and Latinos, who are mostly gathered in self-segregated groups. One wall is plastered with what are meant to be inspiring corporate messages in Spanish and English, illustrated with geometric shapes and arrows. The "Cornerstones of Continuous Improvement" are written at each point of a large triangle: "Quality, Process Improvement, Teamwork." Next to this diagram is a more detailed "14 Points of Continuous Improvement," which include quizzical tips like "Drive Out Fear." Workers pass these grand pronouncements without pause, but they take note of a yellow flyer taped to the wall that reads "Taco Soup Wednesday Night."

I'm joined a few minutes later by a white man in a flannel coat who tells me that he's been on the debone line for five months. He snorts when I tell him that I'm impressed he's lasted so long.

"It's work release," he says. "The only reason I'm here is 'cause they locked my ass up." I don't ask what landed him in prison, but he does reveal that after the death of his father, he went on a number of epic alcohol binges. "Can't do that anymore 'cause I'm locked up and got myself a bleeding ulcer. But I'll tell you one thing," he says before I depart, "once I'm free you ain't never gonna see me step foot inside a chicken plant again."

I use the bathroom and manage to find my way back to Kyle and the boxes. He is seated on the rollers, hood pulled even lower on his head to ward off the cold, while a mechanic tries to get the machine back up and working.

LATE IN THE shift, a stocky nineteen-year-old with Popeye forearms joins IQF to cover for Kyle while he takes his break. Though I haven't asked, Popeye relates his recent history to me as we alternate the stacking of boxes. He's been on parole since he was fifteen, for breaking and entering a mobile home. Since then he's spent much of his free time smoking crack and snorting crystal meth. He has a son, which he admits is unfortunate for the son. He hit a cop once—never a good idea—and was promptly arrested. He was found to be carrying a pistol and three ounces of cocaine.

"I'm never going to have drugs or a piece on me if I'm going to be fucking up a cop." I nod as I grab another box of chicken. That seems a wise course to follow.

"So what the fuck are you doing this bullshit work for?" he asks. I tell him I'm traveling and need money to keep going. "Hey, I'm getting myself a good job making fifteen bucks an hour building churches. I'm not staying doing this shit. You should come with me, since you like to travel." I nod again, my eyes focused elsewhere. "They say that we'll be going to Tennessee and Maryland. Maybe some other places after that, if it turns out to be the shit. They even pay for us to stay in motels." He stacks a box and stands up straight, turning around to face me.

"You want to go? I can tell this guy I know, and we can be partners."

I stay quiet, wondering how I got myself into this mess.

"It's like, why *wouldn't* you want to go?" His voice has become serious, and there's a hint of potential aggression.

"Fuck," I say. I know I don't make an impressive tough guy, so when forced to pretend my only real hope is to curse. "Sounds like a good idea. Only thing is that I just paid two months' rent here. But otherwise, I'd be on it in a fucking second." There, that seemed okay.

He seems to accept it. "Fair enough—I get you." We finish up the shift without further discussion. He lasts a few more days at the plant; my last interaction with him is in the break room before the start of a shift. He tells me that he's getting ready to hit the road, and I gently say again that I'm going to stay. I put down the Elmore Leonard mystery I've been reading and wish him good luck.

"What the fuck?!" he yells. I'm not sure how to respond.

"What the fuck, what?"

"What the fuck are you reading a book for, Yankee?"

FOR REASONS THAT aren't explained, IQF is released earlier than other departments. As I walk toward the break room at 7:40 a.m., I meet a stream of men and women heading in the other direction, getting ready to begin the day shift. I swipe my ID card to sign out, am hit by the bright sunshine of another scorching day, hop on my bike, and pedal home. Kyle has agreed to pick me up tonight, so I don't have to worry about getting run over by a chicken truck. Back in my trailer I eat a quick breakfast of cereal and a peanut butter and jelly sandwich, type up my notes, and lay down. The sun is streaming through the window, my trailer shakes each time a truck loaded with live chickens passes, and my neighbor's roosters are engaged with a dog in some sort of noise competition. I can't be bothered; I fall asleep instantly.

CHAPTER 7

In 1989, the announcement that a poultry plant would be coming to town was cause for celebration. Russellville and its surrounding communities were desperate for jobs, with the county's unemployment rate holding steady at about 10 percent. Dozens of jubilant stories were filed in the *Franklin County Times*, the local newspaper. Six hundred processing jobs would need to be filled; 300 chicken farmers would be contracted to raise birds; an estimated $40 million would be infused into the economy. "This just may be the shot in the arm our economy has been needing," noted one reporter. A member of the economic development board that helped attract Gold Kist described poultry plant work as "the finest type industry," before adding that many employees would earn $4.35 an hour. Two months later, speaking at the plant's groundbreaking ceremony, Governor Gay Hunt heralded it as a watershed moment for economic development. "Alabama has become a pro-business and pro-jobs state. When we have people working together like you have here, our children won't have to leave the state to find jobs."

Russellville had been in competition with other poor towns, and in order to attract "the finest type industry," taxpayers had to sweeten the pot. The local water, gas, and electric boards made sizable contributions toward the $100,000 used to subsidize the purchase of the land for Gold Kist, and the water board invested another $200,000 in piping to supply the facility. State funds, too, were committed: More than half a million dollars were allocated to upgrade roads leading to the plant and hatchery.[3] Such is the model for much of the economic development that occurs in the American South: Poor regions make large concessions to corporations and are rewarded with minimum-wage jobs in return.[4]

In the late 1990s, with the poultry industry booming, Gold Kist expanded the plant and added another 750 workers. But when VF Jeanswear, maker of Lee Jeans, announced in 2001 that it was shuttering three local plants—resulting in a loss of 1,300 jobs—it became clear that the story of economic development in Franklin County was less about adding jobs than replacing them. Workers at Lee were unionized, earned wages that averaged between $10 and $11 an hour, and had free medical insurance: It was an occupation on which one could build a stable life. Indeed, the loyalty of Lee's workforce put any poultry plant to shame. Nearly a third of the workers at Lee's Russellville plant, which opened in 1972, had been with the company for more than a decade; one in five had been there at least twenty years. "This is a dark day in Franklin Country," remarked a representative of the chamber of commerce. "I can't remember anything this bad happening to us as a community. There are not that many jobs in Franklin County to replace these jobs."[5]

I arrived in town eighteen years after the surge of optimism that followed the opening of the poultry plant. The county's unemployment rate still stood at over 8 percent, and the dream of high-quality jobs had vanished: Poultry processing was soon discovered to be punishing work for poverty wages. Claims of a new day dawning no longer held water, as parents who had stepped foot inside the plant certainly didn't hope their children would one day join them. But while the early hype had died quickly, the plant jobs were still "better than nothing," as one local told me.

As the most important industry in an impoverished region, the chicken company wielded significant power; this was most evident in the positive press it received. Over the years, the *Franklin County Times* ran upbeat articles that profiled the chicken industry, interviewed a few satisfied chicken farmers (obviously hand-picked by the company), and included feel-good statements by plant managers. Most of the articles looked like little more than company press releases. Searching through the paper's archives, I wasn't able to find many attempts to tell the story from the bottom up, through the voices of ordinary workers. On the drive over to the plant on my second night of work, Kyle offers up his perspective on poultry work.

"It's a fucking struggle every night just to get my ass in," he says, the glowing lights of the plant illuminating the cloudy sky. "And when I worked here before, it was the same thing: four years of forcing myself to come in. I don't know how I lasted that long. I was always one point away from getting fired."

"Why'd you quit?" I ask. (After a few more days of work I realize this is the sort of question a poultry plant worker never needs to ask.)

"I just got to a point one night when I couldn't take it. How long can you do work that a trained monkey could do? I didn't even tell my supervisor I was going to the bathroom or nothing. I was stacking boxes: I put a box down and walked out of the plant, right on home in the dark. Had to bang on the door 'cause

Cindy was asleep and I didn't have keys. But she was real cool about it. She said, 'We'll make it through. I don't know how, but we'll make it.'"

During the two-year stretch away from the plant, he collected unemployment and twice worked at Wal-Mart, earning minimum wage. (He is not alone: Many people—like his wife—bounce back and forth between the town's two dead-end jobs.) Though he found Wal-Mart less depressing than the plant, he soon soured on that experience as well. About the mega-retailer he says, "I don't care if they call us 'associates,' they still treat their people like shit. They never gave me enough hours or any regular schedule." So now he was back working with chicken—"for how long, I couldn't tell you." He opens the car door; we are parked in the lot, watching two dozen inmates on work release step out of a de-partment of corrections bus and head into the plant. "Alright, I s'pose we should be heading in. Don't want to, but got to."

TONIGHT I'M AGAIN transferred out of DSI. Barbara tells me that I'll be "making combos," which explains nothing. I follow her to a large room out of sight of DSI and am introduced to a black man who tells me his name is Squirrel. He shows me a com-pleted combo, which turns out to be a chest-high octagonal box made of stiff cardboard that is open at the top—the perfect size for a child to construct a makeshift fort. Here, I learn, they are used for a much less fun purpose: Placed at the end of various lines throughout the plant, they collect everything from chicken nuggets and breasts to skeletal remains.

Combos arrive flat, so the first task is to open the box and seal the bottom by pressing and locking the flaps together. Once this is complete, I take the combo and place it upside down on the ce-ment floor and grab a wooden pallet and toss it on top. Dizziness becomes a factor at this point, because the pallet needs to be connected to the box through the use of enough plastic wrap to immobilize a giant elephant. I walk around the combo in a tight circle a dozen times, holding the tube of wrap in my hands and winding it around the combo, then the pallet, and around the combo again. It's not a particularly hard job, but it does induce vertigo. Each time I complete a combo I need a few seconds to regain my balance before starting another. For the first few hours, as soon as I finish a combo, there is someone who drags it away, so I have no time to rest.

After a few hours of making combos as quickly as dizziness allows, demand slows. I take a seat on a cardboard box and lean back against the cement wall. Sweat has soaked through my T-shirt and is beginning to saturate the cloak that Squirrel has given me to wear. The temperature in the room is much warmer than at IQF, and walking in circles seems to be burning off a decent amount of calories.

For the first time I'm able to take in my surroundings. To my right is the re-hang area. It is called re-hang because it is the second time the birds are hung up: The first is in "live hang," where workers grab live chickens that have been delivered by truck and hang them upside down on metal hooks. Once attached, the heads of the live birds pass through a tank of electrified water, rendering them immobile. They are then beheaded by a mechanical blade and submerged in boiling water to remove their feathers.

When the process works correctly, the chicken becomes unconscious upon hitting the electrified water and is killed by the blades. But, as anyone who has worked in a chicken plant knows, the scale and pace of the operation means that the system rarely operates perfectly. When the water isn't sufficiently charged, the birds remain conscious for the beheading phase. When the mechanical blades miss the chickens' necks, a group of workers known as "kill room attendants" or "backup killers" are on hand to manually slit the birds' throats. Still, each year millions of birds somehow survive the bath and various blades and are boiled alive.[6]

Now dead and de-feathered, the chickens enter the evisceration phase. One way to envision what happens in evisceration (or "Evis," as it is called at the plant) is to read through the job titles, which range from neck breaker and oil sack cutter to giblet harvester and lung vacuumer. Workers stand one next to the other as the birds fly past, each doing their part until, by the end of the line, the result is a disemboweled carcass that moves on to re-hang.

Evisceration is out of my line of sight, but I have a clear view of re-hang, and it looks like a particularly unpleasant job. At present there are twelve men in re-hang, all Latinos except for one African American. (Although the plant workforce is diverse, with roughly an equal number of whites, blacks, and Latinos, it's becoming clear that immigrants dominate the most arduous jobs.) The men stand shoulder to shoulder on an elevated platform in a U-shaped design, facing a waist-high metal moat that is overflowing with featherless chickens. The chickens look like what you'd find in a butcher shop, except for the presence of long spinal cords, which give them a particularly macabre look. The workers stick their hands into the pile of moist chickens, grabbing carcasses by the legs, and slide what I guess are the chicken's ankles through metal hangers that pass quickly at forehead level. After one bird is hung, they immediately stick their hands in the pile of chicken for another; in re-hang there is no time for breaks.

Squirrel has been at the plant for many years and previously worked in re-hang. He's glad to be out. "You have to hang twenty-eight birds a minute," he says, joining me on a nearby cardboard box. "They will stand by you with a stopwatch to make sure. When you first start, it tires out your shoulders, until you get used to it." Indeed, at the moment there is a supervisor's assistant—identifiable by his blue hairnet—walking back and forth in front of the workers, pausing occasionally to assess an individual's output.*

When I tire of watching re-hang, my attention turns to an area that Squirrel tells me is called leg quarters, located in the same rectangular room where we assemble combos. Here the bottom half of a chicken, still hanging from hooks ten feet in the air, is sliced down the middle by a circular saw. Once cut, the legs fall into a funnel-like contraption. Boxes travel along a conveyor belt below the funnel, and every few minutes, the funnel opens and shoots out the legs in a movement that resembles violent defecation. Most of the plant's chicken is sold in the United States, but the dark meat of leg quarters is shipped to Russia and China. (China is also the market for the plant's "Paw" department—chicken feet—a cuisine that hasn't yet developed a following in the States.)

Once the funnel shoots out a load of legs, the full box is weighed, taped, labeled, and stacked on pallets to be loaded onto trucks. My attention turns to a man standing directly in front of me, about twenty feet away. He is white, probably in his fifties, and wearing a flannel coat, tattered work boots, and large red headphones to keep out the noise.

His role is to place lids on the boxes that pass by. There is simply no way to describe his task in a manner that is interesting. He grabs lids that are on a platform running at eye level and puts them on the boxes that pass by at waist level. He does this over and over again, without shifting his gaze. Other people on the line are out of earshot, so he has no one to talk to. As the lull in demand for combos continues, I remain seated on my cardboard box and enter a sort of twilight zone, transfixed by the man's repetitive

---

* The hairnets (*mayas* in Spanish) are color-coded: white for regular workers, red for cleanup workers, and blue for assistant supervisors. Supervisors wear blue hard hats.

motions. Grab a lid, put it on. Grab a lid, put it on. How long do I watch him? I have no idea. Long enough to see him put on hundreds of lids, without pausing or even shuffling his feet. Leaning forward so my elbows rest on my knees, I start dipping my head with each lid. The spell is finally broken when a woman comes to pick up three combos, and I rise to replenish my stock.

I'VE DONE A number of less-than-glamorous jobs in my life, from delivering pizzas and filing papers to selling electronics at K-Mart and installing drywall. Still, none of those low-wage jobs are adequate preparation for what I've just witnessed. For people who have never worked at a fast-paced, low-skilled factory job, it is difficult to communicate through words the weight of the endeavor. The usual adjectives—*monotonous* or *boring* or *endless*—point in the general direction, but are much too mild.

Paradoxically it's the mindlessness of the jobs that can make them so difficult. Think of a task you can complete with minimal concentration. As I later reflected on the man placing lids on boxes, the task that came to mind involved a giant arithmetic workbook. Imagine that your job is to complete the workbook, which is full of simple addition problems like $8 + 6 =$ ___ or $3 + 9 =$ ___. Perhaps there are fifty such problems on each page and 500 pages in the workbook. The first few minutes might be fun—it feels good to be able to breeze through the pages—but the problems quickly start to repeat. There is muted satisfaction in finishing the first workbook, but it is short-lived: Another takes its place. In no time the game has grown old, you're tired and bored, and you never want to be asked the sum of $2 + 3$ again.

Which is too bad, because if you're stuck in a place like Russellville, you just might spend the next twenty years of your life in a job whose primary task is as meaningful and challenging as noting that $2 + 3 = 5$. I'm not arguing that people in the plant would prefer work that is physically or mentally taxing. But we all like to learn new things, find some purpose in what we do, and be at least occasionally challenged. This is an elementary observation, but it's easy to forget how many people never get that chance. Early on, Kyle asked me what my father did for a living. I told him that he runs his own nonprofit organization working to improve youth sports. "You know, that sounds interesting," Kyle said. "Does he like it?"

"He loves it."

Kyle got a dreamlike look, as if I was describing something exotic, like the contours of the planet Mars. "Huh. I always wondered what that would be like, you know, to enjoy what you do. Never did like what I was doing. Don't know nobody else who does, neither."

I GET MY first taste of true line-work monotony the following evening, when I'm told to stay in DSI. Since DSI deals directly with fresh chicken meat—unlike IQF or the combo department—for the first time I put on the standard plant uniform: a cheap blue plastic smock no thicker than a single piece of paper, a pair of cotton gloves under a pair of plastic ones, and a white hairnet.

At this point DSI remains a mystery. I don't know what the acronym stands for, or what it does. I do see two lines running parallel to each other, with workers standing on either side. Since keeping workers totally in the dark seems to be part of the business model at Pilgrim's Pride, I'm not surprised when Barbara tells me to follow her without explanation. We leave the twenty or so other DSI workers and walk up a low platform, where another short belt runs at waist level. I'm now standing above the workers.

"You————————before?" Barbara asks. There are words in between that I can't hear. I pull out my earplugs and the noise of the plant rushes in.

"What's that?" I shout.

"I said, you ever tear chicken breasts?" She's now shouting too.

"Not really."

"Okay, good. Stay here and when the breasts come by, tear them in half."

Tear them in half? With my hands? I turn around in time to see her walking away and I put my plugs back in. This should be interesting.

I stand at the perch for several minutes, waiting nervously for chicken breasts. From this angle I have a view of a large section of the plant floor, looking out on both DSI and debone, but it's just too complex to make sense of. I realize that while workers are slaving away on the ground, an intricate system of machinery is constantly churning above us. I am reminded of those plastic marble sets of childhood, in which you placed a marble and then followed its progress along a circuitous path until it eventually landed at the bottom. Wherever I look I see chicken meat flying off belts, spinning around gears, dropping from one moving plane to another.

"What's going on, Gabriel?" Kyle ambles up the steps, wearing his hooded Alabama sweatshirt. "Looks like we're fixin' to be partners."

"You know what we're doing here?"

"Chicken breasts. You tear them in half, they come to me, and I put them in boxes."

Just as Kyle takes a position to my right, the first few chicken breasts begin dropping from a belt ten feet in the air. They land on another belt with a plop and travel directly past my station.

The breasts are pink, slippery, heart-shaped, and much larger than I expected.* A line of sinew connects the two halves of each

---

* Industrial chickens, I later learn, are selectively bred to develop outsized breasts. This artificial tinkering is profitable for companies like Pilgrim's Pride; less so for the chickens. Along with suffering from broken

breast, which is what Kyle says I must tear through. Some rip easily, needing no more strength that what is required to tear through
a thin stack of papers. Others are stubborn and take a second effort to separate; for these I dig my fingers and thumbs deep into
the flesh and yank hard. Some, in fact, are connected so strongly
by the sinew that I actually tear right through the breast muscle.
Tonight the whole breasts don't give off much of a smell, but each
time I tear through the dense muscle, a nauseating whiff of meat
is released.

For a few minutes my vegetarian self is aware that this task is
pretty gross. A number of the breasts are coated in coagulated
purple blood. Others have a film covering the muscle that makes
the meat hard to hold, and a few go squirting out of my hands
onto the cement floor. Gobs of fat cling to the breasts; the fat is
whitish and could easily be confused with scrambled eggs. When
I tear the breasts, pieces of fat come flying at me, and within minutes they cover my blue smock. Other pieces are sent sailing at my
face, landing on my cheeks and forehead.

As disgusting as this task is, it doesn't take very long for a routine to set in. Within an hour I've torn up the breasts of nearly a
thousand birds that were recently slaughtered, but I'm no longer
even thinking about chicken. I'm bored, my wrists are beginning
to hurt, and my thumbs are locking up.

"This sucks," I shout over to Kyle.

He grins. "Welcome to Pilgrim's Pride!"

---

legs that are unable to support their top-heavy physiques, many chickens
have lungs and hearts that can't keep pace with the growth of their
breasts, and the birds succumb to heart failure. It sounds like a freakish
event—chickens felled by heart attacks?—but every year millions of birds
perish precisely this way before reaching slaughter weight. Heart attacks
have become so prevalent that the industry has even created a euphemistic
name for the phenomenon: flip-over syndrome. This syndrome is virtually
unknown among non-factory-farmed chickens.

Breasts have been dropping from above one at a time. Now, entire groups are tumbling down. Whole breasts start getting past me, so I use my right arm as a wall to drag back the intact breasts before they get to Kyle. Of course, the time I spend dragging them back is time I'm not tearing them, and it's not long before I've got a massive collection of breasts in front of me that I am, essentially, hugging. A few tumble off the line and land at my feet. I kick them to the ground.

As I'm wondering what to do, a woman walks by wearing the blue hairnet of an assistant supervisor. "Hey, we could use some more help!" I shout to her. She turns to me.

"What?"

"We could use some help! I can't keep up!" She gives a faint nod and keeps on walking.

"Just let some go," Kyle says. "Fuck it if we can't get them all." That sounds like a good idea. I remove the barricade my arm has created. Kyle lets hundreds of whole breasts glide past him and into the boxes, which will be delivered to customers whole instead of divided. We fill up a number of boxes before the pace slows and I'm able to regain my rhythm. I glance around furtively, waiting for an outraged supervisor. But no one is watching. Hanging from the break room wall is a framed document reminding us of the three cornerstones of continual improvement: quality, process improvement, and teamwork. Out here in the real world of the processing floor, Kyle and I have just demonstrated teamwork in order to reach a process improvement that has completely undermined quality. When you're working in a plant that can slaughter and process more than 250,000 chickens a day, quality just doesn't stand a chance.

We work until 1:45 a.m. Due to the din of the machinery, Barbara communicates that it is break time by holding both hands in front of her chest and miming the breaking of a stick. Kyle and I discard our smocks, which are torn and covered in chicken muck, and toss them in the trash. As a result of my mind roaming over the last hour, I've come to the conclusion that the breasts resemble nothing so much as the rear ends of newborn babies. This is my insight for the day. Later in the shift I am moved to a different part of the line, doing the same work next to a black woman who has been at the plant for four months. As we tear breasts I share this observation. Her response: "You have something wrong in your head." After a few minutes of silently tearing breasts, she comes around. "It does, kinda. The butt of a white baby."

I SPEND THE following week tearing breasts. I figure a conservative estimate has me going through a breast every four seconds, or 7,200 breasts a shift. I arrive home each morning with throbbing hands, sleep fitfully throughout the day (I never manage to sleep more than five hours at a time), eat some food, take my ibuprofen, and wait for Kyle to pick me up to start all over again. I begin taking notes by hand, as typing on the computer hurts. My right ring finger, still not completely recovered from Yuma, is popping again when I bend it. I occasionally think about going outside for a walk or bike ride, but when I open the door I am reminded that I'm in Alabama and it's summertime. There are a number of trailers nearby—home to either Mexican or Guatemalan immigrants—but when I stop by to socialize, nobody is home; they are working the day shift. So I lie back down or read a book. Without TV, radio, or the Internet, it makes for a strange existence: My world has shrunk to the inside of my trailer and the confines of the plant.

Inside the plant I am finally beginning to understand how DSI functions. The department consists of two parallel conveyor belts, with workers assigned specific tasks to complete at various points along the belts. Pushed up against the head of each belt is a large metal bin that stands on four posts, not unlike a deep sink. To begin the action, a worker dumps a plastic tub of chicken breasts into the bin, another worker stands at the bin tearing the breasts in half, while a third places the separated breasts onto the belt.

From here the breasts pass through a machine that cuts a section off the top with a high-powered stream of water (I never quite understood why this is done; I suppose it makes the breast meat flatter and therefore more easily positioned between two buns). A worker stands directly behind this machine, grabbing the separated top and tossing it into a nearby bin, while the rest of the breast drops onto a much wider belt. Four women line up the center of the breasts along a laser beam before the breasts disappear into a large rectangular contraption made of metal. Several seconds later the meat reemerges, now transformed into chicken strips, nuggets, and patties for fast-food chains. These rectangular machines are the centerpieces of DSI, precisely cutting the breasts with a series of fine, high-pressure water streams. Another group of workers snatch the sliced pieces and toss them onto another belt running at eye level. These belts in turn head to other workers, who collect the pieces in plastic containers that, when full, are placed on yet another belt. The full container ends up at the stack-off area, where it is weighed, labeled, and stacked on pallets. As soon as a pallet is completed, a pallet driver pulls up and carries it away to be shipped off.

The many steps makes it a confusing process to describe, but essentially workers are stationed at various points along a series of conveyor belts where they perform a very specific task over and over again, usually without moving their feet. The noise of the plant makes it very difficult to strike up a conversation, and during the first week the only people I've hung out with during breaks are Kyle and Ben. But Barbara eventually puts me at the front of the line, where I spend the shift tearing up chicken breasts. Here it is slightly quieter, allowing for communication as long as we yell into each other's ears. Which is how I get to know Jesús.

Thirty-eight years old and five and a half feet tall, Jesús has the type of stocky frame that suggests rugged athleticism, with scars along his forearms and hands that indicate a tolerance for pain. Along with a hairnet he also wears a beard net over his chin to cover a large goatee. I stay quiet for the first few hours, tearing breasts and tossing them to his side of the bin. He stands opposite me, tearing breasts, but he is also responsible for placing the separated meat on the belt. It doesn't take long to understand why Barbara has placed Jesús at the front of the line: He works at a very fast pace and never seems to tire. The bin fills with a combination of ice, water, blood, and breasts. I stop occasionally—when the supervisors aren't around—to open and close my freezing hands. I wait for Jesús to do the same, but he just keeps chugging along, tearing breasts and throwing them on the belt at a rate of at least one per second.

After our first break, I yell across the bin and introduce myself. He looks up. "You speak Spanish?" I nod and ask if he's from Mexico. He shakes his head. "Guatemala."

"How long have you been here?"

"Ten years."

"How much longer do you think you'll be able to take this?" I ask.

"What do you mean?" He looks confused.

"I mean, survive working at the chicken plant."

"Oh, a long time, for sure. This is good work because it's slow." (Jesús is the only person I hear who characterizes chicken plant work as "slow.")

"Feels pretty fast to me."

He smiles. "But not like picking tomatoes."

Over the next several nights, socializing across a bin of chicken breasts, Jesús tells me how he ended up in Russellville. In the process he corrects a key misconception at the plant: The immigrant workforce is not overwhelmingly Mexican but rather Guatemalan. Most Mexicans, it seems, have graduated to better jobs: Many are employed at various mobile home factories, while others, like Sabrina, have opened small businesses. Today, the vast majority of the immigrant workers at Pilgrim's Pride are from Guatemala. Like Jesús, they are indigenous and generally from one of two northern provinces: Huehuetenango and Quiché. As a child, Jesús grew beans and corn with his family near the town of San Miguel in Huehuetenango. He was fifteen years old in 1985 when he fled the country's civil war, but he doesn't go into detail except to say, "We suffered a little, I suppose." (Like many of the older immigrants, Jesús eventually gained political asylum; the recent arrivals are more likely to be undocumented.)

He first arrived in the potato fields of Idaho, traveling with an older friend who had already spent several years working for the same farmer. He spoke only Q'anjob'al, an Indian dialect. He spent six months in Idaho, working fourteen-hour days earning $3.50 an hour. One day, a coworker in Idaho who had a green card and a car asked if he wanted to head to Florida. A week later, Jesús was picking tomatoes for Dubois Farms in the Florida farming community of Indiantown. A few years later, Jesús's wife, Leticia, arrived, and the couple spent the next decade picking tomatoes and oranges in Florida and blueberries in Maine and New Jersey. Like many Guatemalans, Jesús learned Spanish while working with Mexicans in the fields, although his wife still feels more comfortable conversing in her native Q'anjob'al.

Eventually farmwork began to take a toll, especially on his back. "They have you running all day carrying buckets of tomatoes,"

Jesús says. Several of his relatives had moved to Russellville and told him to come along. Ten years later, he has only good things to say about the decision. With their combined incomes—Leticia works in debone—and some help from family, they have been able to purchase two homes, and their seven-year-old daughter is getting the sort of education her parents could only dream about. "We've traveled enough," Jesús says. "We're in Russellville to stay."

Talking with Jesús helps the time pass, but after three nights of tearing breasts at the bin, my hands have had enough. I can deal with the soreness; the cold is what drives me crazy. We're standing in one place, moving only occasionally to let a man named Guillermo dump more chickens into the bin, and the temperature feels like it must be in the low forties. Despite an extra sweatshirt and two pairs of socks, my body is uncomfortably cold, but it is my hands that suffer the most.

The bins that hold the chicken breasts have four holes in the bottom so the icy and bloody water can drain out, but these holes are quickly plugged by pieces of chicken muscle and fat. For this reason, much of the time that I am grabbing for breasts I am also bathing my hands in frigid water, and the thin cotton gloves that I wear beneath thin plastic gloves don't provide much insulation. Occasionally, when I'm feeling adventurous, I drive my hand down through several feet of breasts and bloody water in order to try and clear the holes, and for a few minutes bloody water will come pouring out at my feet, but another clog soon develops.

During one break I turn in my damp pair of cotton gloves to the smock room and ask for two in return, so I can double up. The woman behind the counter shakes her head. "You can only have one at a time—you give me a dirty one, I give you a clean one."

"My hands are cold."

"Then you need to talk to your supervisor."

"Look, can you just give me one extra pair? My hands are freezing." I'm getting annoyed, as these gloves are, as I'm sure Pilgrim's Pride would admit, cheap pieces of shit.

"No."

When I complain to Jesús, he shows me where DSI keeps a stash of gloves I can dip into. Still, it is one of the small but memorable slights that remind us how little power we have. I am a very insignificant cog in a very large machine—replaceable by design—and shouldn't be surprised when I'm treated accordingly. When I tell Kyle about the glove incident on the drive home, he bursts into laughter. (Not that the story was even funny, but on the drive home, having just been released from the plant, I find that we're often giddy.)

"Shit, Gabriel—you oughta get yourself a collection of those gloves! Bet you can sell 'em for at least a nickel apiece. Fucking chicken plant assholes."

ONE ADVANTAGE TO working nights, I'm told by both managers and coworkers, is that I can get things done during the day. I don't have much to do during the day except try to get at least six hours of sleep, which usually proves impossible, but many of my coworkers have children to care for and errands to run. They leave work in the morning, take their kids to school, buy groceries, and attend a doctor's appointment in the afternoon—without ever having to worry about cutting into their work schedule. This "advantage," though, has an obvious price: When people are taking care of business during the day, they're not sleeping. And even a lack of chores doesn't guarantee a good day's sleep, as I'm finding, for people who are new to night work (which, with the significant turnover at the plant, is a substantial percentage of the workforce). Sleep, therefore, is often treated like a precious commodity, and it's not uncommon to hear one person ask another at the beginning of a shift, "How many hours did you sleep?" in lieu of a more traditional greeting. The question is essentially the same: How are you?

The knot of anxiety around sleep has to do with the need to make it through a shift without going unconscious. While I'm tearing breasts with Jesús, DSI has its first sleep casualty: An African American woman is fired for repeatedly nodding off for thirty seconds at a time. She did this, according to a woman who worked next to her on the line, while standing. She never fell over or leaned on the line for support; she would just tuck her chin into her neck and be out. How she did it, I have no idea. No one is particularly moved by her departure—which occurs sometime after 2:00 a.m.—though a slight sense of excitement builds as a rumor gets passed around that she's going to call in a bomb threat as a parting gift, which could result in our early dismissal (the call is never made).

During a break I sit across the table from the woman who worked alongside the just-fired individual. It turns out that the fired woman has a young son, and though she found someone to watch him during the night, she couldn't afford a sitter during the day. After an eight-hour shift, she was home with a child who was just getting up and ready to play. It strikes me as a tragic situation, but the woman telling the story isn't especially sympathetic. "I have a young child, too, but I don't understand why she can't afford to pay a sitter during the day."

"Really? Making eight bucks an hour? I burn through that without a kid."

She shrugs. "Well, since I just started, I can't afford it, so my mom helps watch my child. But she'd been working here a while. So with all the money she's made, it doesn't make sense."

This lack of solidarity seems stranger as we continue to chat. It turns out that the person I'm speaking with has also been having a hard time staying awake. "On the line no one talks," she complains. Her task has been to separate sliced chicken strips and place them on a line—repeating the motion thirty times a minute. She has started singing to herself in an effort to stay awake, but as the hours go by she isn't always able to keep her eyes open. She'll close them involuntarily, her head will dip, and then she'll catch herself and regain consciousness. Anyone that's been on a long road trip probably knows the feeling. Not fun at all.

Part of the problem is the line work itself, which consists of standing in one place for eight hours and doing the exact same thing over and over again. As long as I'm working next to Jesús away from the loudest area of the line, I'm able to entertain myself with conversation. But for one segment of a shift—probably less than two hours but it felt much longer—I was switched to the task of separating chicken nuggets by hand. The DSI machine can cut the muscular tissue of the chicken breasts into nuggets without a problem, but the fat surrounding the muscle is stubborn. So for who knows how long, I stood apart from the other workers and separated the fat from hundreds of nuggets every minute. Within five minutes of staring at the whirl of meat, tunnel vision set in; within thirty minutes I was shaking my head back and forth and stomping my feet to stay awake. I entered my own little world, as all line workers do. Unfortunately, this world is oppressively boring. "My five-year-old son could do it," is how Kyle describes separating nuggets. It's a testament to the fired woman's work ethic—or sheer economic desperation—that she was able to hold on to the job for even a week.

AT THE END of my second week, I'm switched to a new job dumping tubs. Although I had hoped to get placed on the debone line, and stopped by to inquire about openings with HR—only to be greeted with "You want to do what?" both times—I've come to realize that almost any job at the plant has certain core factors in common. Tub dumping is no exception: It doesn't take much skill, and if you do it for an extended period it's virtually guaranteed to cause an injury.

On DSI's first line, Guillermo has been dumping tubs into the bin for Jesús and me. A young white man has been dumping for the second line but has apparently quit. Guillermo gives me a fifteen-second "training"—which is fifteen seconds longer than I've grown accustomed to. I watch him grab a plastic container from a pallet, pop off the lid, scoop out the ice that has been packed on top of the breasts, and dump the contents into the bin. A middle-aged Latino man with rectangular glasses—who works the line opposite Jesús—stands next to the bin, tearing the chicken breasts and placing them onto the line.

My training complete, I get to work on a new pallet. While tearing breasts with Jesús I hadn't paid much attention to this job but now realize the extent of the workload. Each pallet holds twenty-five tubs—five in a row, five rows high—and in the middle of the top row of tubs is a cardboard wedge with a UPC code that lists the collective weight. I'm about to unload 1,765 pounds of chicken breasts.

The first tub I grab has a sticker stating it weighs seventy-nine pounds. I remove the lid, grab the two handles on either side of the tub, and lean it toward me at an angle in order to scoop out the ice with my hands. As I'm scooping I also watch dumbly as a stream of bloody water pours from the tub directly onto my shoes. I know it's bloody because it's red. I know it lands on my shoes because although I don't bother looking down—since I'm busy scooping ice—I can feel the liquid seeping into my socks as I carry the tub toward the bin.

The distance from the pallet to the bin is only ten feet, but it's treacherous. Despite the extra traction of the overshoes, the cement floor is slick with a combination of ice, water, and chicken fat. I raise the tub to my chest and heave it over the lip of the bin. The seventy-nine pounds of meat land with a plop, squirting liquid in various directions. "*Lo siento*," I say in apology. The man tossing breasts onto the line doesn't even flinch, just smiles and shrugs at me without pausing. I stack the tub and go back for another.

Thirty minutes later I've unloaded the first pallet—nearly a ton of chicken breasts. Sweat is pouring down my face and steam is rising from my head. The overshoes have provided little protection, and as liquid swishes between my toes, I do my best not to fixate on the fact that my feet are bathed in a mix of water and chicken blood. My biceps are burning: To raise each tub above the lip of the bin, one uses essentially the same motion as a bicep curl. My disposable plastic smock is already full of holes, causing liquid to seep into my sweatshirt. And though the top four rows of the tubs weren't too hard to pick up, the last row of five tubs sits only several inches off the ground. Each weighed between seventy-five and seventy-nine pounds, and by the final tub my back is starting to complain. If there is a job that should require a back brace, this is it.

But what is most frustrating is that as I start tearing off the plastic wrap on another pallet, I can see that the bin is nearly empty. Although I've been dumping as fast as possible, my partner, who tells me his name is Mario, is emptying the bin just as quickly—apparently trying to keep pace with Jesús on the other line. "It's moving fast," he says of the belt speed, which is set by our supervisors and can vary according to demand. "It's not always like this." He guesses the machine is slicing up a breast every second.

Halfway through my second pallet the machine starts making a grinding sound and Barbara yells for Mario to stop. I dump several more tubs and join Mario, who is at his station with his forearms hanging over the lip of the bin, as if standing at a bar. I just dumped hundreds of raw and pretty smelly chicken breasts that he's choosing to hover over, but such is life at the plant. You either become desensitized or you go home.

"We've got six more minutes," he tells me.

"Exactly six?"

"Six. I can see what's wrong." He pulls out a watch from his pocket, checks the time, and puts it back. "It's midnight right now. One more minute before the mechanics show up, then five minutes to fix it. Time to rest."

A minute later two white men with tools jangling from their belts rush by. "*Los mecánicos*," says Mario, nodding.

The mechanical breakdown provides a chance for conversation. Mario tells me he is fifty years old and, like Jesús, from a small village in Huehuetenango. In 1989, he left Guatemala for Los Angeles, where he found a job sewing waistbands into jeans at a Calvin Klein factory. It was piecework—fifteen cents a jean—but he was a fast worker and could put out a hundred jeans an hour. In 1999 the factory shut down and relocated to Mexico. An old friend from Guatemala, who was working at the chicken plant, told him to come over and he'd be guaranteed a job. Plus, life in Russellville was easy—rent was cheap, the town was quiet. Ten years later, Mario doesn't regret leaving Los Angeles, and he plans on putting in another twelve years in DSI before retiring.

"And what is your story?" he asks. "I know you aren't from here." I'm thinking of how to answer when the belt turns back on and Barbara shouts at us to get started. Mario pulls out his watch and turns its face to me. It reads 12:06 a.m. He taps his head twice with his index finger and grins, revealing a silver-capped front tooth. Despite having gobs of chicken fat stuck to his smock, he has something of a professorial air about him: I get the feeling he has a lot to teach me, about the chicken plant and otherwise.

By the time we reach our first break, at 1:45 a.m., I've dumped five pallets of breasts—about four and a half tons. I tear off what little remains of my smock, which by now is shredded from bracing the edges of the tubs against my chest. My shoes, jeans, and sweat-shirt are all soaked with water and chicken juice. I've noticed that the tub dumper on the other line, Guillermo, is wearing a longer smock and galoshes that nearly reach his knees, and I complain to Barbara that I need the same. She has the gear waiting for me when I get back from the break. "You keep this smock all week," she says. "Take it home each night and wash it so it doesn't start smelling. Next week you'll get a new one—it's only for the tub dumpers." I realize that I've just unintentionally committed my-self to the position.

WHEN I WAKE up at noon I slowly realize that it's Friday—which means I've got a weekend to recuperate. I bike into town for groceries and while standing in line at a Subway sandwich shop in Russellville—located within Wal-Mart—I hear someone call my name. Kyle is sitting in a booth with his son, Andy, a five-year-old with straight red hair and bright blue eyes. "I'm just glad the week is finally over," Kyle tells me after I sit down across the table. Last night, he said, one woman even asked him if he was drunk, since he was staggering around with the shovel—adding ice to combos—and didn't seem especially coherent. I hadn't noticed because I'd been dumping tubs at the other end of the line. "I laughed and told her I ain't drunk." He was just very, very tired.

He explains that the problem started on Sunday, when the cen-tral air-conditioning in his trailer went out. Monday was hot and humid; the rest of the week was even more brutal. I had awakened each day at noon in a sweat and cranked up the AC to its highest setting. Kyle was waiting for Friday's paycheck to buy a window unit, so he had to sweat through the five days. "I would try and lay down, but it was too damn hot," he tells me. Today, he's come to Wal-Mart to visit his wife, Cindy, who works in the toy depart-ment, and to figure out which model of air conditioner he wants.

Even with Cindy's employee discount, it'll be a major purchase. "But after what happened this morning, I ain't waiting no more."

This morning he had dropped me off and gone home to find his paycheck in the mail. He ate a quick breakfast and, despite his fatigue, drove into town to cash his check and pay his utilities bill. (I understand his urgency, as they later threatened to cut off my water because I owed $2.90.) On the way home he fell asleep on Highway 724, a two-lane road, and veered across the left lane and into a ditch on the shoulder. He woke up before slamming into anything and was lucky there wasn't oncoming traffic and that his car wasn't damaged. "It scared the shit out of me," he says. "The craziest thing is that I was only a mile from the house when I fell asleep, but I couldn't stay awake. I must have been like a zombie."

In retrospect, I could attest that he *was* a bit like a zombie at work. But the graveyard shift at the chicken plant is full of zombies. By two in the morning, nearly everyone on DSI's line looks half-dead, with eyelids drooping and faces devoid of expression. Had he come into a typical office looking the way he did on any given day this week, he'd have been sent home immediately. But I'd already grown so accustomed to the look of sleep deprivation—and my own lack of sleep probably dulled my observations—that Kyle hadn't appeared any more tired than usual. He had picked me up, we mumbled our hellos, and we sat in silence in the car.

I walk with Kyle and Andy to the air-conditioner aisle. He points out the model he is considering, which costs $167; with Cindy's 10 percent employee discount it will run him about $150. That's half his paycheck, money he could definitely use for the rent that's coming due or to patch up his leaky car. But more than anything, he needs to sleep. I pick up the box and admire it, pretending I know what I'm looking at. "I'm going to have it up so high I'll be shivering," he tells me.

BEFORE FALLING ASLEEP back at my trailer, I take stock of my first two weeks as an employee at the plant. I've met one woman from orientation now working an eighty-hour week to support her family. Another mother, exhausted because she can't afford child-care, is fired after being unable to stay awake while separating chicken strips. Now my neighbor has nearly killed himself because he didn't have enough money to pay for an air conditioner.

I don't consider myself naive when it comes to poverty. I know millions of people struggle every day for things I take for granted. I spent five years organizing tenants on the brink of eviction in Brooklyn, and another three years reporting on issues related to poverty. But I'm still not prepared for what I've encountered in Alabama. I've come to write about the lives of immigrants but have been blindsided by the degree of rural poverty suffered by U.S. citizens. I am reminded of how Barbara Ehrenreich charac-terized poverty in *Nickel and Dimed*. Forget about poverty as something sad but sustainable, she argued; instead, poverty must be recognized as "acute distress" and "a state of emergency."[7]

The grinding, deadening work; the workplace diet of sodas and candy bars; the sleep deprivation; the frequent health emergencies; the complete lack of savings: *Unsustainable* is one of the first words that come to mind when I consider the lives of my English-speaking coworkers. (The immigrants in the plant seem better off—both mentally and physically—probably because they can fa-vorably compare the wages and working conditions to what they have left behind in Guatemala.) To understand the nature of the distress, it helps to have access to the facts of their lives—to know about the car driven into a ditch and the son who wakes up just as a mother is ready to collapse. But the *presence* of distress is a more public affair: It is written across each face. The first thing an outsider at the plant will notice—it is impossible not to—is that every American worker over forty is missing some front teeth; and the gummy smiles, combined with the thick creases that carve up cheeks and foreheads, make people look decades older. I often felt, on learning someone's age, that I had been transported back to the harsh frontier life of the early 1800s. An overweight, gray-haired man with a bent back and chronic cough, who I imagine must be nearing retirement, turns out to be forty-two. Before I can catch myself, I think: *He probably won't be alive in a decade.*

"Working the night shift makes you old quick," Kyle tells me. I won't be here long enough to feel its full effect, but my lack of premature aging is regularly noted. I've never been told that I look particularly young for my age, but at the chicken plant people are genuinely astounded when I tell them I am thirty years old; everyone assumes I recently graduated high school. Some people refuse to believe I am telling the truth after I insist upon my age. "If you don't want to tell me your real age you don't have to," one woman laughs, before asking me for the second time what I have to hide. I eventually say that I am twenty-two just to change the subject. I have felt fortunate for many things—economic stability, access to a college education, work that I enjoy—but it's never occurred to me to be thankful for the sum of all these good fortunes: Life isn't "making me old quick."

The Charlotte Observer/John D. Simmons

CHAPTER 8

It is challenging to work at a poultry plant. It is also challenging
to write about the work in a way that remains interesting. It felt
like each day in Yuma I learned something new—about technique,
about various types of lettuce, about the lives of my coworkers.
But how to write about a job that consists of one simple task repeated endlessly, that requires little skill except a willingness to
punish one's body, and that is performed amidst noise that makes
it difficult to hold sustained conversations? I spend another week
dumping tubs; here are snippets from my notes:

*Sunday–Dump tubs all shift, machine breaks down once for fifteen
minutes. Throw out my back again at the end, reaching down
to grab tub from bottom row. Hurts like hell, switch places with
Mario for last hour: He dumps and I tear breasts and put them
on line. He moves pretty well for a guy in his fifties. My hands
get really cold.*

Monday–Another day of dumping tubs. My right forearm and wrist feel weak, have this pain that runs up my arm just at the moment I'm raising the tub. Machine doesn't break down (sucks). Ben is now dumping tubs for other line—someone quit. Doesn't complain but looks like he's dying. Sweating even more than me. I see down the line that Kyle is having trouble staying awake. Lucky no one sees him.

Tuesday–Kyle doesn't show up at my trailer tonight. Could bike in but fuck it. Call plant and leave a message with my ID number saying I won't make it. Spend an hour staring out my window at trucks passing with chickens, read a little, fall asleep around midnight.

Wednesday–Kyle picked me up tonight; said he was too tired last night. Cindy's ankle got really swollen and blue from standing all day at Wal-Mart, and since she has a history of blood clots he took her to the hospital. Spent all day waiting for a doctor, so he didn't sleep. Says she might have to go on disability. Kyle angry because when he called Wal-Mart to say Cindy was injured, a manager told him he'd have to "write her up." At work still dumping tubs. Almost fall on my face when I slip on ice. Mario guesses that I'm dumping two bins a minute tonight, which seems about right. Bins tonight are almost all about 70 pounds each. That means I'm lifting 140 pounds worth of chicken breast every minute; 8,400 pounds an hour; 67,200 pounds during a shift. Feel like crap when I finally get off. Sign posted in break room says that DSI has to work Friday, so I'll be able to make up for missed day.

Thursday–Dump tubs most of night, but toward end of shift spend an hour catching chicken bits in cardboard boxes. I have to keep boxes beneath two metal chutes—chicken comes sliding down chute and leaves streaks of fat on metal. I don't like the job cause I have to stir the chicken meat with my hands in the box to make

*it fill up evenly. Lots of fat on the meat. When the boxes are full
I stick them on a belt and put another box in its place.*
Friday–*Dump all shift. Machine going really fast for some reason.
Too tired to talk much with Mario tonight. Hands and forearms
are hurting. Ben still hanging in and dumping for Jesús on
other line—now wearing brace on right wrist. Says his mom used
it when she worked on debone line and that it helps relieve pressure. "My hands are numb, like they're asleep," he tells me.*

I'm beginning to appreciate the sheer willpower it takes to complete this type of job day after day. In a single shift I could be asked
to tear through more than 7,000 chicken breasts or lift, carry, and
dump more than thirty tons of meat. This is not the sort of work
one wants to read a minute-by-minute description of, any more
than one wants to engage in the activity itself. By now I have written fifteen pages of notes about dumping tubs and tearing breasts,
but when I read them over, they strike me as repetitive and mind-
numbing. Back hurts; my hands get cold; machine breaks down:
These aren't the sorts of nuanced insights I'm looking for. Journalist
Héctor Tobar, who was briefly employed at a poultry plant in Ash-
land, Alabama, wrote that the work "erases portions of your memory
if you do it too long."[8] I feel like it's also erasing my creativity.

IN A TOWN crowded with churches, I find my salvation at the
public library, which provides a needed refuge from my lonely
trailer and the monotony of the plant. I met the head librarian,
Deborah Barnett, during my first weekend in town. In order to
receive a library card, I presented my New York driver's license.
"What are you doing all the way out here?" she asked. I told her
that I was traveling around to "see the country" and working at
the chicken plant. "You must be writing a book," she replied. I
shook my head, thinking: Librarians are smart. Eventually I told

her about my project and we became fast friends. She ordered my previous books for the library, put me in touch with a local journalist, and let me check out as many items as I wanted.

Although Barnett has lived in Russellville for twenty-two years, she remains something of an outsider. "People know I'm from California, so I can get away with saying things that others can't," she told me with a smile. She grew up on the coast in Ventura, later moved to Oregon with her husband, and in the 1980s, after their two children had moved out, came to Russellville to be closer to her husband's parents. Her friends thought she was crazy. "They told me it would be like the movie *Deliverance*," she says between chuckles. "It's different from the rest of the country, but it's not like *that*."

With short brown hair and a playful glint in her eyes, the sixty-one-year-old brought much-needed energy to what had become a woefully dated library collection. With persistent fund-raising she has been able to quintuple the library's budget and increase the collection, and is currently seeking funding for a Hispanic heritage section. A perennial challenge at the library has been to maintain diversity. "Everyone wants to donate Christian books or inspirational fiction, but we've already got too much of that," she tells me. In order to secure space for books not dealing with Jesus Christ, Barnett came up with a strategy. "When people tell me that they have Christian books to donate, I say, 'Great, but I also need you to donate a book on Judaism or Islam so that we can have balance.'" Not many people in Russellville have books on Judaism or Islam in their collection; I would bet a decent number have never met a Jew or a Muslim. So Barnett has the space to order a wide array of secular books, some even with a left-of-center perspective. "This is probably the most liberal library in the state of Alabama," she says proudly.

Barnett arrived in Russellville several years before the chicken plant opened and so has witnessed its role in the dramatic transformation of the town. The library itself, a white brick structure that had been a greasy spoon café and pool hall, is located in an area of downtown referred to as "little Mexico." Across the street is a row of immigrant-owned shops selling groceries, furniture, and clothing. Single-family homes line the side streets, many housing Guatemalans and Mexicans. "Latinos are responsible for most of the revitalization going on," she says. "Before, many of the downtown shops had been boarded up. We didn't even like to have evening activities here, because the area was so deserted that it didn't feel safe."

Along with staffing an institution in the middle of a growing immigrant community, Barnett's position as head librarian has allowed her to gauge the mood of locals. As she reminds me, "This is the closest thing we have to a bar in town." For years the immigrant community was a topic that didn't elicit a whole lot of controversy. When people complained, they typically did so in private settings, using quiet voices. Certainly there could be an undercurrent of racism, but those who complained had to acknowledge the benefits of the new arrivals, who literally brought life into a dying area: Between 2000 and 2007, the number of immigrants in Franklin County increased by 1,500, while the overall population actually declined by 800.[9] Many of the long-abandoned storefronts were cleaned and reopened, such as El Quetzal, a large grocery store several blocks from the library, named after Guatemala's national bird. "It was an auto parts store many years before," said thirty-seven-year-old owner Pascual Mateo, who purchased the vacant building in 2001. "The front windows were broken and trees had started branching into the store. The first thing we did was clear out the trash. We used a van and carted away seventy loads." The same process occurred in run-down residences, with families moving into empty homes and fixing them up. Immigrants were, of course, also providing a steady stream of workers to the plant. According to John Hicks, Barnett's friend and a staff writer at the weekly *Franklin Free Press,* "Anyone with their head on straight knows that without those workers, the plant would go belly up."

Over the years, the complaint Barnett heard most frequently was that immigrants didn't pay taxes. Putting aside the fact that immigrants—even undocumented immigrants—pay all sorts of taxes, this is an ironic criticism to make in Alabama, where residents are proud of their low tax rate. (Barnett and her husband, for example, pay $1.25 a year in property tax for the three acres they own.)* People also expressed a belief that immigrants had access to a wide range of services not available to citizens, a complaint I would also hear from several coworkers at the chicken plant. That no one can point to these services is natural, since they don't exist. Still, I can understand the frustration: Workers earning poverty wages at the chicken plant need more social services and resources. They needed them before immigrants arrived, and they need them today.

Despite such complaints, it seems that until several years before my arrival there was relative tranquility in Russellville in regards to the immigration question. Some people, like the man from Russellville I met at the CCC conference, certainly harbored racist ideas but seemed to understand that such thinking wasn't safe for public expression. And unlike some towns faced with a rapid influx of newcomers, local politicians didn't propose anti-immigrant laws or try to launch careers based on scapegoating the new arrivals.

---

* Undocumented immigrants pay sales tax and, as renters, effectively pay property tax. Immigrants working with Individual Tax ID Numbers (ITINs) pay income taxes, while those using fake Social Security numbers pay between $6 and $7 billion into the retirement system; as this is money they will never be able to use, it serves as a subsidy to cover retirement paychecks for American workers.

Hicks explained that the politicians of Russellville prefer to avoid any topics even slightly controversial. When I was in town, I read through many candidate statements for an upcoming election for city council and mayor. Most candidates ran on an identical platform, promising to repair sidewalks, attract more business to the area, and clean up downtown. I never once saw any reference to the immigrant community. And although this reticence to address the issue meant that immigrants weren't being officially targeted, it also meant that no politicians were proposing events to encourage interaction, like holding cross-cultural festivities or offering English classes. If anything, the growing immigrant community was ignored. Guatemalans and Mexicans had their own shops and social networks, and in general knew as little about the locals as the locals knew about them. Despite the lack of interaction, it certainly helped that the two groups shared a belief in fundamentalist Christianity, and that immigrants—while undeniably transforming Russellville—didn't draw undue attention to themselves. Immigrants were seen as compliant, quiet, and God-fearing. They kept their heads down and they worked hard; they were grateful to the United States of America, and to Russellville, for the opportunities they had been granted.

So when millions of immigrants across the country took to the streets on April 10, 2006, it seemed to have little to do with small, conservative, rural Russellville. That night, images on television showed large protests in dozens of cities; these immigrants were loud and angry and making demands. In Russellville, the day had passed like any other, quietly and without fanfare. But the quiet didn't last long. The following day, Barnett tells me, a group of immigrants marched downtown, passing by the library. "That is when people really started freaking out," she says. "After that day, people would come into the library and tell me, 'I'm moving out of here.' I thought, good luck—where are you going to go?"

IT TAKES ME very little time to track down the prime organizer of the immigrant march. The catalyst was a Guatemalan named Dagoberto, a diminutive man whose preference for baggy shorts and oversized T-shirts makes him appear smaller still. Conveniently, he happens to live in a house next door to my trailer, and had recently left a position in debone to visit Guatemala. Now back in Alabama, he is doing whatever odd jobs he can find until he can return to the plant. (In an attempt to discourage turnover, workers who quit Pilgrim's Pride must wait one year before reapplying.) When there's no work, he spends his free time feeding the chickens in his backyard coop or relaxing on a chair under the shade provided by the entryway awning. On a few lazy afternoons I take up an adjacent seat, eventually revealing that I'm a journalist. He allows me to take notes as we talk and sip soda, interrupted occasionally by trucks of live chickens heading toward the plant, which never fail to leave a stream of feathers flying in their wake.

Like Jesús, Dagoberto and his wife, Martha, are from the Guatemalan town of San Miguel. In 1990, they crossed through Mexico to arrive in Florida, where they quickly found work picking tomatoes in Immokalee and Indiantown, often working in the same fields as Jesús. When the tomato season finished they traveled to Georgia and harvested eggplant. After eggplant came tobacco—again in Georgia—then back to Florida for tomatoes, a return to Georgia for two years of debone work in a poultry plant, and finally, in 1997, he and his family, which now included a son and daughter, moved to Russellville.

In describing his work experiences, Dagoberto is like many immigrants I meet. I ask him about picking tomatoes in Immokalee and he barely raises an eyebrow. (Immokalee is infamous for its brutal working conditions; some bosses have even held their workers in slavery, as documented by the Coalition of Immokalee Workers.) "It could be hard some days," is the most I ever get out of him. The job entailed picking tomatoes as fast as possible to fill up buckets that weighed more than thirty pounds, running with the bucket on his shoulders, dumping its contents into a truck, and dashing back to do it all over again. It's the kind of work, like lettuce harvesting, that can age a person quickly. "*Pues, era normal*," he explains. It was normal, nothing special. Hard, certainly—but what work isn't?

But he wants to tell me about tobacco. "Tobacco is suffering," he says, shaking his head. He earned $70 for a day's work, filling trailers with tobacco leaves that he would carry under his armpits. Even when wearing long-sleeve shirts, his skin would flare up, leaving his torso and armpits covered in rashes. "It felt like my body was on fire," he says of the combination of sweat and raw skin. At night he took baths with talcum powder to provide some relief, but when the harvest finished he resolved never to set foot in a tobacco field again. "I'm not sure why, but I felt bad a lot of the time."*

When he moved to Russellville, Dagoberto was a heavy drinker and smoker, two habits that ended when, for the first time, he entered a church. He is now a lay leader with the Good Shepherd Catholic Church (*Buen Pastor*), which consumes much of his time. Three nights a week different church bands play in his

---

* Many tobacco workers, and this likely included Dagoberto, suffer from green tobacco sickness (GTS), referred to as the "green monster." GTS occurs when nicotine enters the bloodstream through the skin, resulting in acute poisoning with symptoms that begin with headaches and dizziness and can lead to sunstroke and even death. In one study of farmworkers in North Carolina, nearly 15 percent were found to be suffering from GTS. "By the end of the season, non-smoking workers had nicotine levels equivalent to regular smokers," the authors of the report concluded. Although providing workers with waterproof outfits could minimize their exposure to nicotine, these would cost money. Instead, growers encouraged workers to begin smoking in order to build up a tolerance to nicotine.

garage, and on Friday evenings the garage hosts an informal prayer service. On Saturday nights, a Spanish-language service—mostly singing—is held at Good Shepherd, in addition to the Sunday Mass. Dagoberto credits church with giving him the courage to speak up and organize the rallies. He and Martha were granted political asylum due to Guatemala's civil war, and so didn't worry about being deported. Still, he dealt with a gnawing sense that he was inferior to white Americans. "It's hard to explain," he says. "I just had the feeling that Americans were smarter and somehow better than me."

Church changed all that. "When you get to know God, you quickly learn that *all* of us are his children. I'm no better than you, and you're no better than me." If Dagoberto found in Christianity a religion that confirms the worth of everyone—including undocumented immigrants—he saw an opportunity to reinforce that belief with action in 2006. Immigrants were organizing around the country in support of legalization and against a proposed bill in the House of Representatives that would turn undocumented immigrants into felons. When Dagoberto heard on a Spanish radio station that a protest was being organized for Monday, April 10, in Albertville—about one hundred miles west of Russellville—he convinced a group of several dozen Guatemalans and Mexicans to come along.

One of the organizers in Albertville, upon seeing the number of folks from Russellville, asked why they weren't organizing their own march. Why come so far when, as everyone knew, Russellville had plenty of immigrants? The thought immediately appealed to Dagoberto. Of course they should have a march! "I knew a lot of people—at the church and the plant—who were afraid to stand up, but at some point we had to do something." What Russellville's immigrant community needed was a coming-out party, an event to bring people together and—if nothing else—assert their presence and humanity. As Dagoberto marched with the group, he announced to his companions that he wanted to organize a rally in Russellville.

"When?" a friend asked.

For Dagoberto, the answer was obvious. "Why not tomorrow?"

They returned to Russellville that afternoon and got to work. Dagoberto and a few others went to the police station to inform them of the march, but were told that they needed to request a parade permit fifteen days prior to the event. For some reason—perhaps they realized that Dagoberto would not accept no for an answer—the officers eventually conceded and allowed the group to march through downtown. Dagoberto enlisted the help of a young man named Martin, who made signs announcing the march. The pair arrived at the chicken plant in time to catch the workers departing from the day shift. At the same time, key movers in the immigrant community were mobilizing. At Mama's Kitchen, Sabrina was talking to customers and spreading the word; in town, Pascual Mateo was doing the same at El Quetzal, the Guatemalan grocery store.

The next morning no one knew what to expect. "We had people spreading rumors that immigration agents were going to be at the march to arrest everyone," says Dagoberto. Having worked as an organizer, I know how hard it can be to get even two dozen people to a demonstration, and we usually had weeks if not months to do outreach. With less than twenty-four hours to plan, chances were good that the event would be a bust.

Instead, 500 people marched through downtown to show their support for immigration reform and highlight the contributions that the immigrant community had made to Russellville. Storeowners stepped outside to watch the procession; residents left their porches to see the cause of so much noise. At the Eastside Park, where a rally was held, white onlookers stood at the edge of the grass. "Where did all these people come from?" many asked, echoing the question on the lips of people across the country in the wake of the immigrant protests. Locals knew, of course, that immigrants were working at the chicken plant, but many lived silent and separate existences, spending their time in trailer parks on the outskirts of town. They'd certainly never gathered and chanted and waved Guatemalan and Mexican flags. It was the largest political rally Russellville had seen in years, if not decades. It was also the first time that many people heard directly from immigrants, and the words they heard weren't ones of gratitude.

"People say we are dirty, that we are carrying diseases to this nation and killing people," Dagoberto's friend Martin told the *Franklin County Times*. "But we pay taxes like everyone else. Most of the people who work for Gold Kist are Hispanic. We are the motor of this city. Gold Kist makes money off us, the city is getting bigger because of us; we're making everyone richer." (It wasn't until later that year that Pilgrim's Pride purchased Gold Kist.)

The march made many people furious. "You had people carrying Mexican flags," says Barnett. "Mexican flags in the South? That's not a good idea." To make matters worse, the newspaper ran a front-page photograph of the rally; clearly visible in the frame was an American flag held upside down.

The paper asked readers: "Do you think Hispanic residents had reason to march through downtown Russellville?" Of those polled, 92.9 percent said no. One man wrote into the paper complaining that he had watched "this city and county be invaded with an overflow of the Hispanic population," and that the demonstration showed him "how much Hispanics are not needed in this country." He went on to ask: "Do you really think you are doing jobs that we will not do? Who did the work before you came?"

There was not, of course, a chicken plant before they came.

LOCAL CONTEXT IS necessary to understand the psychic impact of that first protest. Russellville is not a town accustomed to demonstrations. When searching through nearly two decades of archives of the *Franklin County Times* I found only one other instance of political activism—and the manner in which it was dealt with is illuminating. In 1991, while the paper was running story after story in support of the first Gulf War, Russellville resident Barry Carpenter and his wife, Cheryl, passed out antiwar fliers downtown. Carpenter also wrote a message in chalk on the sidewalk outside a church that read, "And God said, 'Thou shall not kill.'" The police arrested the Carpenters, charging them with criminal mischief, desecration of a building, criminal littering, and endangering the welfare of a child (Cheryl was holding their eighteen-month-old child while passing out fliers). After they found a flag in Barry's pocket in a "wadded condition," they charged him with desecration of a venerable object as well.

ON MAY 1, two weeks after the initial protest, a smaller group of immigrants and their children—this time careful to hoist only American flags—again paraded through downtown, this time in coordination with rallies across the country. The next day, in response, a group of 200 locals held a "Take Back America" rally on the steps of the Franklin County Courthouse. The rally was organized by local radio personality Tommy "Hutty" Hutcheson, who handed out bright red T-shirts meant to symbolize patriotism (and not, as one might think, communism). One anti-immigrant protester was photographed wearing a red shirt and carrying a sign with the Mexican flag crossed out. Speakers highlighted the need to "take back each city and county" in what amounted to nothing less than "a fight for the very soul of America." In a touching, inadvertent display of interconnectivity, the red T-shirts worn by the patriots working to "take America back" were made in Mexico.

It was the third political rally in less than a month, a burst of activity unlike anything people could recall, but thus far it was a local affair. Days later, however, the immigration drama playing out in tiny Russellville would be broadcast across the state, because the Ku Klux Klan had come to town.

"Klan Takes to City Streets," proclaimed the newspaper headline. Fifty people marched through downtown to arrive at the courthouse steps, a handful of them wearing white, red, and green robes. Eventually a crowd of about 300 gathered to listen to folks like "Brother Billy," a Klan leader from Birmingham. "This is our nation," Billy argued. "If they don't like our laws, they can leave. America was founded as a Christian nation by a Christian race, not a mud race."

Also on hand was Imperial Wizard Ray Larsen of South Bend, Indiana, who hoped that the growing anger over immigration would serve as a recruitment mechanism for the Klan. Larsen added a touch of levity to the occasion when he tried to find common cause with the very "mud race" the KKK had once lynched. After stating that illegal immigrants stole American jobs, he added, "And I'm talking about blacks and whites. They want you out of here because they want this as their land." One hopes he at least took off his hood to deliver this message of unity.

John Hicks was reporting at the rally. "The mood in the crowd was one of curiosity," he tells me in his office in downtown Russellville. "As far as I could tell, none of the people who spoke were locals." While people in robes with ridiculous pseudonyms complained about a mud race, several dozen counterprotesters held signs with messages like "All One People" and "Free Your Mind." And when speakers on the steps shouted, "white power!" at the crowd, a few African Americans shouted back, "black power!" Television cameras and journalists from across the state were on hand to record every moment. As the *Franklin County Times* editorialized, "We're sure the pictures from that event will look nice on the next 'Welcome to Russellville' brochure."

"It was like they were watching a freak show," says Hicks, referring to the crowd. Still, despite the circuslike atmosphere, a fair number of the onlookers applauded the Klan's anti-immigrant message.

Spring 2006 marked the moment when many Americans woke up to the rapidly changing demographics of our country. In large cities the number of marchers was overwhelming; but in small anonymous towns like Russellville, the impact was more profound. After fifteen years of silence, immigrants gathered hundreds strong to demand respect and an acknowledgment of their labor. Some whites who before might have only muttered under their breath about the "illegal invasion" were now certain that the time had come to "take America back." And when the KKK arrived, it found—for once—an audience containing more supporters than protesters. In Russellville it seemed like much more conflict was assured, and that violence wasn't out of the question.

INSTEAD, AFTER THE departure of the KKK, is seems like life went back to normal. Two years later, as I wandered around town, I certainly didn't see or hear anything to suggest relations between immigrants and locals were threatening to boil over. Occasionally I would pick up on a whispered comment like "illegals are everywhere" or, when walking down supermarket aisles, something about the injustice of bilingual labels. But this is hardly unique territory: I've heard such comments in all sorts of places. And when I gently raised the subject of immigrants in town—by telling a cashier, for example, that I was surprised that so many immigrants were employed at the plant—the reaction was always the same. "That's because they'll do the jobs we don't want. You would never catch me inside that plant."

Schools are often a flashpoint of anger and tension, but in Russellville the dramatic growth of Latino students seems to have been taken in stride. "In 1991, we had three Hispanic students in the entire district," says George Harper, who is in charge of special education and English learning programs. Today, of the 2,500 students, 31 percent are Latino. At lower grades, that percentage is even higher: 42 percent of the 2009 kindergarten class was Spanish speaking. But what is most remarkable is how quickly Latino students adapt. By fifth grade, Latino students are at the same level as whites and blacks in reading, writing, and math. "I don't know if they're legal or illegal," says Harper, who oversees a staff of bilingual parent liaisons and has hired several bilingual teachers. "What I know is that we're going to educate these children, because if we don't we're going to pay for it down the road. Some school systems discourage their immigrant parents and children from coming to them; others open their arms to students. We've tried to be one of the latter."

When I asked my immigrant coworkers if they had ever experienced racism, no one had any particular anecdotes. "I have never had a problem here," Mario told me. I asked him if people had called him names or in some way made him feel unwelcome, but again he shook his head. "Everything is very calm here, especially compared to Los Angeles." Jesús, too, didn't seem to have had any problem settling in. When I sit with groups of immigrants from other departments during breaks, I don't hear any horror stories. If anything, people don't pay enough attention to them to say anything racist. They are allowed to go about their lives in peace.

I should underscore the limited nature of my exploration of racism. I bopped around town and tried to gauge local feelings, but it was a highly unscientific endeavor. Most of my waking hours were spent in the plant. It is also quite possible that immigrants didn't feel comfortable divulging stories to me; it is undoubtedly true that I got to know only perhaps two dozen people. For all I know, hundreds of immigrants have faced insults and felt targeted while going about their business in town.

But what I can report with more confidence is the surprising lack of tension between Americans—both black and white—and immigrants at the plant itself. Each group makes up about one-third of the workforce; the whites and Latinos are more likely to live nearby, while the African Americans tend to make the thirty-minute drive south from "the Shoals," an area that includes the towns of Florence, Muscle Shoals, Tuscumbia, and Sheffield, with a total population of about 150,000. Compared to Russellville, the Shoals is lively and cosmopolitan: It has music festivals, a Renaissance faire, a major school in the University of North Alabama, and laws that allow for the sale of alcohol. Early on, I asked one of my black coworkers if she was from Russellville, and she looked at me as if I were insane. "I've never even *stopped* in Russellville," she said. (Indeed, I never met a black worker from Russellville—nor did I see many around town—which was odd since they make up more than 10 percent of the city's population.)

During breaks most workers sat in self-segregated groups, but there was enough mixing that no one, for example, thought it particularly strange that I often sat with Guatemalans (although people did think it odd I spoke Spanish). Folks stopped by booths to banter and share snacks and bitch, and on the processing floor there was plenty of friendly, if sometimes confused, interaction. Two of the African American women in DSI, when they helped Mario and Jesús tear chicken breasts, asked questions about Guatemala, and while dumping tubs I served as translator. Men taught each other curse words in the other's language, and I even knew of a few cross-cultural relationships that had developed at the plant—each between a Guatemalan man and a white woman.

But the formation of deep relationships was rare: Language created a real barrier, and most folks didn't stick around long enough. What was more common was simple curiosity: My American-born coworkers wanted to know who these people were. It felt like a junior high class reacting to the arrival of a foreign student from an unknown country. I got the sense that Ben, for example, had never actually been in the same room as someone who didn't speak English. He was amazed by how short the Mexicans were. After I explained that the "Mexicans" were actually from Guatemala, he wanted to know if all Guatemalans were so short.

"Maybe not all," I told him, "but most of them are pretty short."

"Someday I'm going to travel to Guatemala just so I can walk around and feel tall," he said, giggling. "I like feeling tall. And maybe I'll learn Spanish." This was an admittedly silly comment: It's not the sort of evidence one would point to in developing a sophisticated analysis of relations toward immigrants in the American South. But it was the sort of question I heard people, black and white, wonder amongst themselves. Why were they short? How did they get so strong? Where did they come from, exactly? They were very basic questions, very human questions, and they lacked hostility.

I had expected to find more anger. One of the most common complaints, after all, is that immigrants are taking jobs meant for Americans. In Russellville the main source of jobs is the poultry plant. But no American laboring within the four walls of the plant felt that his or her job was in danger of being "stolen." The jobs at the plant come easy: I was hired within a week. It is surviving the work that is hard. People lose their jobs at the plant because they quit, not because an immigrant takes their position.

The one person I knew who occasionally complained about immigrants was Kyle. But his complaints were abstract and based mostly on misinformation. Driving back from the plant one day, he told me that he didn't have anything against immigrants who came over to better their lives. "Hell, I would do the same thing in a second if I needed to help my family, whether it was legal or not. But what I don't think is right, Gabriel, is that they come over here and get treated better than Americans. We give them all these benefits that you and me, as citizens, can't touch." When I asked what benefits he was referring to, the conversation quickly dried up.

I also noticed that for all the Fox News talking points that Kyle carried around in his head, he reserved his real anger for supervisors. During one break he sat down at a table with Mario and me; we were speaking in Spanish about the fast speed of the line. "What'd he say?" Kyle asked me after Mario had finished his sentence.

"We're bitching about Debbie. She came over today and told me to tell Mario in Spanish that she needed him to work as fast as possible."

Kyle scowled. "What do they think this is, a matter of national security? We're tearing up soggy chicken meat, and they give us some bullshit about working as fast as possible?" I translated his comment for Mario, who nodded and smiled.

CHAPTER 9

After three weeks at the plant, I have grown to share Kyle's dislike of our supervisors. In Yuma, I initially found Pedro to be an intimidating and imposing figure, but as time went on, my feelings toward him warmed. He worked impossibly long hours, showing up at the fields before sunrise and leaving well after dark. Though he did at times violate my personal space, his heart was in the right place. As a result I respected Pedro, as did the rest of the crew.

At the chicken plant I feel no respect for our two supervisors, Barbara and Debbie, and even develop a special antipathy for Debbie. While both seem to do little more than walk around and tell us to work faster before disappearing for yet another smoke break, Barbara can at least hold her own: When she stops by the bin she'll tear through breasts as quickly as anyone. Debbie, on the other hand, prefers not to get her hands dirty, and when she does help out, she tears the breasts at a pace far slower than what she herself would permit. She also has an irritating habit of yelling "*¡Ándale!*" at Jesús and Mario when she strolls by, telling them to hurry up. The first time I hear this it's just weird; the second time it's annoying; after that, it's hard not to shout something rude in return.

Occasionally Debbie seems to remember that the bodies working the line aren't cogs but human beings, but her perky "How's everybody doing today?" serves only to alienate us further. We play along, smiling and saying that we're doing fine, then look at each other when she's out of earshot to ask, *What the fuck is her problem?*

One night, after grimacing through another round of Debbie's "*¡Ándales!*" I ask Mario what he thinks about getting a union in the plant. "It would be good," he says, telling me that he voted for the union in 2006. That drive, organized by the United Food and Commercial Workers, didn't go so well: 486 employees voted for representation, while 844 voted against. Mario says the only positive development to come from the effort was that the company changed its position regarding equipment. Before the union drive, the company, then owned by Gold Kist, would give workers a week's supply of gloves and hairnets; if any ripped or were lost over the course of the week, the replacement cost was taken out of the employee's paycheck. The union promised to fight for free equipment if they won, arguing it was unfair to penalize workers for poorly made supplies (my gloves tore a number of times, for which I would have been charged earlier). Despite the union's loss, the company decided to change their policy, probably in response to widespread worker complaint.

But there were larger issues than nickel and diming workers over cheap supplies. Pilgrim's Pride employees can opt to pay for their insurance through Blue Cross and Blue Shield of Texas, though a number of workers told me they couldn't afford the premiums, which for Kyle came to about $60 a month. "Didn't help none, either," he says, explaining that his visits to the doctor for

a back problem cost him nearly $2,000, which the insurance de-
nied because it was a preexisting condition. In fact, the best health
care for poultry workers is reserved for their children. Even
though Kyle and Cindy were both working, they were still poor
enough for their children to be covered by Medicaid.

Along with poverty wages and insurance premiums that failed
to cover many health problems, another critical area that needed
improvement was the quality of the medical care provided by the
plant's nurse, a regular criticism among workers in the poultry
industry. In Russellville, the most dramatic example of inadequate
care occurred in 2004, when a woman named Delores Smith
slipped and fell to the floor. In considerable pain and having trouble walking, she went to the nurse, who, without even looking at
the worker's ankle, told her to take some ibuprofen and go home.
When Delores got to her car, she looked down and saw bones
sticking through her socks. Her ankle was broken in three
places.[10]

Still, despite low wages, a grueling pace, and horror stories like
that of Delores Smith, two-thirds of the workers voted against the
union. Since the plant has such high turnover, most of the people
I socialized with during breaks hadn't been around during the
union drive. This fact points to one difficulty in organizing at the
plant: High turnover prevents the development of solidarity
among workers. Many stick around for a few weeks or months and
see the plant as an emergency work measure that they'll soon leave
behind. But I did learn that two people I knew, Dagoberto and
Kyle, had voted in the election—and both had cast a vote against
the union. Each illustrates the unique challenges, and promises,
of organizing in the traditionally unorganized South.

Dagoberto, the spark for the immigrant marches in Russellville,
would seem a natural candidate to lead a union drive. He was
clearly connected, respected, and not afraid to stick his neck out.

"To be honest, at the time I didn't really know what the union was," he explains. For immigrants like Dagoberto, who tells me he didn't have meaningful contact with the union, plant management had free rein to define the function of organized labor: Enrich union officials by skimming off the paychecks of workers. What did change his perspective—he tells me that he'll vote for the union if there's another election—is what happened after the vote on the debone line. "They sped up the line speed," he says. "It was running thirty-five birds a minute. When the union lost, they increased it to thirty-eight to forty birds."

There is a widespread belief that Latinos at the plant, too afraid to go against management because of their immigration status, were the reason that the union drive failed. "In any plant, they really do go after the immigrants," says Joe Parks, a union official with the UFCW local that attempted to organize Russellville. "Their goal is to strike fear in the Hispanic workers, because they know the majority of them are undocumented."

The secret ballot vote makes such a claim impossible to corroborate. But what is indisputably true is that unions need to do a better job of reaching out to and connecting with immigrant workers. A union drive that isn't able to identify and activate the natural fighters like Dagoberto has very little chance of success. Management is certainly prepared to expend whatever resources necessary to get their point across to all workers, no matter what language they speak.

At the plant in the weeks leading up to the vote, every worker was called off the line several times, in shifts, to the room where I had my orientation. In these sessions they listened to bilingual management representatives—brought in from Atlanta—and watched videos that, in Kyle's words, made the antiunion video I saw during orientation seem tame. "The manager always made sure to say, 'Now, I'm not telling you how to vote,'" Kyle says. "Then they'd show some video that made it seem like the union was some sort of Antichrist." (Gold Kist, in combating an earlier union drive at a plant in Georgia, had been found to break labor laws by monitoring the activities of pro-union workers and showing videos and affixing posters in the plant that equated unions, none too subtly, with strikes and violence. Vote No Violent Strikes! Vote *No* Union! read one poster, with images of a vehicle riddled with bullet holes, another with shattered windows, and a man in bandages.)

Kyle, who had initially signed a petition requesting an election, was eventually convinced by management that bringing in a union would only mean trouble. "What I remember is that they said with a union, we couldn't go directly to our supervisors if we had a problem. We'd have to do everything through the union. You know how they are—they like to tell us that they have an open-door policy and we can come to them with our complaints." Still, Kyle wasn't entirely comfortable with his decision. His brother, after all, worked at a Saturn plant in Tennessee and was a member of the United Auto Workers; he earned $30 an hour. And his wife, Cindy, who was working days on the debone line at the time, was leaning toward voting yes.

"They have an open-door policy with closed ears," Cindy tells me. She worked three different times at the plant, beginning in 1990, and wasn't impressed with how supervisors treated the workers. "They all have their favorites and if you're on their good side then you can do whatever you want." A union could mean uniform treatment, she figured. Still, Kyle was eventually able to convince her to vote against the union.

"I'll admit when I'm wrong," Kyle tells me. "They suckered my ass, but if they have another vote I'll go for the union. The way I think about it now, there is strength in numbers." While I was at the plant, however, there was very little talk about a union—unless I brought the subject up.

What seems to have made a lasting impression on Kyle was what happened on the night of the vote. Work was slow and at a certain point his supervisor said that he could observe the counting of ballots in the orientation room. He remembers that Debbie, our supervisor, was hanging around the room as well. When it was determined, sometime around daybreak, that the union had lost, the disappointed officials got into their cars and headed for the exit. Debbie, according to Kyle, followed them outside. "She was out there yelling, 'Get off our property!'" Kyle remembers. "I couldn't believe how freaking immature she was acting. You won, you know, show some class. The union came in and tried something and they lost—you didn't see them acting unprofessionally."

And what happened next really got under Kyle's skin. That morning, on the way out the door, workers were in for a special treat. "Supervisors were just smiling and handing out Krispy Kreme donuts," Kyle says. "That's what we got for voting the union down: a single fucking donut. Like we're nothing but little kids."

Parks, the union official, wouldn't reveal whether another union drive was being considered for Russellville. He did tell me that Local 1996 represented about 1,300 poultry workers at plants in Alabama and Tennessee for such companies as Tyson, Wayne Farms, and Koch Foods. "Typically, there's about a 30 percent combined difference in pay and benefits between organized and unorganized plants," he says, noting that the organized workers receive vacation and severance pay along with more generous health insurance. "That's where the real difference comes in, with benefits. And that as a union worker I can disagree with my employer without fear of being fired. In a non-union place, it's their way or the highway. Personally, that means more than anything to me."

UNLIKE MEATPACKING, WHICH has its origins in north-
ern cities like Chicago, and where for a time militant labor activism
carved middle-class jobs out of the carving of meat, poultry has
always been a poor person's occupation. The first chicken farmers
emerged in the 1920s in the Delmarva Peninsula (the combined
eastern shores of Delaware, Maryland, and Virginia); chickens
were seen as a means for hardscrabble farmers to hedge their bets
in case of a poor vegetable season, and were delivered live to markets in cities like New York and Philadelphia.

Government intervention during World War II dramatically increased the amount of chicken consumed in the country, while
shifting its center from Delmarva to the South. Beef was rationed;
the source of protein was seen as something best saved for the
troops. "Raising and eating chicken were now patriotic duties and
a matter of national security," writes Steve Striffler in *Chicken*, his
book about the industry. At the same time, the government com-
mandeered the entire supply of chicken meat from the Delmarva
Peninsula for federal food programs. "This wartime policy," notes
Striffler, "effectively meant that the premier poultry-producing region in the country, a region that produced over half of the country's commercial broilers, was suddenly removed from the
market."[11]

Southern entrepreneurs like John Tyson of Arkansas stepped in
to fill the vacuum, and the South has been the center of the poultry
industry ever since. It has two key advantages: an unorganized
workforce and low labor costs, along with a ready supply of desper-
ately poor farmers eager to switch to raising chickens. Eventually
the model became one of vertical integration, with large companies
like Pilgrim's Pride controlling everything from the hatcheries to
the feed to the processing plants. The one aspect they left "independent" was the growers—the farmers—who signed contracts,
were given chicks, and expected to deliver slaughter-weight birds.

Keeping the growers as independent contractors ensured that companies weren't responsible for investing the capital to build the growing sheds. As a result, growers took on debt and were especially vulnerable to market forces, as well as the dictates of the company, since without a contract their sheds became worthless.

Poultry officially entered the modern era in 1983, when McDonald's introduced the Chicken McNugget. Chicken lost its identity as a bird and became a deep-fried industrial creation. Over the following decade, American consumption of chicken outpaced beef. Today, the average American consumes eighty-six pounds of chicken a year, the equivalent of 262 chicken breasts. Originally touted for its health benefits, much of this chicken is consumed as nuggets, strips, and patties in a "further processed" form—fried in oil and breaded—resulting in a product that could be twice as fatty as a hamburger.

IT TAKES LESS than a month for my body to start breaking down under the strain of feeding America's appetite for chicken. As in Yuma, the pain is primarily focused in my hands and wrists, though the lifting of tubs is starting to wear on my forearms and back as well. I dealt with the pain early on by taking ibuprofen before and during each shift—two pills at 10:30 p.m., two more at 2:30 a.m.—but now I start taking painkillers even when I'm not working. Jars of pasta sauce are becoming difficult to open, and the throbbing in my hands is starting to wake me up when I'm sleeping.

From what I can tell, the most common method of dealing with pain is to quit. One person has already left tub dumping after two months, and Ben, whose hands hurt when he opens and closes them, will depart in a matter of weeks. I have no doubt that despite being a healthy thirty-year-old, something in my body—my hands or my back—would most certainly give out within the year.

By the time Kyle's wife, Cindy, departed the debone line, she tells me that she was having problems even holding on to a glass of water, an indicator of carpal tunnel syndrome. It took some time to recover, but she did; the real damage occurs when an employee perseveres and attempts to work through the pain.

One worker whose hands were destroyed by line work is Roxanne, a middle-aged woman who lives in a modest house near the plant. When I interview her over the telephone, she tells me that she spent twelve years in various departments, including four years on the debone line, and along with increasingly painful arthritis, she saw the joint in her left thumb deteriorate. In 2006, her doctor recommended surgery. He also recommended that she not set foot again in the plant, and so she quit and paid for the surgery out of her pocket. "The workman's comp over there is rotten—if you have surgery one day, they expect you to come back the next," she says in a hushed voice. "The doctor told me that the joint in my thumb was almost completely worn away, so they took an extra vein in my leg that I didn't need and wrapped it around my thumb. Over time that's supposed to form a gristle." In effect, the vein will eventually replace the cartilage of the thumb joint.

"My hand still hurts; they say it will never be like it was. But it wasn't just me—everybody on the line had hand problems. When you work over there, I guess you have to accept that you're gonna hurt. But if you tell them that you're hurting, all they say is to take more Tylenol and go home." (In a passing comment, a human resources employee at Pilgrim's Pride later tells me, "Everyone on the debone line complains about their hands.")

Sabrina's mother worked four years in the evisceration department and has three surgeries to show for it, each paid for by the plant. Each shift she made thousands of cutting and squeezing motions, causing the tendons in both her wrists to become inflamed;

one wrist had to be operated on twice. After the last surgery she returned to work for a few months, but when her wrists started hurting again, her husband convinced her to quit. Even years later, Sabrina says that her mother's hands "still aren't normal," pointing to a recent attempt to make tamales that was cut short by wrist pain.

Dr. Don Beach, whose office is in the town of Moulton, about thirty miles east of Russellville, sees a lot of poultry workers. His patients come from three states—Alabama, Mississippi, and Tennessee—traveling considerable distances because Dr. Beach speaks Spanish. He's been a doctor in the area for sixteen years and nearly one-fifth of his patients are immigrants. "The most common problem for line workers that I see—especially the debone workers—is carpal tunnel," he tells me when I visit his office.

But during breaks people don't often talk about ailments, and most of the positions on DSI place much less stress on the hands than debone. Although line workers are using their hands, many of the tasks in DSI—lining up breasts on a belt or snatching sections of nuggets and strips—are easier than the thousands of cuts debone workers make with knives and scissors. During breaks I see men and women from debone flexing their hands and massaging their wrists as they sit in booths, but it seems like folks deal with the pain in the same way that Ben does: privately, without complaint, and with painkillers.

OFFICIAL GOVERNMENT STATISTICS paint a very different picture of working in the poultry industry. According to the Labor Department, it is very unlikely that a poultry plant worker will develop a musculoskeletal disorder (MSD) such as carpal tunnel or tendonitis. In 2006, only 20.8 of every 10,000 poultry workers missed work due to an MSD. By comparison, toy store employees were more than twice as likely to miss work due to an MSD.

To account for the low incidence of MSDs, which were four times higher for poultry workers a decade ago, the industry points to improvements like more ergonomic workstations, the rotation of jobs, and the introduction of machinery to replace some line workers. In the words of Richard Lobb, the National Chicken Council spokesperson, "Workplace safety is a key objective and core value for all poultry processing companies."

But this "core value" and government statistics are called into question by recent reports. A Duke University study, published in 2007, interviewed nearly 300 female workers at two poultry plants in North Carolina. They found that 43 percent reported symptoms of MSDs. The study blamed the high rate of MSDs in part on the lack of workplace safety regulation. The maximum line speed, for example, is set by the USDA—and takes into consideration only food safety, without worrying about whether such speeds are safe for workers.

"Since the USDA began setting line speeds in 1968, the pace has increased from less than 20 birds a minute to the current maximum of 91 birds a minute," says Hester Lipscomb, an associate professor of occupational and environmental medicine at Duke and the study's senior author. Lipscomb believes that the women didn't complain or seek treatment for their injuries because they were worried about losing their jobs. (It's worth mentioning that these weren't undocumented immigrants; all the women in the study were African American.)[12]

In 2008, the *Charlotte Observer* published "The Cruelest Cuts," a weeklong series on the poultry industry.[13] During a twenty-two-month investigation, they interviewed workers from thirteen plants and various companies, focusing especially on the House of Raeford, a chicken and turkey processor with seven plants in the Carolinas. On paper, House of Raeford was an extremely safe place to work: Over a four-year period at their 800-employee plant in West Columbia, South Carolina, not a single worker suffered from an MSD, while another of their plants had a five-year streak without a lost time accident.

But these statistics contradicted what reporters heard from doctors and workers. "I don't know a single worker who doesn't have some sort of pain in their hand," Dr. Jorge Garcia, who has seen an estimated 1,000 poultry workers in South Carolina, told the paper. The *Observer* interviewed more than 130 workers who said they had been injured on the job; three-fourths of these injuries were to their hands and wrists. Some complained they were denied a request to see doctors; others contended that they were fired after being injured. The *Observer* eventually obtained internal injury log reports for three House of Raeford plants, and soon discovered the reason for the company's stellar safety streak: They failed to report more than half the injuries to OSHA. When they did record injuries, they often rushed workers back to the plant floor just hours after surgery so that they wouldn't have to report a missed day.

Bob Whitmore, who has directed OSHA's record-keeping system for twenty years, was presented with the *Observer*'s findings—most backed up by medical documents from injured workers—along with the injury log reports. He concluded that House of Raeford brazenly broke workplace laws, and went on the record to admit that the injury rates for poultry processors are likely two to three times higher than official government figures indicate.

In response to the series, North Carolina's Occupational Safety and Health division launched an investigation that found 49 serious safety violations at one of the company's plants and proposed $178,000 in fines. The federal government also indicted a plant manager and a head of human resources, along with about a dozen supervisors, for knowingly hiring undocumented workers.

Unfortunately for many of the workers, they also raided one of the plants and arrested more than 330 immigrants. Most were deported, while dozens are serving prison time for using false documents or reentering the country illegally.

The *Observer* also found that OSHA inspections of poultry plants were at a fifteen-year low and that federal guidelines written in 2002 made it easier for companies to hide MSDs in the injury logs (when they bothered to report injuries). It was a neat feedback loop: Weakened federal guidelines and enforcement allowed companies to underreport injuries; a company that reported low injury rates was less likely to be inspected. Companies saved money. Poultry plants were safer than toy stores. The only people not prospering from the arrangement were the people it was putatively designed to protect: workers.

I'VE STOPPED BY human resources twice to ask Bill, the overnight HR manager, about a transfer to debone, so I figure this persistence has paid off when Barbara tells me at the beginning of the week that I'm needed elsewhere. Instead, I'm told to make combos again. This time I am working with a partner. David is a recent high school graduate from Haleyville who has been at the plant less than a month, and judging by his physique could be training for a triathlon. As we're waiting for the combo supplies to be delivered, I comment on the size of his arms. "Been working out?"

"Lifting weights every day." He looks at me with curiosity. "You don't talk like you're from around here. Mind if I ask what you're doing?" I tell him my story about liking to travel, and he nods his head. "I'm the same way. I want more than what I can get in Haleyville. That's why I'm going to sign up for the air force." He hopes to join the special forces and teach fighting and survival skills, which would mean, according to what he's heard, that he wouldn't be deployed anywhere "unless it gets real bad." I think of Iraq and Afghanistan but say nothing.

With two people doing what I previously did alone, we work for only about three hours the first night. Most of the time we sit around on boxes, David chewing his Grizzly wintergreen tobacco and me staring at the same man placing the same lids on the same boxes. It's a wonder he hasn't gone crazy.

Day two is even slower. The plant just isn't using that many combos right now, and once we've got a dozen made, the area becomes crowded, so we have to wait for them to be picked up. It feels like we're doing something wrong by sitting around, so I try to keep busy, but there's really not much to do. I sweep up a little—totally unnecessary—and engage in a host of pointless tasks like polishing the handles of a scissor with my shirtsleeve. I also start making the combos very deliberately, walking around the cardboard containers with the plastic wrap as slowly as possible. I usually walk around the combos in a counterclockwise direction but start switching this up: This counts as my entertainment for the night.

By the third evening I don't even try to look busy. I want to transfer out of here; I want a supervisor to realize that Pilgrim's Pride is wasting money and put me into debone, or DSI, or anywhere that actually has something for me to do. In a plant that pushes its workers to keep up a fast pace, I've somehow found the one job in which I can literally do nothing. It may seem strange to complain, but the truth is that a night of sitting around and freezing my ass off passes a lot more slowly than one in which I'm actually doing something. Ever have a day at the office where you didn't have a single thing to do? Remember how long that day lasted? That's how I'm feeling, except my office doesn't have an Internet connection and is located in a walk-in freezer, so I'm also shivering like mad and tapping out songs on my knees and occasionally jumping up and down.

So I start walking around. Not to be rebellious or for journalistic purposes—I've already seen most areas of the plant—but simply because I need something to do. I walk circles around DSI, I stroll past the debone line, I make repeated and unnecessary trips to the bathroom. I say hi to Kyle as he shovels ice into combos, I check in on Mario and Jesús, I observe Ben struggling with a few heavy tubs. But it's cold just standing around and gawking, so I saunter around the much warmer break room and then figure what the hell and buy a coffee and drink it in a booth. It's not break time but no one says anything, so I put my head down and fall asleep for who knows how long, then walk back to my station and see that we still have thirteen combos waiting to be picked up. David is sitting on a box staring at the ground. When he sees me, he shrugs then spits tobacco juice into a bottle he has tucked away in a shirt pocket. So I make another round. By Thursday, workers in rehang, who have watched me do very little as they keep up a frantic pace, make a sign of rubbing their fingers with their thumb when I pass: easy money.

"*Dinero fácil,*" Mario tells me during break, echoing their sentiments. Maybe so, but I can't take this much longer. I complain to Barbara that I have nothing to do, but she says that I'm to stay put. I stop by the HR office but Bill isn't around. Finally, on one of my strolls I try to circumvent the bureaucracy by asking the debone supervisor, a Mexican immigrant named Carlos, if he needs any help. He looks at me, confused for a moment, but says he'll see what he can do. I would bet quite a bit of money this is the first time a worker has requested a transfer to his department.

On the last night of work for the week, I meet Fernando, a Guatemalan in the rehang department. I've seen him give me the easy money gesture a number of times, and during a break he calls me over. He's sitting alone in his booth, and is surprised to learn I speak Spanish and have traveled through Guatemala. He tells me that he never went to school—not even grade school—and harvested sugar cane as a kid. He was eighteen when he came to the United States in 1999. For some reason he seems to trust me instantly, and without prodding reveals that he spent five months on the border in Nogales, Mexico, working in construction to earn money to pay a smuggler to guide him across.

"But how did you get a job here?" I ask. "They checked out my Social Security number and everything." This is something I've been curious about but afraid to ask.

He smiles. "It's a real number; it just belongs to someone else. I paid for it after I came here." He doesn't know the owner of the number and doesn't appear particularly interested in finding out.

"Supposedly he's Puerto Rican. Where are you staying?" I describe my trailer's location. "I know that trailer. I live nearby. If you want sometime you could go to church with me. Do you go to church?"

"No, not normally. But I'd go with you." As people start heading back we exchange phone numbers.

"I go to services on Saturday night," he says. "If you want to go, give me a call and I'll pick you up."

RELIGION IS VERY important in Russellville, and a more determined reporter would already have spent his weekends visiting different congregations instead of camped out in the library. Even though I have yet to step inside a church, I've nonetheless been struck by the degree to which they dominate the landscape. On one of my walking tours of downtown, the first place of worship I noticed was Faith Outreach Mission, its name freshly emblazoned in a bright red font over a modern black façade. Two red-and-orange flame decals were affixed to its glass windows, along with an image of Jesus, a crown of thorns atop his head. The effect was dramatic and aggressive.

Next door I noticed the Church of God, which was within sight of My Father's House Church, which was near Iglesia Pentecostes.

Storefronts on the next block included The Church on the Street, Ministerio Emmanuel, and Igelsia Bethel del Congreso. The string of churches was broken up by a Spanish bookstore and the Eagle's Nest Youth Center. In the bookstore, every title was about Jesus; the youth center was a space for teenagers "where living for Jesus is cool." One block north was the First United Baptist Church, followed by the First United Methodist Church, which was across the street from the Church of Christ, which was near the Casa del Padre, which sat directly opposite the New Beginning Worship Center (which was looking for musicians to join its praise and worship team).

I call Fernando on Saturday afternoon and a few hours later he pulls into my driveway, his eighteen-month-old son, Ricky, in a car seat in the back. Fernando's evangelical church is located in the eastern section of Russellville, not far from the highway, and when we enter, thirty people are already seated on folding chairs and singing. The crowd seems to be entirely Guatemalan except for a bearded white man named Jimmy, who doesn't speak Spanish but later says that he enjoys the energy of the group.

And there is a lot of energy: The church's amplification system seems more appropriate for a large hall with hundreds of congregants. We take seats in the fourth row, about twenty feet from the stage, where eight speakers are lined up, each five feet tall. A guitarist strums one chord repeatedly, the bassist plucks two notes, and a drummer keeps up a steady four-beat rhythm. None of their efforts are easy to hear, as they are drowned out by the cacophony created by two very enthusiastic men on keyboards. While they occasionally tap out simple melodies, the pair prefers the dizzying number of special effects generated by their machines, and at times the results sound less like music than a fireworks display. "Jesus Christ is everywhere!" Ba-boom! "From Guatemala to Alabama!" Ba-da-boom! I'm not much of a singer, but it doesn't take long for me to get into the act, standing and clapping with the group.

As the singing continues the audience grows livelier. In the pauses between words, people start shouting "Hallelujah!" and "¡*Cristo vive!*" (Christ lives). We keep this up for sixty minutes until the guest pastor—a short man with dark skin and a white double-breasted suit—takes the microphone. His sermon emphasizes the idea that if we follow Jesus we will meet him in heaven.

Once he has finished speaking, we reach a period called free time, which I assumed was set aside for mingling and drinking coffee. Instead it is a chance for members to come up and share their stories. Tonight's speaker is a solidly built Guatemalan man dressed in jeans and a flannel shirt, by far the least formally attired person present (many of the congregants are wearing suits and dresses). He speaks eloquently about coming to the United States as a teenager to better his life and then succumbing to alcohol. It is a brutally honest account—he mentions visiting prostitutes while working in the fields of California and "doing other things that I knew I shouldn't do, but that I didn't seem able to stop." In Russellville he has sobered up, found God, and "become more honest and less ashamed." By the time he finishes, tears are streaming down his face. The audience stands and applauds loudly, then begins another song.

Once the service concludes, we move to another room for a quick meal of tortillas, rice, and chicken. On the way home, Fernando tells me that he too had a problem with alcohol when he arrived. Like many American teenagers, it seems that he started drinking out of boredom. He didn't know very many people, he was away from his family, and there wasn't a whole lot to do in Russellville. Like Dagoberto, the rally organizer, and the man who made the church presentation, Fernando credits church with helping him swear off alcohol, because "at the church you have people who look after you and care for you."

When I was young, I remember church as a sterile place where I had to sit down and stay quiet, but in Russellville the institution appears to play an opposite role, providing a space where people can let their guards down. Walking around downtown, the immigrants I pass often look serious and even apprehensive. Church, on the other hand, is a forum where folks can talk and laugh and sing, a place where they can share the many stresses that come with being an immigrant in a new land and receive critical moral support. I later attend an overflowing crowd at Good Shepherd Catholic Church, where I recognize dozens of faces from the plant. The mood at Good Shepherd, like Fernando's church, is celebratory.

"When I arrived they held a great welcoming party for me," says Father Jim Hedderman. Hedderman, who stands 6 foot 3 inches tall and weighs "255 pounds and going down," recently arrived in town from Huntsville. Known as Father Jaime, he is a jolly presence who takes a more lighthearted approach to Catholicism: He describes his perspective as, "No guilt, no guilt—we've had enough guilt already!" With a church of 400 families—350 of them immigrant—he loves the new assignment. "It is so *fun*," he says, laughing. "We have a soccer field behind the church, people playing all sorts of games—there's a spirit of youth and energy here." He speaks Spanish but also hears confessions in various indigenous languages like Quiché and Q'anjob'al.

"You don't find as much isolation among the Hispanic culture as you do among Anglos," he tells me. Along with strong family ties, it is the church that plays the central role in creating a sense of community. Although many of his immigrant parishioners are earning poverty wages, they usually have large support systems of friends and relatives. "The majority of people coming to the church for financial assistance are whites," he says. "They are the ones who can feel very alone."

CHAPTER 10

On Sunday night a debone supervisor stands in our path as we head onto the processing floor. "Everybody stop and wash your hands!" she shouts, motioning to a long sink against the wall that is typically ignored. I am walking in with Ben, and like everyone else we grumble and wonder what's going on, but do as we're told. Already waiting at DSI, Kyle has heard a rumor that "the Russians are coming." Apparently one of the company's Russian clients will be inspecting the plant before renewing a leg meat contract, and so for a few days we are to put on a show and act as if we always wash our hands at this station. "This happens every time someone important comes," Kyle says.

The news about the Russians provides a momentary distraction from what is usually the most punishing night of the week. Sundays are the hardest for me—and many others—because we've returned to a normal sleep schedule over the weekend. This wasn't my original plan; I figured that I would become a night owl and maintain a daytime sleeping schedule even on my days off. But after a week of fitful sleep, I find that I need the weekend to recharge, and often sleep twelve hours a night.

During the first break I put my head down but am awakened by a tap on the shoulder. "You eat hot dogs?" Kyle asks. I shake my head. Cindy has packed him a lunch of franks but he's no longer hungry: He just spent three hours in a department called MSC (mechanically separated chicken). "They take the chicken skeletons and grind them up in a machine," he says. "They come out the other side like franks in this brown paste. I sit there looking for foreign objects in the bones before they are ground up." He shivers.

"Foreign objects like what?"

"Anything, I guess. Plastic, pieces of tape. I've been finding tape—found maybe fifteen so far."

"And if you miss one?"

"Then I guess someone will be eating tape in their hot dog. I saw a chicken eye pass by, didn't touch that. You want my hot dogs?"

"Nope."

"Maybe if I worked here for a couple of weeks I'd get used to it. But I don't think I can eat these right now." I mentally add a walk-through of MSC to my list of areas I want to visit before I leave the plant; my agenda already includes a tour of the live hang floor and paw (chicken feet) department, where I hope to surreptitiously snap a couple of photos. I'm saving this mission for my last week of work—I have two left—just in case a supervisor catches me and asks what the hell I'm doing.

There is some amusement tonight on the line, thanks to Debbie. After the break, while I am dumping for Mario, he slows the pace in which he places the breasts on the line.

"¿Qué pasa?" I shout.

"It's not cutting right," Mario says. He points at the spot where the first slice is made to lop off the top. "If I go quicker the machine won't be able to keep up." I can't see what he is referring to, but am happy nonetheless: The slower pace means I don't have to dump as many tubs. After a few minutes he stops entirely. "It's not working."

Debbie passes by, pauses at the bin, and shouts, "*¡Ándale, Mario!*" Mario looks at her and points to the machine, starting to say something. "Hurry, Mario. *¡Ándale!*" With Debbie still hovering, he shrugs and starts throwing the breasts on the belt, trying to hide a growing smile. Satisfied, she walks away.

"Stop! Mario, stop!" Less than a minute later the machine has jammed, incorrectly cutting a bunch of breasts that will now be discarded. Mario, usually sober-faced, is grinning widely. We pull off our gloves and wait for the mechanics. One of the women lining up the breasts calls me over angrily.

"Who told you to start up again?"

"Debbie."

"Aaargh! I knew it! She doesn't have a clue. If I—"

"Hey, what's wrong?" Debbie has popped out from behind the slicing contraption. "You doing okay?"

The woman grabs her back. "Oh, nothing. Just my back is hurting."

Standing next to the bin with Mario, I say, "You should be a supervisor. You know more than her, for sure."

"I can't. You need a GED." If that's true, it's nonsense—though it might explain why, in a plant where at least one-third of the workers are immigrants, there is only one Latino supervisor, the Mexican immigrant in the debone department whom I spoke to about transferring.

I rest for a few more moments and then join Ben in dumping tubs for the other line, which is running smoothly. As always, his cheeks are bright red and sweat is pouring down his face. "What's up, loser?" he asks, glad for the help. Five minutes later, Barbara yells for us to stop this line, as well.

For the next thirty minutes no one is doing anything. Jesús goes to the bathroom; Ben leans against the wall, recuperating and flexing his right wrist, still with a brace around it; the six women who line up breasts are talking to each other. I toss a few pieces of ice at Kyle, who is standing across the line and leaning on the shovel he uses to deposit dry ice in combos. My throws sail wide and he doesn't notice: He's in another animated conversation with someone about the prospects of the University of Alabama's football team this year. The only people not enjoying the break are Debbie and Barbara, who are staring at the machine while the mechanics go to work, probably with no better understanding of what is wrong than we have, though making a point of scrunching up their faces as if in deep concentration. Debbie in particular seems distraught by the malfunctions, and walks back and forth along the line in agitation.

"She's pissed that we're resting," I say to Mario.

"She always gets upset when the machine breaks. One time she even started crying."

I ponder this as I join Ben in leaning against the wall. In my mind, Debbie has grown to embody everything that is wrong with bosses: all-powerful, demanding, condescending. I've even started to think of her as some sort of big shot that needs to be taken down a level. But she cried when the machine broke down? Imagining tears streaking down her face as she pounds the machine in frustration triggers a realization: She isn't too high above us. A typical plant worker earns less than $17,000 a year; I doubt Debbie makes more than $25,000. Sure, her work is less dangerous and less repetitive, but she's earning working-class wages. And unlike many of my coworkers and me, she is very emotionally invested in the work. I resolve to try and think nicer thoughts about her.

Ah, but how quickly sympathy disappears! Once the line is back up and running, she comes over as I'm lifting an eighty-pound tub. "I don't want Mario taking any breaks," she says. "You need to make sure the tub is always completely full so that he doesn't have to reach. *No reaching.*" I grunt as I raise the tub to my chest and dump the meat over the lip of the bin. When Mario works quickly, he can sometimes clear out the section of the bin nearest him, and so he reaches across to pull breasts stacked on the other side. Over the course of an eight-hour shift, there is no way that this movement could use more than a minute's time.

"No breaks, Mario," she says as she walks away. "*Ándale.*"

I tell Mario about the no reaching rule, and he scoffs. "She thinks this is easy, but I'd like to see her come do it," he says. "It's very easy when all you have to do is talk."

At 7:40 a.m., when I've dumped the last tub and Mario is finishing up, Debbie walks over, evidently concerned that she hasn't caused enough trouble. "*Ándale*, Mario!" After a long shift and several visits from Debbie, Mario has finally reached the limits of his tolerance, and he does the unthinkable: He begins to slow his pace. The message is obvious—get out of my face and let me do my work—but a smiling Debbie doesn't seem to get it. "Come on, Mario!" Mario keeps up the slower pace until he places the last chicken breast on the belt, all the while listening to Debbie's encouragement. Once the tub is empty she actually starts clapping.

I SLEEP UNTIL noon and wake up both restless and groggy. It is a testament to the vertiginous nature of the night shift at a chicken plant that, entering my second month, I simultaneously feel as if my time in Alabama is rushing past in a blur, creating few distinct memories while hidden within every blurry day are stubborn hours that refuse to pass normally, stretching so long as to nearly stand still. Add the intense daytime heat and humidity with the frigid nighttime temperatures of the processing plant—along with varying degrees of sleep deprivation—and the most precise description of my state of mind is discombobulated.

I tell myself that I should get out more during the day. With two weeks left, I am growing convinced that I need to augment my work experiences with more traditional reporting. Up to this point I have purposely kept a low profile so as not to attract undue attention, and I have told only a few select people about my book. I've been in Russellville for seven weeks and I've settled in nicely—now is the time to start exploring. And I already know my first goal. I want somehow to gain access to the inside of a chicken farm.

Hundreds of thousands of live chickens are trucked in every day to be slaughtered and processed, many passing within a hundred feet of my trailer. But though I watch the birds on their journey, and help turn them into fattening finger food, I know about only the last hour of their life. I want to walk through a factory farm where the chickens spend about six miserable weeks before reaching slaughter weight (fifty years ago, without the benefit of growth-enhancing drugs or high doses of antibiotics, this "growing" process took more than three months). I've read horror stories about these farms, where tens of thousands of birds are stuffed into cramped sheds reeking of ammonia from chicken shit, frequently collapse on broken legs that can't support their enormous breasts, and see the light of day only when they make their short trip to the slaughterhouse. But during my bike rides around the countryside, I have yet to see a single farm.

Ironically, McDonald's is the only place in Russellville that I've found with public Internet access, aside from a Christian bookstore that keeps irregular hours. After some online exploring, I'm able to download a list of factory farms in Alabama from the Environmental Protection Agency. There are dozens in Franklin County, and I select one of the nearest, which looks to be about ten miles east of my trailer.

The following afternoon I head out to the chicken farm, cycling past Mama's Kitchen and turning east. The ride takes me through miles of hilly countryside occasionally interrupted by collapsing farmhouses and trailers, which are set back from the narrow road and often obscured by brush. Some of the structures are evidently still inhabited, as twice I find—with no warning barks—a large canine sprinting several paces behind me, trying to tear off my ankles.*

I arrive at my destination—an impressive two-story brick house—in forty-five minutes, without passing a single car. Six long and low buildings are off to the left, down a dirt path: These are the sheds where the chickens are kept. I expected them to be noisy, but I don't even hear the proverbial peep. At the head of the dirt path is a sign with the Pilgrim's Pride logo, and another with some sort of bio-safety emblem and a warning not to trespass. A truck is in the driveway and as I approach the door of the house, I prepare my rap. I need to explain who I am and what I am doing as concisely and innocently as possible. I can't imagine the farmer has many unannounced visitors, and I'm probably the first adult who has ever biked up to his house to say hello. I'm also from out of town, and a journalist, and covered in sweat. I sop up the moisture from my forehead with the sleeve of my T-shirt. I hear someone approaching and take a deep breath.

---

* This is a recurring event—it happens nearly every time I ride into Russellville—that never fails to deliver at least several seconds of sheer terror. There is nothing quite like cycling through peaceful pastures, only to be set upon by a rabid-looking dog gnashing its teeth as it tries to pull you from your bike and, presumably, devour you.

A slender blond-haired woman, probably in her forties, opens the door. "Hello?"

"Hi, how are you doing?" I introduce myself as a journalist from New York City who is writing about the poultry industry. "I was riding by and saw the sign for Pilgrim's Pride and thought maybe you all raised chickens here." As I talk I do my best to read her face but find it hard to know what she is thinking. If anything, she looks skeptical.

"It's my husband that takes care of that," she says, "and he's not here."

I immediately fill the awkward silence that follows her declarative statement with talk. Friendly talk; ingratiating talk. I explain that I decided to move to Russellville for two months in order to complete a book that deals, in part, with the poultry industry. "I'm hoping to learn as much as possible—about how chickens are raised and killed and processed. I already know it's one of those industries that we all depend on but that very few people really know anything about." Still nothing—I keep talking. "So I've been working for a while at the plant and have learned how hard that work can be. But I thought it would be good to also tour a farm and interview a farmer, you know, 'cause the work they do, I'm sure, is just as hard, and I want to be able to explain that side of things."

As I'm rambling her face seems to soften. "I'm sure my husband wouldn't mind showing you around," she eventually says. "He feeds the chickens every morning at 8:30. You can stop by then if you want." I thank her and say I'll be by in the morning, then decide to give her my name and phone number so that her husband can call if anything comes up. And indeed, while I'm taking a nap that evening, he leaves me a message on my cell phone. Though he'd like to help me out, he can't give me a tour.

He tells me that as a chicken farmer he's too concerned about bio-safety; I might have a cold and pass the germs along to his chickens.

I'm frustrated, but at least I still have a long list of farms within biking distance that I can check out. Eventually I'll get lucky.

But the following day is simply too hot, so instead of going in search of another farm I decide to eat lunch at Mama's Kitchen. With my time winding down, I have been meaning to stop by and tell Sabrina that I'm a journalist. I know she won't blow my cover, and she'll probably get a kick out of the project. Also, there is something in me that wants to divulge my secret, to explain my project to other people.

Thus far in Alabama, when I've told someone that I'm a reporter—which I consider to be very important news—they are completely unmoved. But Sabrina's reaction is dramatic. Standing behind the store's counter, she lets out a relieved sigh and breaks into a wide grin. I stand there proudly: She is evidently impressed that I've written books and articles.

"Gabriel, I was sure you were immigration."

The pride turns to shock. She believed I was an undercover federal agent with Immigration and Customs Enforcement (ICE).

"I thought you were here to get a job and investigate and deport the workers. You're a journalist? I have to tell my friend!" She goes into the kitchen and returns with a newspaper clipping about a new deportation scheme by the U.S. government, speaking into her phone rapidly. I hear her tell the person on the other end about me. "He works with the union—he's in Postville right now," she says after hanging up. Three months earlier, ICE conducted a massive raid at Agriprocessors Inc.'s kosher slaughterhouse in Postville, Iowa, and arrested 389 undocumented immigrants. About 300 of the immigrants, primarily from Guatemala, were convicted of identity fraud in speedy trials and sentenced to five months in federal prison, in what was the largest immigration enforcement operation at a single workplace. (Later that year, in August, an even larger raid in Laurel, Mississippi, would result in the arrest of 595 undocumented immigrants working at a Howard Industries transformer plant.)

In retrospect, the fact that I might have been an immigration agent was an obvious possibility. I knew that in April 2008, while I was planning out the details of the trip, ICE had raided five Pilgrim's Pride plants—in Arkansas, Tennessee, Florida, West Virginia, and Texas—and took 400 workers into custody. Although they hadn't targeted Russellville, workers had undoubtedly been following the news closely. But I naively figured that once I started speaking Spanish and displaying my sympathies, people would trust me.

Sabrina evidently did trust me, at the outset—at least enough to rent me her trailer. But I learn that she started wondering about me and speaking to her friends, and became convinced I had an ulterior motive (which I did—just not to deport immigrants). Why else would an American citizen who spoke perfect English and passable Spanish—and who lived in New York City—wind up renting a broken-down trailer and working the graveyard shift? I recall, too, her exact words when describing the trailer:

"You should know that there are only Mexicans and Guatemalans living around it."

And my reaction: "*Perfecto*."

For weeks now, Sabrina, an ardent defender of immigrants, believed that she was renting a trailer to an immigration agent. Earlier, she had invited me to her daughter's fifteenth-birthday celebration—her *quinceanera*. Now I understand why she had retracted the invitation: She figured it was an intelligence-gathering activity.

Biking back to the trailer, I feel like a fool. Do most of the immigrants at the plant think I'm with immigration? Does Jesús? Or Mario? I was certain that I had a rapport with both of them, but I was certain that Sabrina and I had a rapport too. I'm the friendly white guy who speaks Spanish and is interested in hearing details about the lives of immigrants. What sounded innocent now seems pretty damn suspicious. I decide to tell Jesús and Mario tonight about my book.

AS I'M TIEING on my smock and noticing a long tear down one side, Barbara comes up to me.

"HR says they want to see you."

"About what?"

"Don't know. They just said for me to bring you." After more than a month of requesting a move to debone, maybe they're finally taking me up on the offer. I'm glad, but also annoyed, since I'm eager to divulge my secret to Mario and Jesús. I suppose it doesn't matter; I can tell them during break.

I follow Barbara back through the plant and down a series of offices. We turn into one room, where a white man with wispy brown hair is seated behind a desk. He looks to be in his late thirties. A younger Latina woman is perched on a chair to his right.

"You don't need me, right?" Barbara asks before heading back.

"Have a seat. I'm Eric," the man behind the desk says. He explains that he is the head of human resources for the plant. I have the first flash of anxiety. "This is a complicated story, and we have a lot of questions, but we should probably start first at one point and then go backward. We've been speaking to corporate and our lawyers, and we decided that in today's environment, we're going to have to let you go."

I hear the words clearly, but they seem far away. "Let me go?"

"We got a call from one of our farmers. He said a journalist wanted to get a tour of the farm, and that he was working at the plant. So we pulled your file. We went on your Web site and read your writings."

The pace of events has exceeded my ability to make sense of them, as if someone has smothered my brain with a pillow. "Uhhh . . . oh?" I look up to see Bill, the HR night manager, standing in the doorway.

"Hey, Bill, you know Gabriel, right?" He nods a hello and steps into the room. Eric tells me that he's been given a list of items from the attorneys of Pilgrim's Pride that he has to go through. If I've taken photographs or video in the plant, I need to turn in the footage. (I haven't done either, as I was saving any documentation for next week.) Eric has me surrender my ID card—which I had hoped to save as a memento—and explains that had I contacted Pilgrim's Pride as a journalist, perhaps something could have been worked out in terms of me working at the plant. There's no reason to argue the point, though it's obviously false. Pilgrim's Pride wouldn't have acceded to my request to work at the plant with knowledge that I was a journalist for the same reason they are now firing me.*

"Okay, I think that's everything the lawyers wanted me to say," Eric says, sounding relieved. "This has gone much better than we expected." Thus far I've listened quietly. Did they anticipate that

---

* The following week, Trevor Stokes, a reporter with the *Times Daily*, a paper out of the nearby town of Florence, visited the plant in an attempt to get a comment for a story he was writing about immigration in Franklin County. His brief "interview" went poorly: The plant manager ushered him off the property and refused even to give her name. So I think it is safe to say that the company would not have "worked something out" with me had I been up front about my identity and project.

I would jump up and angrily denounce my firing? "Now that that's out of the way," Eric continues, "I'm hoping we can just talk. We've all been scratching our heads over here since we found out. I mean, I've only been here three weeks, and I find out there's a guy here from Brooklyn, and this is how I have to meet him?" It turns out Eric is a new hire, having arrived not long after me, and is originally from upstate New York.

Since receiving the farmer's phone call, Eric has read a number of my articles and ordered both of my books from Amazon. "I'm fascinated by what you've been writing," he tells me. "I almost signed up for your newsletter, but I figured that would be strange to do before we met. Can you tell us what exactly you're doing?" By now I'm mentally caught up with what's happening, so I'm able to give my five-minute marketing pitch: I'm writing about immigrant work by actually doing jobs alongside immigrants.

"I'm sorry I never got you a job in debone," Bill says once I'm finished, sounding like he means it.

"That's okay—dumping tubs was hard enough. I didn't want to push too much, 'cause I knew it was a strange request."

The Latina woman, whose name I don't catch, laughs. "That's right—no one wants to be transferred to debone." Like Eric, she's been reading my articles. "I really admire the work that you're doing," she says. This is getting weird, but I'm starting to enjoy it: I've got a mini fan club in human resources. On later reflection, I realize that I've probably provided some intrigue and relief from a job that—like the processing work—must get pretty monotonous and mind-numbing: endless orientations and worker interviews and everything else that constitutes the constant struggle to keep a poultry plant staffed. I would have imagined that this scene—being caught and fired—would be more hostile, but instead the room has a feeling of camaraderie.

And so, fifteen minutes after the firing business has been completed, I'm sitting in the same chair, feeling quite comfortable and chatting it up with the trio. Eric asks if I've read *The Omnivore's Dilemma* by Michael Pollan—I have—and points out the book on a shelf. It's not a title I'd expect to find in a plant of the largest poultry company in the world, but Eric tells me that his old job was at Petaluma Poultry, the organic chicken company that Pollan profiles. (It's not a very positive portrayal: Pollan finds 20,000 "free range" chickens crowded into a shed with very little room to move—much like factory-farmed chickens.)

I tell them my next stop on the immigrant work circuit will be New York City. "Let me know if you need a reference," Eric jokes, before the others file out and he gives me a ride to my trailer. I type up the notes of what happened and call my parents to tell them the news. "Can they just do that?" my mom asks. "Is it legal for them to fire you?" In the heat of the moment the question hadn't occurred to me. Either way, I explain that with my cover blown, I didn't feel like sticking around. I wanted to know what it was like to work at a poultry plant, which required that the company not know I was a journalist. (I later learn that since I was an "at will" employee, Pilgrim's Pride could legally fire me without cause.)

"You don't sound too upset," my father says. He's right. It took several minutes to recover from the initial shock of being discovered. Once I did, I was able to enjoy what should have been an awkward and unpleasant post-firing interview. Instead, it turned into a nice little chat—cheery even. While I was doing my best to remember each line that was said, in order to report it as accurately as possible, I was also distracted by a thought that kept surfacing every few minutes. With each repetition, a wave of relief washed over me: This means I don't have to dump tubs tonight. This means I don't have to dump tubs tonight.

Kyle stops by my trailer the next morning. "Where'd they put you last night? I didn't see you at break and couldn't find you when we got out." He listens to my story about being fired and about my real occupation. He is quiet and interested.

Finally, he says: "Gabriel, you're one slick motherfucker." It's one of the best compliments I've ever received.*

———————

* Although clearly false: A slick motherfucker wouldn't get caught and fired.

Part Three

FLOWERS AND FOOD

October–December, New York, New York

GETTING THE JOB

In October I'm ready to begin searching for work in my place of residence, New York City. Yuma and Russellville made the selection of work easy: Each had one major industry in town, and I just hoped they'd hire me. Here, one of my difficulties is deciding what type of work to seek out. New York is a city of immigrants: They clean our clothes and care for our children; build our homes and vacuum our offices; drive the taxis we hail; and cook the food we order. With 36 percent of New York City's residents foreign-born, one would be hard-pressed to find an industry that wasn't in some way dependent on their labor. So what should I aim for?

This question is tied up with another challenge of my project's new locale: Many low-wage immigrants find work in the city's sprawling underground economy. Here, employers are generally much smaller than Dole or Pilgrim's Pride—they might be a one-man construction company or a single, non-chain restaurant. Almost none of the dozens of undocumented immigrants I've known, either through my organizing work or as a journalist, had what we would call a traditional work arrangement. Instead, they are paid off the books, usually in cash, with no overtime and frequently earning less than the minimum wage. Many find jobs through informal references—someone tells a boss that their sister needs work—or unlicensed labor agencies. Manual laborers gather on corners hoping to be picked up for a day's work. I don't stand a chance on the corners, I'm likely to elicit suspicion if I entered a labor agency in an immigrant neighborhood, and I don't have any Mexican siblings to vouch for my dependability to their boss.

The third complication is that many workplaces are segregated by ethnicity. A construction foreman might want only Mexican workers; the head of a dry cleaner could prefer Chinese employees. At root, the informal referral systems and segregated workforces are a direct result of an employer's preference for a docile workforce. The bosses are breaking the law, day after day after day. They hope to find undocumented workers that they can exploit by paying sub-minimum wages and avoiding overtime.* "How do

---

* In response, some immigrants who are legally authorized to work instead present their employer with obviously forged immigration papers they have purchased on the black market. Because they know that the boss prefers to hire undocumented workers, their status as a legal immigrant, in such situations, becomes a guarded secret.

you plan on getting someone to hire you?" one of my friends asks, to which I have no real answer.

I'M PUZZLING OVER this riddle in my study when I hear snippets of Spanish. I prop open a window and lean out from the fourth floor. A crew of Ecuadorian workers, installing new windows, is perched precariously on wooden scaffolding held up by a primitive-looking system of ropes and pulleys. I ask about work and they tell me to speak to their Indian boss, who can be found at a midtown Manhattan worksite early each weekday morning. He pays cash, $100 a day.

I'm not able to track down the boss, but while cycling through Manhattan I nearly collide with a restaurant delivery worker who is blasting down Sixth Avenue against traffic. He apologizes to me for nearly ending my life, but the episode, and the sheer number of immigrant delivery workers I encounter on the street, leads me to spend the next week trying for a restaurant job, especially as I have read several stories about construction work drying up with the downswing in the economy. Without being able to think of a better strategy, I spend my days pedaling up to delivery workers to ask if they know whether their restaurant is hiring, explaining that I'm hoping for a job in dishwashing or delivery. This tactic surprises a few people; one older man, when I turn to ask my question as we're coasting up Eighth Avenue, flinches so dramatically that he nearly falls over. I decide to approach people at red lights.

A handful of men tell me that their restaurants are short delivery workers. When I show up, however, the bosses—who thus far are white, Latino, or Asian—look at me skeptically and tell me the position has just been filled. I don't believe them. I finally come close to being hired at a trendy Asian fusion restaurant near Union

Square, after spending ten minutes doing my best to convince a young Thai manager that I can handle delivery.

"But it's very, very hard," he says, arguing that I should consider a waiter position instead. "The Mexicans do the delivery, and you're not Mexican."

This is hard to refute. He finally hands me a card and tells me to stop by the next week. "Maybe the Mexicans will say yes, we'll see," he says, as if the delivery workers make the hiring decisions.

I inquire about jobs at twenty or so other restaurants over the next two days, without success. One morning, as I'm biking up a busy avenue in Chelsea to check out a few eateries near Central Park, I'm forced to slam on my brakes. A virtual forest has been planted in the bike lane. Hundreds of long branches, tied together with twine, are leaning against each other. Next to the branches are buckets of colorful flowers, and next to the flowers are potted plants that are overflowing into the traffic.

Cars are zipping by on my right at thirty miles per hour. As I'm standing over my bike, impatiently waiting for traffic to thin, I notice that two Latino men are frantically tossing bales of branches into the back of a large white commercial truck. Three other men, who are speaking Spanish to each other, come out of a storefront and join in. It slowly dawns on me that I've just entered New York's flower district.

"*¿Su jefe necesita gente? Estoy buscando trabajo.*" I ask the men if their boss needs any help.

One of them turns toward me; he is wearing a Guns 'N Roses *Appetite for Destruction* T-shirt. I take this as a good omen. "I don't know. You should go talk to the Greek inside."

I lock up my bike and walk into a storefront jammed with plants and trees. I squeeze through a narrow pathway to the back, where I find the "Greek," a man named Tony, sitting on a wooden stool and talking rapidly into a telephone. He is wearing jeans and a stained short-sleeve shirt with a drooping collar, and while his gray hair is thinning on the top, there is still enough on the sides to be unruly, giving the impression that he recently rolled out of bed. "Yes, beautiful maple, sir, best maple you can find," he says. "Come pick it up. Yes, sir, yes . . . okay." He hangs up.

"How can I help you, young man?"

"I'm looking for work."

"What kind of work?"

"Anything."

"Good, that's good, young man," he says approvingly; I almost expect him to pat me on the head. He writes down my name and phone number and sticks it on the wall. "The woman is out right now but I'll talk to her. Come back tomorrow. Maybe we can get you something." This feels very old-school, very mom-and-pop. It could provide a nice contrast to my last two jobs, both within multinational corporations.

"I have a really good feeling about the job," I tell my partner Daniella that night. "For some reason it feels like home to me."

I stop by the following day, but "the woman" is still out. "Come back tomorrow, young man," Tony tells me between phone calls. While I observe him during these brief interactions, he strikes me as the quintessential New Yorker: fast-moving, gruff, no-nonsense. Outside the shop I chat with one of the workers, Lucas, who keeps his long black hair in a ponytail and is wearing a blue tank top that reveals powerful arms. He's confused when I explain that I'm looking for work, thinking instead that I'm searching for a certain kind of plant.

"Oh, if you want a job, he [Tony] won't help you. He doesn't make any decisions. The real person in charge is Helen."

"That's what Tony told me. He said to come back tomorrow."

"But you don't want a job here."

"Sure I do. Why not? At least I can practice my Spanish."

"Well, maybe. But I don't think you'll like it."

"Is it that hard?" I ask.

"A little," is what I think I hear him say. Later I'll wonder about that, because *un poco* (a little) sounds similar to *es loco* (it's crazy).

I MAKE TWO more trips to the shop until I finally meet "the woman." Helen appears to be in her fifties and has blond hair; when she looks me over, her face—already tense—becomes even more pinched and pointed. I'm guessing it's been a long time since she's taken a deep breath.

"Where are you working now?" she asks. I tell her I'm unemployed.

"Where have you worked before?"

"I've done a lot of work. I've cut lettuce, construction, delivered pizzas—"

"What's the problem, you can't keep a job?"

"A lot of the jobs are seasonal, like lettuce. So they have work for only a few months."

"Where do you live?"

"Crown Heights, Brooklyn."

"Do you have a car?"

"No."

"How much rent do you pay?" A weird question, but I tell her.

"Who do you live with?"

There is no way this can be a legal question to ask a potential employee. Still, I comply: I want the job.

"What does your girlfriend do?"

A few more questions like this and she finally focuses her glare on something other than my face. She shrugs at Tony. "Okay, come by tomorrow at five in the morning. We'll see how you work."

"Before I leave, could you tell me, like, what I'll be doing or how much you pay?"

"You do whatever Tony tells you to do," she snaps. "I can't tell you money. We'll try you for a week and see what we think, then we talk about money."

CHAPTER 11

My alarm wakes me at 3:45 a.m. Thirty minutes and a shot of espresso later, I'm out the door. New York City at this hour is a magical place: deserted, quiet, manageable. It feels like my private metropolis as I cruise through downtown Brooklyn and across the Manhattan Bridge.

Lucas is in the shop with a white woman I haven't yet met; she writes up a time card for me and tells me to do whatever Lucas does. "The first thing we do is move all this stuff outside," he says. The storefront is even more claustrophobic than I remember, and as I follow Lucas deeper into the store, we have to push our way through branches as if we're bushwhacking. We spend the first fifteen minutes carrying bales of oak and maple branches outside, leaning them against the store's front window. Several other immigrant workers sleepily punch in and join us.

It's a pretty calm work environment until Tony arrives. I'm in the process of dragging two bales of birch through the front door.

"Morning," I say.

"Look at all those leaves, mister." I turn in the direction he is pointing, my early-morning brain still foggy. Leaves are strewn around the sidewalk. "Clean that up, mister. Get string and tie it up. Throw it away!" He dashes into the store.

It's not clear what I'm supposed to do. Tie up leaves with string? I tell Lucas, who is rushing past with a large plant, what Tony has said. "*Su abuelito es loco*," he replies. He's saying that Tony, whom he's calling my grandfather evidently because we're both white, is crazy.

After a few minutes of searching I finally come across a ball of twine and scissors. Tony is on the phone taking an order, so I don't bother him with questions. I cut several sections of twine and head back outside. As I'm looking at the leaves, still trying to formulate a plan, Tony rushes up to me.

"Mister!" he yells into my face. He hasn't brushed his teeth. "Mister, take the pear and put it in the corner." He points north, in the general direction of a white truck, and is off.

I stick the twine in my pocket, wondering what the branches of a pear tree might look like. Have I missed some sort of orientation? By now there are dozens of bales leaning against the storefront window. I stare at them for several seconds, until another worker passes by and points out the pear. I pick up the bale and hoist it over my right shoulder. "Put it in the corner," Tony has told me. I assume he means in the corner of the truck. I walk to the truck and am about to heave it in when I decide that it wouldn't hurt to double-check. I turn back and see Tony standing outside the store, staring at me.

"You want it in the corner of the truck?" I yell. He doesn't respond. "You want it here, in the corner of the truck?" Again, nothing. I'm sure he can hear me. Okay. I toss the pear bale in the truck. Tony walks over quickly.

"Mister, what are you doing? Mister, why didn't you listen to me? I said put it *in the corner*." I look at him blankly.

"Forget it. Hand it to me." I step inside the truck and pass him the branches. "In the corner, in the corner. That's what I told you, mister. You need to use common sense." He mutters to himself as he carries the branches up the street to the corner, dumping them in the middle of the sidewalk. Apparently someone is coming to pick them up. "Common sense, mister," he tells me when he returns. "In. The. Corner."

I WILL FOREVER remember the next five hours as being one of the most stressful periods in my life. If there is a system to the organization of the shop, I can't discern it. Tony paces back and forth, his faded jeans drooping low and the grimace on his face indicating the likelihood of cardiac arrest. His managerial style combines maximum intensity—just being in his presence causes my shirt to become soaked in sweat—with a reliance on enigmatic instructions. There is nothing here that should be so difficult: We are moving bales of branches outside, arranging plant and flower displays on the sidewalk for customers to peruse, and loading and unloading trucks. But with Tony as my boss, even the simplest task becomes damn near impossible to understand.

"We're looking sloppy out there!" he shouts in my face as I'm carrying two bales of oak, one over each shoulder. I nod. We cross paths again. This time, I'm lugging a massive pumpkin, which must weigh at least sixty pounds. Halloween is approaching. "Mister, we're looking really sloppy out there!" I have absolutely no idea what he is talking about.

Seeing my confusion, Lucas explains that when Tony shouts, "We're looking really sloppy out there!" he is actually instructing me to grab a broom and sweep the sidewalk. My task explained, I dig out a broom that is wedged between bales of magnolia. As I'm sweeping the leaves into a pile, Tony shouts from behind, "Wake up!" I turn around just in time to prevent a bale of branches from falling on me. "Wake up, mister! Put these in the truck. Gotta stay awake." I grab the branches, which have red berries hanging from them, to discover they are covered in thorns. (Later in the day I ask Lucas about gloves. "If you want them you have to buy them," he explains.)

Within an hour I'm alternating between waves of paranoia and fury. No matter what activity I am engaged in, Tony finds time to come up and make comments like, "Mister, what are you *doing?*" Often I am doing exactly what he had instructed me to do not five minutes earlier. I come to realize, after this happens a dozen times within twenty minutes, that he doesn't even seem aware that he is asking a question. Instead, he has developed two verbal tics. The first is to address everyone, incessantly, as mister. This is maddening enough; it is made worse by the fact that some of the other workers have picked up the habit. The second is that anytime he comes across workers—a frequent occurrence, as we are in a tight space—he automatically asks us what we're doing. As the boss, it would appear, his job is to accuse.

"You can't let your grandfather bother you," Lucas tells me at 9:00 a.m. We're standing behind the truck stripping leaves from birch branches, out of Tony's line of sight. "He's always like this. No one knows what he's talking about."

A tall white guy, who apparently knows Lucas, shouts out, "You've got a new guy!" Lucas nods.

"Just started," I say.

"Welcome to the jungle!" the man yells. "You learn quick enough it's crazy here."

As the morning wears on, I am relieved to see that Tony isn't singling me out; it's a jungle for everyone. By now I am working with four others, all immigrants: Lucas, Israel, and Carlos, in their late thirties or early forties, are from southern Mexico; and Antonio, a powerfully built twenty-seven-year-old, is from Honduras. None is safe from Tony's tirades, but though they make faces to each other when Tony isn't looking, they seem to be taking it in stride.

They have grown accustomed to a workday in which nothing is ever sufficiently explained, in which they are expected to jump from one random activity to another whenever Tony opens his mouth. I realize that I'm going to need to develop thick skin, and quickly.

"Right now it's good, because he can't see us," Lucas says as we continue to pull leaves from birch branches. "But the secret is to stay busy. Don't forget—they are always watching." He opens his eyes wide and moves his head back and forth, mimicking Big Brother. "If you don't know what to do, grab the broom. If they see that you are a good worker," he flexes his large right bicep, "then you shouldn't have any problems."

"Any idea how much money they will pay me?"

When he started, Lucas explains, he made between $300 and $350 a week for sixty hours of work—Sunday is the only day off. That comes to about $5 an hour. "But like I said, if they see you're a good worker they might pay more." At home that night I do the calculations. New York's minimum wage is $7.15 an hour. Factor in twenty hours of overtime, and an employer like Tony— if he's interested in complying with U.S. labor laws—owes each worker $500 before taxes.

As I'm moving goods back and forth between the store and the sidewalk, customers browse through our selection. It doesn't take long to learn to identify the basic branches: oak, maple, curly willow, birch, pear, and magnolia. My least favorite is the Washington hawthorn, with its red berries and sharp thorns. The customers, who seem mostly to be interior decorators, are of the sleek and skinny sort with spiked hair and too-tan skin; they could have walked directly into the shop from an MTV set. Some are quite nice, but a few are pushy and whiny and make no effort to get out of our way when we're balancing heavy loads. Twice I spin ever so slightly after passing customers of this type, giving a gentle tap to their heads with the back end of whatever I'm carrying over my shoulder.

RELIEF FINALLY COMES at 1:00 p.m., when Tony tells me to hop in a truck to make deliveries. The driver, Hector, is from Puerto Rico and has been working for the company for years. "How's it going, Junior?" he asks as we pull away. "This is your first day, right?"

"Yeah. This place is a little crazy."

"Don't worry about it. You can't let Tony bother you—he's always like this."

Over the next ninety minutes we make a half-dozen deliveries. Several smaller loads are for boutique flower shops; the others are large deliveries of branches for private parties ($750, for example, for magnolia and maple branches for the Union Club on the Upper East Side). The final stop is a residence near the Museum of Modern Art, where I use three different service elevators to bring a bale of pear and magnolia to an apartment on the forty-sixth floor. I'm in and out in a hurry but glimpse enough of a massive living room with a sweeping view to realize I am bringing branches to a very wealthy man (I later see a listing for a three-bedroom apartment in the building for $8.9 million).

As we're driving back to the shop, I ask Hector about the origin of the branches. He tells me that Tony has land in New Jersey where many of the trees are grown, and that a group of workers are responsible for cutting and loading the branches each day. Like lettuce, a bale of branches begins to die immediately after being cut, and so the product must be moved quickly in order to arrive looking like something you'd want to gaze on as you're sipping wine and discussing the most recent issue of the *New Yorker*.

"You getting hungry?" Hector asks.

"Yeah, was thinking about taking my break when we get back." I've been going nonstop for nearly nine hours now.

"Break?" He laughs. "They don't give you any breaks here, Junior. But if you're doing a delivery, you can grab something. Just make sure to finish it before we get back." We stop at a pizza joint and I gobble up two slices. It's 2:30 p.m. by the time we arrive back at the shop and the day is winding down—the flower district opens very early and is largely shuttered by the afternoon. After an hour of moving branches inside and sweeping up, I'm dismissed.

THE NEXT DAY I spend most of the morning hours making deliveries around the flower district—one dozen bales of various branches to G. Page Wholesale Flowers, a large shop located in the heart of the district on Twenty-eighth Street; large pumpkins to an advertising agency on Twenty-sixth Street; a collection of flowers for a nearby floral stylist.

I was too busy yesterday to get much of a sense of the flower district, though I had done some reading overnight and learned that the once sprawling region has been shrinking. In the 1960s the district was home to more than a hundred wholesalers, but today there are only about two dozen running along Twenty-eighth Street from Seventh Avenue to Broadway. (When it was formed in the mid-1890s, the district's borders went from Twenty-sixth Street to Twenty-ninth). Still, these two blocks are unlike anywhere else in the city; the urban bustle remains, but pedestrians pass beneath archways of ferns, forming single-file lines as they snake through endless rows of cut flowers and potted plants.

The main threat to the flower district has been real estate, especially since the 1990s, when the area was rezoned to make it easier to build residential buildings. As luxury buildings and hotels have displaced merchants, some advocated relocating the district to a cheaper neighborhood. A couple of years ago, the Flower Market Association—headed by Gary Page of G. Page Wholesale Flowers—believed they had enough support to move to Queens, but some merchants refused, forcing the association to scuttle the plan. As a result, Chelsea still has a couple of blocks left that remain interesting and eccentric, a reminder of what the city was like before the proliferation of generic luxury developments.

When I make my first delivery to G. Page Wholesale Flowers, it's not yet 6:00 a.m., but already dozens of Latino workers—mostly men—are frantically arranging bouquets and wrapping up flowers for customers. I make my way toward the rear with two bales of maple, passing rows of flowers bursting with color. (I am not a flower person, but I later log on to the G. Page Web site, which testifies to the global economy of cut flowers: They sell hydrangeas from Colombia, echeveria from New Zealand, roses from Ecuador, and orchids from Vietnam and Malaysia. The workforce is also geographically diverse: I speak briefly with men from Mexico, Ecuador, and Guatemala.)

Once I've completed the deliveries it's back to the same routine of trying to decipher Tony's orders. Around 10:00 a.m. one of the commercial trucks pulls in, driven by Helen, who shouts at Lucas and me to begin unloading. I walk to the back with Lucas, who pulls the rear door open. "Stay here and I'll hand the bales to you," he says.

Five seconds later, as Lucas is climbing into the truck, Helen rushes up. "What are you doing?" she shrieks at me. "Grab these, grab these!" She pulls out two bales, nearly tripping up Lucas, who is now standing in the truck, and slams them over my shoulder. "Go! Go!" I turn around and notice a black man standing several feet from me, waiting to cross the street.

"Whoa," he says softly. "What's up with her?"

I wonder the same question the rest of the day. As tiresome as Tony can be, he is no match for the sheer meanness of Helen. After we've unloaded the truck as quickly as humanly possible, I carry two bales of maple into the walk-in cooler in the back of the store.

"You need to take the trash out of the cooler," she orders as I pass.

I drop the maple in the cooler, step into the very back—and into three inches of icy water—and grab two soaked bags of trash. As I'm carrying the bags to the front, Carlos, who is standing on one of the wooden tables to my right, asks me to take a bale of magnolia that he is holding.

I place the bags of trash to my side so I don't completely block the only pathway through the store, a movement that takes anywhere from one to two seconds. I mention the elapsed time because such details are necessary to appreciate the extent to which Helen monitors our activity. "Wake up and help!" she yells, upset at the fraction of a second that I needed to position the heavy bags of sopping trash. As I'm carrying the magnolia out I hear her repeat the call for me to "wake up!" I wonder if she is on speed.

In the afternoon I feel fortunate when Helen orders me to accompany Lucas on a large walking delivery to a store on Twenty-eighth Street. The delivery includes boxes of lemon leaves and moss and bales of magnolia, which we place on a large dolly. The dolly, however, keeps wanting to swerve right—into oncoming traffic—so we have to walk slowly, and when we arrive at the building we're forced to wait several minutes for the service elevator.

As we're walking back we find Helen angrily pacing toward us. "Where have you been?" she roars, coming at us with frightening speed. I half expect her to clock Lucas and me in the face. "It took you thirty minutes to make a delivery!" It hasn't been anywhere near thirty minutes. I could also mention the broken dolly and the elevator delay, but instead follow Lucas's lead and stay silent. She turns and, now nearly running, heads back to the store. Lucas curses her in Spanish.

"He's crazy . . . she's crazy. I don't know why you want to work here. If I was an American—if I had papers—I would move on to something else." He's been at the shop for several years and, like the other Latino workers, he is undocumented.

I have to admit that the possibility of a quick exit has already entered my mind. Yesterday evening, as I lay exhausted on the couch and recounted the day, Daniella said that she didn't see how I'd last one month—much less the two months I set as my goal for each occupation. I was starting to wonder that myself. By now I knew that I could handle hard physical labor and had learned to put my head down and grit through tough shifts. But what I wasn't accustomed to was the relentless verbal harassment *while* I worked. This was an entirely new experience, and it left me drained and feeling defeated.

BY 4:00 P.M. the store is closed and the workers have gathered inside, drinking Coronas and trying to figure out what to do on this Friday afternoon. After an eleven-hour day without a break I'm exhausted and ready to head home, but I'm waiting in the doorway of the office. Helen is sitting in the cramped space with another woman, evidently the bookkeeper. At Helen's desk is a checkbook, in her hand a pen. "I'm having a problem because we didn't decide on how much to pay you." She sighs, grimaces, and sighs again, as if this is a burden I ungraciously placed on her shoulders. I've been standing in the doorway for at least two minutes, watching her agonize over my payment.

"A lot of the time you look lost, like you don't know what to do." She continues to finger the checkbook. Finally she writes out $150 for my 21.5 hours. That's less than $7 an hour; minimum wage in New York is $7.15. "Maybe if it was the summertime . . ."

I start to realize that I'm being fired. "I'm all set to come in tomorrow, just tell me what time," I say, trying to change the direction of the dialogue. "I'm still learning, but I'm getting it."

"But I can tell that you are not made for this work." Helen looks over at the bookkeeper as if for assurance. "You're like a happy chicken out there. Always smiling."

What the fuck is a happy chicken? I leave the question unasked. "That's just how I am. It doesn't matter what I'm doing, I'm going to try and enjoy it." She shakes her head slowly.

"If it was summertime and slower maybe we could use you."

Now I'm shifting from shock to anger. "How am I supposed to know everything? It might seem like common sense to you and Tony but I've been here only two days. When I started I didn't even know what a magnolia tree looked like."

She shakes her head again. "It's not just the magnolia trees. If you don't know something, you should ask Tony."

Hysterical. What world is this woman living in? I quickly learned that asking Tony a question—any question—was useless. He ignored my questions; only once did he actually answer. Yesterday afternoon he told me to sweep trash into a bag. I did, and then made the mistake of asking where he wanted the trash placed.

"What should you do with the trash?" he asked. "You should call UPS and have them pick it up. Come on, mister—common sense!"

"You must know that Tony doesn't answer questions," I tell Helen. I consider reciting a list of the responses Tony has given me—beginning with the UPS anecdote—but can already sense the futility of arguing with her.

"You just don't fit in here. You can call Tony tomorrow and see what he says." I stand up, wanting to curse her out. Instead I walk away, tell the workers I've been fired—they are all equally incredulous—and bike home. I call Tony the next day and plead to be rehired, but he doesn't budge.

OVER THE WEEKEND I process the two-day experience. After surviving in lettuce fields and a poultry plant, I certainly didn't expect to be fired from a flower shop of all places. It was difficult to explain the firing to friends. Why, they wondered, would this store—in violation of so many labor laws—even hire

me? And once they decided to hire me, and saw that I was a dili-
gent employee, why let me go so soon? It would have been one
thing had I loafed or talked back. But I worked *hard* in the shop.
I held my tongue when yelled at; I learned to remain silent and
keep my eyes down when Tony or Helen went off. I didn't even
complain about not having a lunch break, or ask for gloves to
protect my hands. When I was given a task I did it, as quickly as
possible. On my second day another new worker showed up,
from Ecuador. I helped him out as much as I could, but he was
having an even more difficult time than I in keeping up. This
man, I later learned, kept the job.

The issue, I came to believe, wasn't about "work ethics" or "following instructions" or any other concrete criticism a boss might
make. It was about power and submission. Tony and Helen, the
rulers of their little fiefdom, had a very particular notion of how a
worker ought to comport themselves. They should hang their
heads, look miserable, and extract very little enjoyment out of the
experience. In my case, they were mostly successful: I hated being
at the shop. But I still did my best to keep up a friendly banter with
coworkers and maintain an incongruous smile on my face throughout much of the day. It was a means to mentally distance myself
from the place, to assert some small measure of levity into an environment that felt like a sweatshop. While I was on the clock they
owned me—as they did everyone else—but my "happy chicken"
antics evidently made this sense of ownership less secure. What if
the other workers started smiling? That could be dangerous.

IN 2007 THE Brennan Center for Justice, a progressive think
tank, published a report on the unregulated economy in New York
City. Although the underground economy is vast, they wrote, it
is "a world of work that lies outside the experience and imagination of many Americans":

It is a world where jobs pay less than the minimum wage, and sometimes nothing at all; where employers do not pay overtime for 60-hour weeks, and deny meal breaks that are required by law; where vital health and safety regulations are routinely ignored, even after injuries occur; and where workers are subject to blatant discrimination, and retaliated against for speaking up or trying to organize.[1]

I found low wages and grueling conditions in Yuma and Russellville, and judging the work by degree of difficulty alone, the flower shop was an "easier" job. I wasn't stooped over in the sun or lifting and dumping tons of chicken breasts. But there is something qualitatively different about my short-lived stint in the flower district. They didn't pay overtime or grant lunch breaks— and paid me less than the minimum wage—but these are not the abuses I will remember. What leaves a lasting impression is the incessant string of accusatory comments, the assumption that we, as workers, merited zero respect. In sum, I will remember being in an environment where the workers were treated as chattel—a more difficult phenomenon to quantify with statistics than wages, but a key component of the work experience for many undocumented immigrants. Just as certain occupations are physically unsafe, certain workplaces are psychologically unhealthy (often, of course, they are both). On some level, then, I ought to be grateful to Tony and Helen for granting me direct access to a world hidden to most Americans—if only for a brief period. But gratitude isn't the first word that springs to mind.

And either way, Tony and Helen are now behind me. I've been fired twice in the last three months, and I'm back where I started: in need of a job.

CHAPTER 12

Less than a week after getting fired at the flower shop, I'm sitting in the lounge of a Mexican restaurant that I'll call Azteca, flipping through the most recent issue of *Portfolio*. The magazine's placement on the table is clearly a status signifier: Azteca aims to be the kind of place that people who read *Portfolio* go to eat, the sorts of folks who, even in an economic downturn, will gladly shell out $14 for an order of guacamole.

After a weekend spent recovering from the flower shop, I spent the first part of the week visiting another half-dozen restaurants, leaving my name and number with noncommittal managers. Azteca holds some promise, because Daniella saw a listing on Craigslist for various positions, including dishwashers and delivery workers. A manager named Greg, wearing a sleek dark suit, invites me to join him at a table in the bar area. Six feet tall and with closely cropped gray hair, he gives a cursory glance over my application and offers me a job in delivery. "We're adding more workers now 'cause we're going to get slammed soon, once we sign up for Seamless Web." Seamless Web, he explains, will allow customers to place delivery orders online.

"I could see you becoming the delivery team leader," he tells me. Thus far, I've shaken his hand and said hello.

"Thanks," I say, not knowing how else to respond.

He nods. "It will be nice to have someone who speaks English. I try to tell people things and they can't understand me." Ah, there's my leadership quality.

Greg doesn't ask many questions during the short interview, or seem surprised that I am interested in doing a job that is normally done by immigrants. He asks briefly about my work experience, and I tell him that I'm coming from a nearby flower shop—"It didn't work out so well"—and have done a variety of nonprofit work for my trusty reference, Artemio. Neither seems to raise any red flags. In fact, once I've accepted the job, Greg is too distracted to focus on the interview; his eyes dart around the mostly empty restaurant, giving the sense that he's got important work left undone. He tells me to come back tomorrow with my Social Security card and driver's license. "Once we get that, you will have a day-long orientation and trail a person for two days." Like the flower shop, there is no discussion of pay, although they do check my license and Social Security card.

The following day Greg is out, but a young Latina at the hostess station is expecting me. I follow her through the double doors of the kitchen, where a handful of people are chopping vegetables, and down a flight of stairs to a small office. She copies my documents and hands me an orientation packet, which includes photos of the thirty or so meals that Azteca delivers. I'm to bring the packet for my first shift, and show up wearing all black. While in training I'll earn $7.50 an hour but won't get to keep any tips. After the training is over, my pay will be $4.60 an hour and I'll split the tips with the other workers. This sounds low to me, even for a position that receives tips, but that evening I learn it is New York's minimum wage for delivery workers.

"Greg mentioned I was supposed to go to an orientation somewhere," I tell her before leaving. Orientations, as I learned in Russellville, can be inadvertently instructive. "Do you know anything about that?"

"He said that?" She shrugs and picks up the phone. "I don't think the delivery boys have to go to the orientation, because you're just . . . the delivery boys." She's on the phone for a few minutes. "No, you don't have to go. Greg says come back tomorrow at five to start your training."

ON THE MORNING that I am to begin work, the *New York Times* publishes another article by Steven Greenhouse that catches my eye: "For $2-an-Hour Restaurant Deliverymen, a $4.6 Million Judgment."

The story involves a group of workers from Saigon Grill, a Vietnamese restaurant with locations on the Upper West Side and in the West Village (the West Village location is not far from Azteca). I already knew that there had been a boycott of the restaurant—complete with noisy protests that certainly scared away a few customers—along with a lawsuit against its owners, Simon and Michelle Nget. The *Times* reported that a federal judge, Michael H. Dolinger, had ruled in favor of thirty-six workers—all Chinese immigrants—finding that over an eight-year period they regularly worked thirteen-hour days, six days a week, for less than $2 an hour. Along with back pay, the judge awarded the deliverymen substantial damages, citing the fact that they were illegally fined up to $200 by the restaurant for such crimes as letting the door slam behind them as they rushed out. "At a minimum, Simon

Nget and Michelle Nget showed no regard whatsoever for legal requirements in connection with their wage policies," Dolinger concluded.

As a result of the lawsuit, a woman with Justice Will Be Served, a group that organizes restaurant workers, said that some businesses, fearful of another high-profile boycott, had already increased wages. It was a remarkable ruling: From earning $2 an hour, a number of the deliverymen were awarded more than $300,000 apiece. One of the workers, Yu Guan Ke, said that the first thing he would do with the money was purchase health insurance for his family. "It was worth the fight because we were treated badly for so long," he said. "I never imagined we would receive so much money."

When I arrive at Azteca, Greg shows me how to clock in using a computer touch screen—my ID number is 6905—and gives me a quick tour of the kitchen. The delivery area includes a counter space and sink, and is on the immediate right after walking through the swinging doors from the restaurant floor. A short man with spiky black hair stands at the counter making guacamole in a stone bowl. His left arm ends at the elbow, an apparent birth defect, but the lightning-quick speed with which he slices the avocado and stirs in spoonfuls of tomatoes and onions is truly impressive. "This is Guillermo," Greg says, introducing me to the senior delivery worker, whose name is not, in fact, Guillermo. (Names are a challenge for Greg; he will call me "Gable" for the first several weeks. Here in the book I'll follow Greg's lead and stick with Guillermo.)

The kitchen is pretty quiet at the moment, as it's too early for dinner. A long grill and stovetop run along the rear wall, where two cooks stand and chat in Spanish. In the far corner is the dishwashing station, where I can see the outline of a man behind a wall of steam. Opposite the delivery counter is the dessert and salad area. As I take in the scene, Greg rattles off a list of things to know while waving his arms about the kitchen—hang jackets here, get sodas from there, receipts print downstairs—at a pace that seems designed to confuse.

I follow Greg past the food preparation counters to the exit door, which leads down a corridor and onto the street that runs behind Azteca. This is how I am to come and go from deliveries. Near the exit is a set of stairs that leads to a small storage room. Leaning against the stairs is a large black bike with a basket attached to the handlebars, which Greg says I'm to use; another mountain bike, whose paint has been partially stripped, is propped against a wall. "The very first thing you do when you arrive is make sure you're stocked up on containers for the night," Greg explains. "All the containers you'll need are up these stairs. Once you've got the containers stocked, fill up at least ten bags of chips. You'll be fucked if you don't get those ready before the rush."

Back at the station, Greg hands over a set of keys for the bike lock. "Your main tasks tonight are to watch how the kitchen works and study the menu," he says.

"Excuse me, *niñas*," says a stocky man, balancing a tray of food over his head with one hand and grabbing a collapsible stand leaning against the counter. He just called Greg and me girls. The man, with a shaved head and puffy nose, brushes past us and sends the double doors flying open with a vigorous front kick. I make a mental note to enter the kitchen carefully.

"Fucking asshole," Greg says. "Okay, you're set. Any questions, ask Guillermo." He leaves, following the trail of the karate kid.

There's another person standing next to Guillermo. Rafael is also in training—this is his third day—and at six feet he towers over most of the kitchen workers. He grew up in the Bronx and is of Dominican descent. "Didn't ever think I'd be doing this," he tells me. The economic slowdown caused his employer, a marketing firm, to slash his hours, and he came across the opening on Craigslist as well. "I told myself that I'd give this two weeks," he says, sounding doubtful. "It was the only job I could find. Getting really hard to make an honest dollar out here—be so much easier to just sell drugs."

"Delivery!" yells a heavyset white woman—the only non-Latino in the kitchen besides me. Guillermo walks over to her and grabs the ticket.

"Since it's your first night, let me give you a word of warning about Greg's bike—the black one," Rafael says. "I call that thing the catapult. First night I was here, take out my very first delivery. Food is in the basket and I hit this little pothole and the containers go flying into the street. Had to come back and take out another order. If you're riding the catapult, make sure to hold the food in the basket with one hand."

Guillermo waves me over. The delivery is for chicken tacos, mole enchiladas, and guacamole. Stacks of containers are on a shelf above the delivery counter; he grabs a container with three compartments for the tacos and a circular one for the enchiladas, placing them on a shelf near the cooks. "You have to watch to make sure they're cooking your order," he instructs. "They like to forget our orders. If it's taking too long you have to tell Becky." He motions to the white woman.

Now that the delivery containers are ready for the cooks, Guillermo grabs two plastic bowls and heads to a station to dish out rice and beans, adding a sprinkling of white cheese onto the beans and cilantro atop the rice. "Enchiladas always get a side of *arroz y frijoles*," he says. "If you forget that, people will call and complain. They'll complain too if you forget tortillas." He puts the rice and beans on the delivery counter and grabs a piece of tin-foil. I follow him across the kitchen to a grill, where two women are making tortillas by hand. "Each order of tacos comes with four tortillas—and four more for the guacamole." He reaches for a metal cylinder that contains a stack of steaming tortillas. One of the tortilla women turns and lightly smacks his hand.

"Don't you rob me!"

Smiling, Guillermo snatches the tortillas. "They're mine now." He crinkles the foil around them. "For the guacamole you need red and green salsas—those are in the fridge over there—and a bag of chips."

Once I've grabbed the salsas from the fridge and a bag of chips from below the counter, Rafael walks me through a guacamole tutorial. On the counter, four small glass bowls sit in a metal pan filled with ice; the bowls contain chopped jalapeño peppers, onions, cilantro, and tomatoes. Next to the pan is a ceramic bowl of salt and a cylinder that holds several knives and spatulas. Rafael grabs a *molcajete* and *tejolote* from a sink—a traditional Mexican stone version of the mortar and pestle—and adds a small scoop of jalapeños along with a spoonful of onions and cilantro and a teaspoon of salt. "Now the fun part." He grinds the mix with the pestle until it forms a green paste, then cuts an avocado in half and places the pit to the side. "Hold on to that—we put it in the guacamole at the end. Supposedly it keeps it fresh." He slices up the avocado, scoops the pieces into the molcajete with a spoon, and adds more salt, onions, and cilantro, along with two scoops of tomatoes. Once it's mixed together he dumps the guacamole into a plastic bowl, plops the pit into the middle of the serving, and snaps on a lid. "That's it. One avocado, fourteen bucks."

By now the tacos and enchilada are ready. Guillermo shows me how to pack the order: tacos on the bottom, then the enchilada, then rice and beans, then guacamole and tortillas and salsa, and finally the bag of chips is stuffed down one side to keep things from moving around. I'm starting to realize how easy it could be to overlook an item: This isn't even a big order.

Rafael volunteers to take the food out, asking and receiving permission to use Guillermo's mountain bike instead of the catapult. He returns fifteen minutes later with scraped hands. "This fucking asshole was walking across the street with a red light," he tells me as he hangs up his jacket. "I know he saw me, but he just kept walking—didn't even try to move." Rafael tugged too hard on the front brake and went face first over the handlebars. Luckily he had already made the delivery and only scraped his hands. He heads to the bathroom to clean up.

"Delivery!" This time I pick up the ticket from Becky: tacos with baby goat meat and an order of guacamole. With Guillermo's guidance I fumble through my first guacamole experiment. He packs the meal and I'm off on my first delivery, to Seventh Avenue and Twenty-seventh Street.

DESPITE INITIALLY STRIKING me as a decent guy, I quickly identify two reasons to believe that Greg wants his deliverymen to be killed. The first is the uniform. I am wearing, as ordered: black socks, black shoes, black pants, black T-shirt, black button-up long-sleeve shirt, and a black windbreaker (the windbreaker is provided by the restaurant). This all-black ensemble makes Azteca's by far the coolest, most quintessentially New York delivery team in Manhattan. At night, it also makes us nearly invisible. On my first trip out I notice that many deliverymen from other restaurants have been given florescent yellow vests, with reflective tape stitched across the front and back. Some even have front lights and bells, as required by law. Safer, sure, but not nearly as sophisticated.

The second dangerous item is the bike itself, a Raleigh that on closer inspection turns out to be a beach cruiser. I stick the bag of food into the basket and walk the bike down a ramp to the street. As soon as I slide onto the seat I realize that I'm in for a completely new experience, despite having cycled throughout New York City for years. It is easily the heaviest bike I've ever ridden—probably weighing more than fifty pounds—and has chopper-style handle-bars that are three feet wide, completely erasing a bike's normal mobility advantage. As I wobble down the street in the bike lane, cars feel like they're inches away. Nearing the first intersection I hit a slight bump and the catapult leaps into action, launching the bag into the air; thankfully the order lands back in the basket. Choosing to steer with one hand while holding the food down in the basket, I come to a red light and press back on the pedals—the bike is equipped with only coaster brakes. Unaccustomed to the distance needed to halt such a boat, I skid through the cross-walk, narrowly dodging a pedestrian who shoots me an angry look. Two minutes on the catapult and I already understand why, of the thousands of crappy delivery bikes I have seen crowding Manhattan's streets, I have never seen anyone, anywhere, rolling along on a beach cruiser.*

Using my own bike, I could easily have made the trip in five minutes, but the girth of the catapult forces me to wait several times with the traffic on Sixth Avenue, as I'm unable to wind around cars crowding the bike lane. More than ten minutes after leaving the restaurant I finally arrive at the corner building and lock the bike to a scaffolding post. What seems to be an unremark-able structure transforms as I pass beneath an archway and enter a long courtyard. I initially believe that the gentle sounds of splashing water are being piped in to induce a sense of peace, until I notice that the entire right wall is an illuminated waterfall. Inside the lobby—which feels like it belongs to a hotel—a large Jackson Pollack–inspired painting hangs on the wall, and I get in

---

* I later look up the bike on the Internet, hoping to learn its weight. While that fact is not revealed, I discover that the bike is called the "Special." The company writes, "Cruising on one of these, you can't help but feel exceptional." Perhaps on a boardwalk; in New York City, it only feels exceptionally stupid.

line behind three other deliverymen at the security desk. When it's my turn I give the guard the apartment number, he makes a call, and I'm allowed up.

A woman who looks to be in her early twenties, evidently a frequent customer, answers the door. "New delivery guy?"

"Yeah, just started." I hand over the food. She signs the bill and closes the door. On the way down I check the tip—$5. Not too bad for a $30 meal. It's official: I'm a deliveryman.

When I arrive back at the kitchen, Guillermo and Rafael are standing at the delivery counter with their hands in their pockets. "Slooow," Rafael says. "It's been like this every night I've been here."

By now the action in the kitchen has picked up. Becky, who I learn is playing the role of expediter, stands in the center of the storm, next to a machine that prints out the orders. Her primary task as expediter is to make sure the cooks know what the orders are, which she does by yelling, and to coordinate large orders so that they are served simultaneously. Three stocky men stand alongside Becky; these are the "runners," who ladle out sides of rice and beans, wipe the edges of the plates clean, and carry out the orders on trays—some quite massive—without breaking a sweat. I find the runners intimidating: One has a large scar running across his face, another calls us "*niñas*" each time he passes, and the third has a habit of hitting Guillermo in the shoulder whenever he gets the chance. Each time they leave for the front of the restaurant, they snatch up one of the folding stands—which they call *burros*, or donkeys—that are leaning against the delivery counter. As a result, we're frequently in their way. All seem to take special pleasure in kicking the double doors with unnecessary force as they exit the kitchen.

While dodging the runners I focus my attention on the cooks. Two men grill meat while two women, farther down the line, heat food in pans over a stovetop. When the food is ready they slide the dish on a shelf running above the counter, where it is kept warm by heat lamps. To the left of the cooks is another stovetop— the tortilla station—where two women roll corn meal into balls, flatten the balls with a metal presser, and place, flip, and remove the tortillas by hand over the heat.

"You getting all this?" Rafael asks.

"Kinda. I think."

"It's hard for me to remember everything 'cause of the stress— already forgot tortillas for one delivery. Too many people running around shouting."

"Yeah, I can see that." It's true that the kitchen has become a beehive of activity. Becky is yelling out orders and cooks are yelling back questions and waiters are wandering in complaining about customers ("Is it just me or was she a total *bitch*?") and burly guys are streaming past while warning us *niñas* to get out of the way. Still, it seems like a manageable place to work. Of course, I'm fresh from the flower shop, so just about anything seems preferable to the constant nagging of Tony and Helen.

"Delivery!" I grab the ticket from Becky: enchiladas, tuna salad, and guacamole. Fifth Avenue between Twenty-sixth and Twenty-seventh. I place the enchilada container on the shelf and dish out rice and beans while Rafael starts mashing the ingredients in the molcajete. Ten minutes later I'm out the door. Ten minutes after that, I'm back at the station with a $4 tip in my pocket. This isn't too bad.

By the end of the five-hour shift, I've made only three deliveries, for a grand total of $13 in tips. The slow night doesn't much matter to me, since I don't keep any tips during training. "Use this time to learn as much as you can," Greg says as I'm preparing to leave. "Once we get Seamless Web hooked up, you won't have any time to stand around."

WHEN I ARRIVE at work the next evening, Greg is engaged in an animated conversation with Guillermo, laying out his vision for Seamless Web. I overhear Greg mention that we're going to have a computer, printer, and fax machine so that orders will come up at our station. "That way it prints right up—bam!—and you can just grab the containers and get moving," he says excitedly. "The fax machine will be used only if for some reason the Web isn't working—that way people can send us a fax directly with the order."

It was my impression that Guillermo, who told me he came to the United States from Mexico about six years ago, didn't speak much English. Indeed, as soon as Greg walks away he turns to me. "What did he say?" I do my best to explain the backup function of the fax machine. Guillermo looks nonplussed, saying, "I don't know how to use a computer, but it will be good if it means more deliveries."

Tonight, again, begins slowly. We stand at the counter for fifteen minutes, waiting for a delivery, until a man wearing a white apron and camouflage pants—who worked the grill yesterday—introduces himself as Armando, one of the head chefs. I ask how he rose through the ranks so quickly, as he looks young.

"I'm only twenty-five." He smiles. "Started as a grill cook, then sous-chef." (Totally ignorant about restaurant jobs and titles, I have to look up sous-chef to learn it is the assistant chef.) He tells me he's from Mexico City, which concludes our time for small talk: He orders us to measure out shredded cheese in the prep area.

The assignment—we fill small bags with 2.5 ounces of shredded cheese—is the sort of mindless work that leads to rambling conversations. I learn that Guillermo, who rents a room in the Queens neighborhood of Astoria, worked for five years at a large restaurant not far from his home, mostly as a prep cook. A fire has temporarily shut down the restaurant, but it's set to reopen next week; Guillermo will then work both jobs. He hopes to return to his regular schedule in Queens, working from six in the morning to five in the afternoon, which will allow him to arrive at Azteca by six o'clock.

"Do you think the other place needs people?" Ideally, I'd like more hours; I'm scheduled to work six nights a week at Azteca, but that comes out to only about thirty hours. He shakes his head. Out of curiosity, I ask how much they pay.

"Three hundred a week, cash. That's pretty good, no?" Pretty good works out to roughly $5 an hour, well below the minimum wage—and doesn't include overtime (as a prep cook, the minimum wage is $7.15, not the $4.60 of deliverymen).

"I know," he says when I point this out. "They have signs up that show the minimum wage." This is a new one: a workplace that posts labor laws while breaking them.

Long after we've finished weighing the cheese, two orders finally come in. Both have guacamole, which I prepare. Guillermo says I can borrow his bike—I'm done experimenting with the catapult—and I string the bags on either handlebar and set off (I can't use my own bike, because its drop-style handlebars don't allow for the hanging of bags).

Guillermo's bike, despite being adjusted for someone about half a foot shorter than me, is a much more pleasant ride. With his narrow handlebars I'm able to weave around traffic, and when I pull on the brakes I actually find myself immediately slowing down. Still, as I'm pedaling down Broadway, I can tell that I'll need time before I feel completely comfortable riding with food.

Both deliveries go to what I will learn are typical buildings for Azteca customers: brightly lit awnings, spotless lobbies complete with flat-screen televisions, doormen, and security desks. Also typical is that very few words are exchanged at the apartment doors.

"How's it going tonight?" I ask. "Good, and you?" "Good."
"Good." "How much is it?" "Forty-five eighty-six." "Here you
go, keep the change." "Thanks, have a good night." "You too."

Back in the kitchen I wander over to the tortilla ladies and introduce myself to Gloria, who has been at Azteca for several
months and makes $8 an hour. She stands over the stovetop the
entire shift, churning out thousands of handmade tortillas each
night. "This is exactly how I made them in Mexico," she says,
showing me how to roll the corn meal into small balls that she
then flattens with a metal press. "I just didn't have to do it all
day."

A compact woman with long hair and a ready laugh, Gloria
grew up in Cuautla, Morelos, just a few blocks from what was
once the home of Emiliano Zapata. She came to the United States
six months ago—her first time north of the border—at the age of
forty-six. Soon after arriving she paid $100 to an employment
agency in Washington Heights, near the apartment she's sharing
with her boyfriend, and was placed in a job cleaning houses. "The
boss said he'd pay me $7 an hour, but only gave me 6," she says,
so she went back to the agency and was sent to Azteca. She knows
very little about New York, beyond the subway route she takes to
and from work, and her only contact is her boyfriend, whom she
met in Cuautla.

In Cuautla, Gloria—a sweet-looking grandmother who may be
just five feet—worked as a security guard for a hospital, earning
two thousand pesos a month while sporting a .22 pistol on her
waist. "It was such a pretty little thing," she says about the handgun in her high-pitched voice. She eventually became a cook at
the hospital, but decided in early 2008—with encouragement
from her boyfriend, who had already emigrated to New York—to
come and join him. She flew from Mexico City to the border and
endured an eight-day trek through Arizona, anticipating a glori-

ous reunion. Instead, she's starting to wonder if she wouldn't have been better off staying put.

"He's acting strange," is how she describes her boyfriend's behavior. Eventually she clarifies the statement: He's seeing other women and drinking too much. She can't imagine a future with the man he has become, but doesn't feel like she's in a position to break it off, as he's the only contact she has in the city. She has friends in the United States, but they all ended up in Los Angeles. "Maybe I'll go there," she says. "If someone would tell me where it is."

By the end of the shift I've made only five deliveries and rolled several hundred balls of corn meal for tortillas. My back isn't sore; my hands are perfectly functional. I could get used to this.

AND THEN COMES Saturday night, marking the official end of my honeymoon with delivery work. The first bad omen occurs before I even arrive at the restaurant. As I'm biking from my apartment it begins to drizzle and swiftly turns into a downpour. I haven't biked in the rain for some time—since Russellville, actually—and I've apparently forgotten that wet ground means slow down, because as I'm veering onto the sidewalk near the Manhattan Bridge, my tires slide out. I slam the right side of my body into the pavement but thankfully discover, once I recover from the accident, that I have avoided doing any serious damage to my body or bike.

Guillermo and Rafael are already at the kitchen when I arrive, with two delivery tickets hanging from the shelf and a third packed and ready to go. I clock in, do my best to wipe the dirt from my pants, and grab the three orders from the counter. Just as I'm walking out the door, Claudia, who takes the delivery orders over the phone, stops me. "The credit card didn't go through for the guy on Irving Place," she says. "Make sure he calls back while you're there." I scribble a note on the ticket and head back into the rain.

In my eight years of cycling around New York City, my general strategy in dealing with cars is to avoid making direct contact. If someone cuts me off, I'll slam on the brakes and mutter to myself. If a driver is moving into the bike lane, I'll slow down and let him take it over. But when one spends five or six hours a night pedaling back and forth in a very congested area, there quickly comes a time when passivity and avoidance are no longer sufficient if one hopes to survive. This is when being a deliveryman becomes a contact sport.

I hit that point riding down the right side of Third Avenue with the three orders of food. A black town car, driving at the same speed that I'm cycling, starts edging into my path. The driver either doesn't see me through the rain or sees me and considers my presence a trivial matter. In response, I drift slightly rightward; moments later, so does the car. By now I can't move any more to the right without launching my body into a row of parked cars. I glance backwards, preparing to slow down, and see a yellow cab bearing down from behind, ready to make a turn at the upcoming light. As the town car continues to list right, I take the only appropriate action and slap the palm of my hand on the passenger-side window. The driver looks over and gives a slight nod of the head, moving several inches back into the lane, as if this is his normal means of determining correct driving position: Wait for the frantic strike. Although the encounter speeds up my heart rate, it also gives me an odd sense of confidence and control. I can slap these cars around if they get out of line.

The first order, on Third Avenue, is for $55. The building is a fourth-floor walk-up, and since I've got two more deliveries to make, I take the steps two at a time. By the time I knock on the door I'm panting and soaking wet. A man comes to the door. "It's raining, huh?" Behind him a movie is playing on a massive flat-screen TV.

"Yep, just started coming down pretty hard." He signs the credit card bill and hands it back to me, which I pocket without looking. As I'm huffing back down the stairs I take out the bill. He's left me a $2 tip.

My next stop is at 1 Irving Place. According to the ticket, it is near Fifteenth Street. I ride down Irving until it ends at Fourteenth Street, but don't see the address, so backtrack to Sixteenth Street. Nothing. Because it's raining, there aren't many people on the street, but I eventually stop a woman walking her dog, who points to a large awning halfway down Fifteenth Street. As I get closer I can see that it's the address I'm looking for.

One Irving Place is by far the largest building I've delivered to thus far. I take one elevator that runs to the seventh floor, then walk through a long hallway, passing a number of people wearing workout gear—the building has a pool and health club—and take another elevator up one of four towers. The man who answers the door has short gray hair, is wearing a suit, and continues speaking rapidly into his cell phone about what sounds like some sort of business deal. I explain politely over his conversation about the credit card number not going through.

"I knew that idiot on the phone would mess up," he snarls. "Look at this"—he holds the bill up to my face—"She didn't even spell my name right! Fucking idiot. No, not you," he says into his phone. "I've got a delivery here. Hold on." He puts the phone into his pocket.

"Sorry about that, sir. Could you just call her back and give—"

"Forget it, I'll pay cash. How much?" I tell him. "Okay, here's the money. Give yourself a five-dollar tip out of it."

"Thanks. I think this is right." I hand over his change. He flips through the bills.

"*Hey*, someone graduated high school," he says before closing the door.

Next up after Mr. Dickhead is a penthouse apartment on Eleventh Street. I check my watch—I've got six minutes to go if I want to make the forty-five-minute window that Greg has said is our goal. I ride east along a congested Fourteenth Street, take a left on Fifth Avenue, and am standing at the door of the penthouse with a minute to spare. The man who answers has a friendly smile, and I can hear his wife in the background, yelling to the kids that dinner is ready. He leaves me a $12 tip, my largest so far.

Back at the kitchen, three more bags are packed near the exit door and ready to be delivered. I snatch them up, noticing that the catapult is gone—poor Rafael—and am off. Since the buildings are nearby, I'm back within twenty minutes. "I forgot tortillas at Eleventh Street," Guillermo tells me, handing over a small bag. "Can you run them over?"

"Anything else to take?"

"No, not right now."

When I ring the buzzer at Eleventh Street, a woman's voice shouts angrily at me through the intercom. "It's too late! We've already finished our meal—*thank* you!" Since I haven't even said anything, I realize that the building must have a hidden camera (good to know: wouldn't want to be picking my nose at the door). By now I'm ready for a quick break and a few tortillas, and take a seat on steps beneath the awning of a nearby building. I open the bag and discover that, in apology, the restaurant has included a large piece of cheesecake (value: $8.50) along with the tortillas. While the rain falls around me and people scurry for shelter, I combine the two items, enjoying four cheesecake tacos.

By the end of the night we've completed twenty-three deliveries. Rafael, riding the slow catapult, took six; Guillermo, responsible for packing, took one; I dropped off sixteen. Together we make nearly $100 in tips, which Guillermo splits evenly with Rafael and me, even though, since this is my last day of training, I'm not supposed to see any of it.

CHAPTER 13

I've worked in two restaurants before coming to Azteca. The first was a relaxed pizza joint in San Jose, California, where I made deliveries in the company pickup. The second was a line cook position at a ski resort in Jackson Hole, Wyoming, where the general goal of the staff, most in their early twenties and with zero interest in things culinary, was to have a good time (my coworkers and even one manager were often drunk, or stoned, or both). Over holiday breaks the lodge could become very busy, but the hectic pace was leavened by the fact that we lacked proper supervision and so could often do as we pleased. One friend, after receiving a complaint that he had overcooked a hamburger, reached over the grill, grabbed the patty from the customer's plate, and slung it against a wall.

Neither experience was especially good training for the culture of a busy, upscale restaurant. Picture the atmosphere of a rush-hour subway station in New York City, late July: Folks are dashing around, muttering to themselves or yelling at others, oozing sweat and stress and in no mood for pleasantries. I've seen a few episodes of those reality cooking shows, where celebrity chefs berate the cooks and the cooks soon turn on each other, acting as if lives hang in the balance. I figured they were over-the-top. They're not.

One night, during a busy stretch, an Ecuadorian waiter named José comes to Becky with a question. Becky, playing the role of expediter, is busy. So Becky says, "José, get the fuck out of my face." José stays put, hoping to get a word in. "I need a tuna salad, *now!*" Becky screams. "*¡Atún!*" (Becky has picked up some Spanish while in the kitchen.) "I need tuna!" shouts the salad preparer in Spanish; the salad is already on a plate, awaiting a grilled tuna from a cook. "The tuna is fucking coming!" yells a cook, standing over a grill jammed with chicken, skewers of shrimp, salmon, and—yes—a tuna steak. Becky turns to grab a bottle of sour cream from the fridge to squeeze onto an enchilada, in the process bumping into José. "José, I can't take your shit right now! Where the fuck is my tuna salad? I need tuna!"

The stress level reaches its highest point when the restaurant hosts large parties, which is often. This is when the screaming and fighting that goes on between cooks and the expediter, or servers and cooks, or runners and servers, or—when there's a true crisis—between just about everyone at the same time, sounds like it will erupt into a full-scale brawl. The beads of sweat, always present on foreheads, start rolling down cheeks. Faces usually pink from the heat turn crimson. But once the rush passes, after the fourteen house salads and five tortilla soups and sixteen racks of lamb have been sorted out and served, the people in the kitchen quickly put the conflict behind them. There is an understanding, it seems, that at rush hour the kitchen is a war zone, and that people behave differently in war zones—so don't take it personally. It's definitely not an environment for everyone, but there's something attractive about the lack of pretense and brutally direct communication. Of course, my ability to enjoy the environment is certainly helped by the fact that as a delivery worker, I'm usually not a target.

Most nights Becky plays expediter, setting the emotional tone of the kitchen. Becky is fun to be around. She has perhaps the foulest mouth I've ever encountered, shares my interest in 1980s punk music, and tells me that she can't stand *Top Chef* because it's "full of pretentious assholes." In her late twenties, she dropped out of culinary school and works between sixty and seventy hours a week while raising a young son. In the kitchen she is fearless: She gets into shouting matches with managers, grill cooks, even the executive chef. One night Azteca has a VIP customer—a vice president of operations for the restaurant chain, or some such title. "We have some feedback," the general manager, a woman given to wearing skintight dresses, tells Becky. "He says it's too salty."

"Fuck that!" Becky shouts. She tastes the sauce. "There's hardly any fucking salt in it! What a fucking dick!" It's hard not to enjoy watching her work.

The one person who seems completely unaffected by the environment is Pancho, a thirty-four-year-old runner from the state of Puebla who has long black hair tied back in a ponytail.* "He says he's from Mexico, but he seems like a total California surfer dude," is how one of the servers puts it to me. Even at the height of kitchen craziness, Pancho always seems to be playing practical jokes. He'll pat Guillermo in a friendly manner, leaving a sticker on his back that stays on through an entire shift, or he'll drop an avocado into the hood of my windbreaker, which I'll discover when I flip it up as I head out the door. When I return from a delivery with a story of

---

* After working in lettuce fields and a chicken plant, where every employee—even the completely bald—was ordered to wear hairnets, it is curious to see that in restaurants, which serve food directly to consumers, plenty of long hair is allowed to dangle over plates.

avocados falling from the sky, he scrunches up his face in determination and says, "You know what, I'll look into who did that."

Across the kitchen from the unflappable Pancho is his polar opposite, a lanky nineteen-year-old cook who left Mexico, he tells me, because his hometown in Guerrero had grown too dangerous due to the drug trade. Called Flaco (skinny) by the other workers, his face seems to have frozen some time ago into a petulant scowl. It doesn't matter what Flaco is doing—grilling up an order of chicken, sucking down a Coke through a straw—he retains the same "what the fuck are you looking at?" expression. When he walks to get a pan of beans, he struts slowly; when someone criticizes something he does, he looks like he's going to explode. Like many young men, he hopes to project an image of toughness, but what comes across instead is a very vulnerable and sensitive boy, far from home and making his way in a foreign country. It also doesn't help that he weighs about 130 pounds and looks like he could be in junior high.

During my second week a stocky white man wearing remarkably unattractive black-and-white pants replaces Becky as expediter. "What the fuck is this?" the man shouts at Flaco. He's holding a plate of food. "Is this how we do rice, *niño*?" Flaco shoots him a look of total disgust and shrugs, remaining silent. "What? What!" The man walks over. "I said, is *this* how we do rice, *niño*?" He dumps the yellow rice back into a metal container. After several more seconds of uncomfortable staring, Flaco finally stirs a bunch of greens into the container of rice—perhaps cilantro, I'm not sure—and puts a serving on the plate. "I will stop calling you *niño* when you start acting like a man," the man with the piebald pants says.

I turn to Guillermo. "What was that about?"

"He's the head chef." Guillermo looks pleased; he often complains to me that Flaco purposely forgets delivery orders, waiting until Becky reminds him.

I'm able to stand around observing the goings-on in the kitchen because after the rush of Saturday the next few shifts are unbelievably slow—so slow that I wonder if Greg has made a mistake in hiring me. With Guillermo coming from his second job in Queens, I'm now arriving an hour before him, so it's my responsibility to set up the station. For the first twenty minutes I fill bags of tortilla chips, replenish the avocado supply from downstairs, fill the glass bowls with tomatoes, jalapeños, cilantro, and onions from the walk-in fridge, and stock needed containers from upstairs. By 5:30 p.m. I'm ready with no place to go.

I soon learn that standing at the delivery counter ensures that I'll keep bumping into the runners as they move in and out of the kitchen. Aside from Pancho, whose lighthearted demeanor I appreciate, my general desire is to steer clear of the runners whenever possible. Felix, who has a prominent facial scar and gravelly voice, is impossible to read. Sometimes he seems to be joking when he tells me to "move it," but other times I'm not so sure; I figure the less he tells me to move it, the better. And Isaac, a broad-shouldered man who refers to everyone on the delivery staff as little girls, is definitely someone I don't want to annoy.

Another reason to give room and respect to the runners is their propensity to purposefully punch people, usually each other. The first time I witnessed this I was convinced that Pancho, who was hit in the ribs by Isaac while hoisting a large tray over his head with one arm, would drop the order. But he simply proceeded onto the restaurant floor as if nothing had happened, and returned the favor to Isaac a few minutes later. On Pancho's prodding, I try to balance a tray holding only two plates overhead and barely get it back on the stand without the food sliding onto the floor. Yet the runners can literally *run* through a crowded kitchen with a full tray balanced high above their heads—often using only their fingertips—while absorbing body shots.

TO FILL THE downtime during the slow week—I make only fourteen deliveries over a three-day period—I take on a variety of jobs in the kitchen, from helping the dishwashers toss out the trash to pulling chicken meat from drumsticks and rolling tortilla balls. While assisting the back-of-the-house staff—all Latino immigrants—it doesn't take long to realize that Azteca suffers from a turnover rate that rivals the poultry plant, at least for the positions that don't receive tips.

Most of the prep cooks and dishwashers have paid storefront referral agencies in immigrant neighborhoods anywhere from $100 to $200 for the job, a common practice within the restaurant industry in staffing the less desirable positions. In recent years, the state attorney general has launched dozens of investigations into employment agencies, often finding that they violate laws by referring immigrant workers to jobs that pay less than the minimum wage. Some of the referred workers have been at Azteca for a few weeks, some a few months, but no one I speak to has a year under his or her belt, and many aren't planning on sticking around much longer. By far, the most disgruntled workers are the dishwashers. "They don't pay enough," says Alvaro, a middle-aged dishwasher from the Galapagos Islands, as we're rolling a heavy dumpster to the curb. Earning $7.50 an hour, he has taken another low-paying job washing dishes at a restaurant called Chop't, and frequently works fourteen-hour days. "They have me running around all night, doing work that should be done by two people," he says. Sweat is trickling down his wide cheeks and his black mustache glistens under the streetlight. "And for what? At the end of the night I have earned almost nothing."

One of Alvaro's dishwashing partners, Antonio, also plans to leave soon. When I ask Antonio how much he makes, he tells me, "No good, no good." One night at the end of the shift I see him staring in concentration at his paycheck.

"Something wrong?"

"I'm missing hours." He tells me that he worked forty-four hours last week, but received payment for only forty hours. "They did that the week before, too," he mutters quietly. Hour shaving is a widespread practice in the restaurant industry; of the more than 500 workers surveyed by the Restaurant Opportunities Center of New York (ROC-NY), for its study "Behind the Kitchen Door," 59 percent reported not being paid overtime hours.[2]

"You should go downstairs and tell a manager," I say. He nods halfheartedly. "Really—if you worked forty-four hours then they should pay you for forty-four. I could even go down there and tell them in English."

He shakes his head. "I'm going to wait and see," he says before leaving. I hope to check in on the situation, but a few days later Alvaro informs me that Antonio quit. A new man takes his place, from a town near Mexico City. He paid a labor agency in Queens $100; thus far, no one has told him how much he'll be making at Azteca. When he learns that Alvaro earns less than $8 an hour, he tells me that he'll probably be gone soon. A week later, I strike up a conversation with a third dishwasher, Javier, in the locker room downstairs as we're changing. He also reports that he's being shorted hours each week, and though he says he might switch jobs, he would rather not complain directly to management, despite being one of the few back-of-the-kitchen staff I've met who has their immigration papers in order.* "If I need to, I'll just switch jobs," he tells me. "That's easier than starting a fight."

Which brings me to something else: There is a certain perversity to the wage scale of restaurant workers. The people earning the

---

* I later learn that this dishwasher is the uncle of Enrique, a friend of mine whose life I chronicled in my first book, *There's No José Here*. When I called Enrique, who worked as a dishwasher when he first arrived in New York, and told him about his uncle's payment problems, he scoffed. "Of course they don't pay all the hours," he said. "I worked sixty hours a week but was paid forty. That is nothing new."

least are the dishwashers, and they have the hardest jobs. They are stationed at one end of the kitchen, obscured behind an always-present wall of steam, coated in sweat and smeared with leftovers. When they emerge from the humidity, pushing heavy carts of clean dishes, they often receive glares, as they inevitably clog up the passageways as they unload plates and bowls. If restaurant kitchens are filled with people who are invisible to the general public, dishwashers are the most invisible. While servers and cooks and delivery people banter amongst themselves and call each other by name, the only time anyone notices the dishwashers is when they're in the way.

On the opposite end of the earning scale are the servers. In less expensive restaurants a server takes an order and returns to the table with the food. But at Azteca, as with most upscale restaurants, a server doesn't usually *serve* anything: They describe the specials, write down the orders, and plug the orders into a touch-screen computer. The task of serving falls on the shoulders of the runners. For this, servers can earn hundreds of dollars a night. Meanwhile, the people who prepare the food, cook the food, and clean the dishes make somewhere between $7.50 and $10.00 an hour. The wide gap in earnings between these two extremes is filled by the restaurant's "middle class," the runners, bussers, and baristas, who are tipped out by servers and seem to average anywhere from $70 to well over $100 a night. As a deliveryman, I suppose I'm part of the lower-middle class, earning more than dishwashers but much less than other tipped positions, while dealing with inclement weather and the dangers of the road.

At Azteca, the servers are generally a nice and funny crew, and in contrast to many upscale restaurants, they are quite diverse.*

---

* Azteca's diverse server staff is unusual for fine-dining establishments in New York City, which are usually segregated by race, with the high-paying positions of servers and bartenders filled almost exclusively by whites. In 2009, the Restaurant Opportunities Center of New

There are white and black and Latino servers, servers born in Ecuador and servers born in Queens. I have no bone to pick with servers; what I find confounding is the system of payment that exists throughout the restaurant industry. By what logic do servers receive tips, and runners receive tips, but not dishwashers or grill cooks? Each job is of comparable importance—whether or not the customer sees the face of the person performing it—as anyone who has received a dirty dish or undercooked meat can attest.

IT'S A RELIEF on slow nights when deliveries finally start rolling in sometime after seven o'clock and I'm able to escape the heat of the kitchen. By now Guillermo and I have reached a working agreement: He packs the orders and I make the deliveries using his bike. I'm glad to hand off the packing responsibilities, because even though my training ended some time ago, I still tend to forget obvious items.

On the streets I'm starting to spot trouble early in what can be a dangerous profession. A 2006 report published by the city found that an average of 23 cyclists were killed each year, with another 400 left seriously injured (the data lumps all cyclists together, and so precise figures on delivery workers aren't available). One of the most frequent dangers occurs when a passenger swings open a car door without looking. When this happens and a cyclist is passing within close range, he plows into the door at full speed, an experience called getting "doored." It happens to just about everyone who spends enough time on a bike—I've been doored twice—and

---

York published the results of a study in which equally qualified applicants—one white and one of color—applied for server positions at more than a hundred Manhattan restaurants. The white applicants were nearly twice as likely to receive a job offer. The report, "The Great Service Divide," is available online (as of April 30, 2009) at www.rocunited.org/files/greatservicedivide.pdf.

it is as unpleasant as it sounds. The worst offenders are taxi passengers: People entering and leaving cabs can be very dangerous, behaving as if they are protected by a force field and not in the middle of a very busy street.

Being doored is one of the predictable dangers; what makes each delivery an adventure are the threats that pop up without warning. Riding along a dark stretch of Nineteenth Street, I hit a huge and invisible pothole. It's nearly as jarring as slamming into a curb, and though I'm able to avoid tumbling over the handlebars, the two orders I'm carrying rip through the bottom of the paper bags and go flying into the street. Containers of shrimp salad and goat tacos and duck breast and guacamole explode, ruining $150 worth of food and ensuring that I'll be making two late deliveries to two upset customers.

Yet another danger to deliverymen, ironically but not surprisingly, are other deliverymen. Many have had little cycling experience before landing the job, and riding around Manhattan on a rickety bike loaded with food is a baptism by fire. Rafael, for instance, had never ridden in the city, and when I went out with him on an early delivery, it was plain that he had no idea what he was doing: He rode against traffic, ventured onto the sidewalk for no apparent reason, and nearly ran into two pedestrians. Of course, Rafael received zero training: Like all deliverymen, he was given an ungainly bike and an address and told to hurry up and go. "It's not rocket science," is how Greg described the work to me one night, with a flippancy that would be erased if he ever tried to make a delivery himself.

Rafael eventually becomes a safer cyclist, but with such a high turnover, there are always beginners on the streets, and over two months I hit three deliverymen who are riding the wrong way and have a handful of extremely close calls. The blogger BikeSnob NYC is exaggerating, but not by much, when he writes about certain rogue deliverymen:

I don't mean to begrudge anybody making a living by bike, and I certainly respect someone who makes a living in a manner as difficult as this. But the fact is, some of these guys are incredibly dangerous and will come at you in ways you'd never expect: from between parked cars; flying off curbs; head-on between two lanes of traffic; and leaping from rooftops and swinging from power lines like Paul Reubens did in *Pee-wee's Big Adventure* during the climactic Warner Brothers studio rampage scene.[3]

But while I'm occasionally spooked by someone pedaling at me like mad from the opposite direction, more often I feel a sense of camaraderie. At some intersections, waiting for the light to change, a team of four or five deliverymen, Latino and Asian, will gather (for whatever reason, it seems to be an entirely male occupation). Some wear rectangular heat-retaining backpacks, some hold pizzas in their baskets, but most use the low-tech method of dangling bags from the handlebars. As we stand and wait, it can feel like I'm a member of a biker gang, and when we zoom off, there are times, especially cruising down Broadway, that our numbers give us the confidence to take over two lanes, at least for a short while.

Now that I'm delivering food, I discover that it's very easy to strike up conversations with fellow deliverymen. Once when I worked on an article for which I needed to interview a deliveryman, I had approached dozens of people in the streets, but after I identified myself as a journalist, they were very hesitant to speak. It took several weeks to find an individual willing to share details about wages and working conditions. Now, whenever I bump into someone, whether we're taking the same elevator or waiting in a lobby, I find that people readily share information, and ask the same questions of me. (My conversations are only with Latino workers; I try conversing with several Asian men but none speaks English.)

What I learn, as far as deliverymen go, is that my minimum wage of $4.60 an hour puts me in the highest income bracket. One Mexican man delivers for an Indian restaurant, and is paid $25 in cash for a twelve-hour shift, which he works six days a week. On a good day he makes $50 in tips. Another, who cooks and delivers for a pizza joint, gets $4 an hour in cash and takes home between $30 and $40 in tips. He also works twelve-hour shifts, six days a week. A nineteen-year-old Ecuadorian I meet while locking up my bike just started at a Thai restaurant; at the end of each day he's given $20 in cash, and earns an additional $40 or so from tips. When I ask how they're able to survive on their income, the answer is always the same: They live in a small apartment with many others.

It quickly becomes obvious that I don't need to "investigate" the prevalence of illegal wages in the food delivery business: That's all there is. The "Behind the Kitchen Door" study of restaurant workers by ROC-NY found that 13 percent of respondents earned less than the minimum wage. For deliverymen, I'm willing to bet that number is more like 95 percent. Over the two months that I deliver food, I speak to perhaps fifty deliverymen about wages, and never meet another person who matches my princely wage of $4.60 an hour, which runs counter to the claim that restaurants increased wages in response to the Saigon Grill decision. That Azteca has decided to comply with minimum-wage laws probably explains why they were willing to hire me. In terms of understanding why Azteca was willing to pay the minimum wage in the first place, the best I could figure was that since it is part of a small corporate chain operating in multiple states, they are more centralized, professionalized, and potentially vulnerable to large-scale lawsuits by workers.

ON THE JOB, I enter buildings that I would never otherwise set foot in, including many in the posh neighborhood of Gramercy

Park. They have doormen and security desks and sign-in protocols. Some require that I wear an ID badge around my neck (Hello, my name is FOOD DELIVERY). At times, guards accompany me into the elevator, even follow me to the resident's door to ensure nothing untoward happens during the transaction. Others tell me to leave the lobby and enter the building around the corner. "*You* use the service elevator"—as if my presence might somehow lower property values.

The city the residents have chosen to live in is noisy, dirty, and rowdy. Their apartment buildings are closely guarded refuges, offering multiple barriers to the unwashed masses, even small children. During the week leading up to Halloween, I see notices posted in various buildings that read something along the lines of: "Halloween is just around the corner! Happy Halloween! If you have people that you would like to allow up to knock on your door for treats, please inform the security desk within three days so we can put their names on our list!"

ON HALLOWEEN, AS I set up the delivery station, Azteca's bar back, who assists the bartender, stops by to say hello. Raimundo is stocky and exceedingly polite—he calls me *caballero* (gentleman) instead of *güe* (sort of like dude)—and worked his way up from delivery. "Last year deliveries on Halloween were very slow," he says.

Greg stops in, and, as usual, his mind is on Seamless Web. "It's going to be up next Tuesday," he says.

My first delivery, which normally should take about ten minutes, is to an apartment on Thirteenth Street between Sixth and Seventh Avenues. As I cruise toward Sixth Avenue, the street becomes increasingly congested with foot traffic, all heading in the direction I'm pedaling. This should tell me something, but I keep plowing forward as the density increases, winding between groups

of revelers decked out in costume. I manage to swerve around
Fred Flintstone before finally dismounting and walking with the
throng. I push my way to the front only to realize that the street
is blocked off by barricades and police officers.

"Sorry, can't get across Sixth here," an officer tells me, sounding sympathetic to my situation: With two bags of food hanging
from my handlebars, I must look pretty helpless. "I'd like to let
you through, but if I do then I'm gonna have a hundred assholes
screaming that they want across too." He tells me that because of
the Halloween parade, Sixth Avenue is blocked all the way up to
Twenty-third Street. To get to the apartment I have to go up ten
blocks, west two blocks, and south ten blocks. Then, to get back
to Azteca, I have to do the entire loop in reverse.

It would be a long detour on any night—I'm cycling an addi-
tional forty-four blocks—but when I turn around I am faced with
thousands of people streaming to get close to the barricades so
they can watch the parade. I begin to pick my way through the
crowd, cursing myself for not remembering the parade (I'd
watched it once before, after all). "It's a delivery guy!" a woman
yells at me, impressed with her powers of observation. Other
people join in. "Hey, delivery guy!" someone shouts to my left. I
turn and look at the man, who is dressed as a marshmallow. *Hello,
idiot.* "That's my delivery!" The marshmallow's buddies laugh
hysterically at this witticism. "Watcha got for us?"

I finally make it through the dense throng and hop back on my
bike, pedaling through a group of mimes playing tennis. I normally
depend on Sixth Avenue to travel north, but since it's shut down,
the only way to Twenty-third Street is to go against traffic on Fifth
Avenue for ten blocks. I have a rule of thumb about going the
wrong way—I'll do it for a maximum of three blocks; otherwise
I'll schlep over to another avenue—but tonight I have little choice.

It proves to be an especially bad time to break my rule, because
Fifth Avenue is a madhouse. The cars are bumper to bumper and

the bike lanes are clogged with drunken revelers spilling over from the sidewalk, along with horse-drawn carriages, which have relocated from their normal territory around Central Park. I pedal very slowly, nodding at a fellow deliveryman who passes me. He looks at me and shakes his head. Forced to stop every several hundred feet, it takes ten minutes to reach Twenty-third Street. From there I bike west to Seventh Avenue, then south to Thirteenth Street. At Seventh Avenue, a police barricade has shut down the street, making it accessible only to people who can prove they live on the block. I get in a long line to show the delivery receipt to a policeman. A man at the front of the line is telling the cop that he's recently moved and his license doesn't yet have his current address, which seems plausible, as people are constantly moving in and out of the city. The cop, though, has apparently been given strict orders, and doesn't let him through. Which leads, predictably, to a shouting match: Ever try telling New Yorkers they can't do something?

An older woman in front of me has a completely different story, explaining that she doesn't believe in carrying identification. The cop lets out a visible sigh, and seeing me with my bags and obvious business tells her to step aside for a moment. As he shoos me through, I hear the woman start to shout about living in a police state.

It's taken me forty-five minutes to arrive at the building, and by now I'm beginning to focus my anger on the true culprit, the customers who placed the order. As residents of the neighborhood, they know that Sixth Avenue is closed for the parade; as patrons of Azteca, they know that the restaurant is located on the *other* side of the parade. They must know, therefore, what I just endured to bring them a double order of guacamole and two enchilada dinners. What asshole would order food to be delivered on the one night when it is nearly impossible to do so?

A white man wearing khakis and a black pullover sweater answers the door. "Hey, what's it like out there?" he asks in a British accent.

I counter his friendliness with a stone face. "Crowded. There's a parade outside your door."

"Yeah, the parade—good fun!"

I hand over the food. "That's one way of looking at it."

"You said it—good fun!" I didn't say that. He signs the credit card receipt and passes me a tip $10, which softens my feelings somewhat.

On the long ride back, I make my first contact with a pedestrian—actually, part of a pedestrian's costume—when I bump into a large inflatable doll. The female doll belongs to a young man and has been tastefully affixed to his body so as to appear that he is on the receiving end of a blow job. Concerned that his creativity will go unnoticed, the man stands at the curb's edge, silently thrusting the doll into the street with his pelvis. It's hard to know what to make of the scene—for one thing, the guy is alone, and there's a certain workmanlike aspect to his thrusts—but I know what to do about the doll in my path, which is to land a sharp elbow and continue down Fifth Avenue.

Throughout the night I see men dressed as women, women dressed as men, adults dressed as babies, babies dressed as puppies, puppies dressed as criminals. With the election looming, many have chosen political motifs, and I can't help but notice that the Sarah Palins wandering the Manhattan streets are by far the most inebriated. It is this drunkenness, especially, of the Palins and others, that turns each trip from the restaurant into a test of reflexes. As anyone who has witnessed a spontaneous bar fight knows, people who are intoxicated tend to be unpredictable, especially when they're roaming in rowdy groups and dressed up as sumo wrestlers. They race each other down the bike lane, hide behind cars, dash into the street, and engage in all sorts of pointless activities fueled by the extra energy of excessive alcohol.

By eight o'clock I've grown weary and start taking more risks, careening through intersections and doing just enough to avoid hitting pedestrians crossing against the light. The only contact I make is with a woman dressed, I believe, as Pippi Longstocking, who darts out from behind a car and into the bike lane. I slam on my brakes and veer into the street, but still gently clip her ankles. As I pass, she lets fly a violent shriek: "Fucker!" she screams at my back. "I was standing here and you just *rode right into me!*" Not my version of events.

While making a delivery on University Place, I'm joined in the elevator by a trio returning from the parade. Each is decked out in wigs and heavy makeup, though I'm not sure who they're meant to be. "Where did you get the idea?"

I'm staring at the elevator door, half listening to their conversation about favorite costumes of the night. "Where did you get the idea?" I realize the woman is speaking to me.

"Me?"

"Wait. Are you a *real* delivery guy?"

"Yeah, there's real food in here and everything."

"That's so cool."

One thing I have certainly not been feeling tonight is cool. "Thanks."

By 10:30 p.m., I've completed fifteen deliveries and made $53 in tips. On the bike ride home I immediately cut east, wanting to get as far from the parade as possible.

CHAPTER 14

Guillermo has a question for me one evening. "In English, how do you say, 'Can you pay me?'" It's been nearly a month since the Queens restaurant has reopened, but he has yet to receive a dime. After I go over the phrase with him, he says that he'll leave the diner if they don't pay him by the end of the week.

By now I've settled into a comfortable routine at Azteca, but Guillermo's question reminds me of one way in which my experience in New York is lacking: I'm still working between thirty and thirty-five hours a week, while many of the back-of-the-kitchen staff are putting in sixty to seventy hours, juggling forty-plus hours at Azteca with another restaurant job elsewhere. I ask Alvaro and several others if their second jobs are hiring, but they shake their heads, explaining that the economic crisis has caused business to slow. (Azteca's business, at least while I'm working there, manages to remain fairly busy despite the deepening recession.)

November brings very unpleasant weather. Twice I get caught in chilly rain while riding to work, and head straight to the bathroom to take off my shoes and wring a cup of dirty water from each of my socks into the sink. Late in the month the rains turn to snow, and for a few days the wind chill drops temperatures into the teens, freezing the water in my bicycle bottle. The one positive of the cold snap is that very few people are out walking around, so the streets are pretty much turned over to cab drivers and delivery workers.

After much delay, Greg finally gets Seamless Web up and running. "You have no idea how much stress this has caused me," he says. Throughout the evening he walks back and forth in front of the computer and printer, a look of deep disappointment on his face. "Why won't they order?" he asks. Finally, toward the end of the shift, two orders come through the system, and a wide grin breaks out on Greg's face. I half suspect that he placed the orders himself, but it turns out that they came from customers in Chelsea. In what will become a pattern, neither leaves very generous tips. As opposed to customers who hand over a cash tip or write it out on a receipt while we wait in full view, Seamless Web users type the tip on a computer, without having to face us, and their tips often sink well below the 10 percent mark.

IN EARLY DECEMBER, for the first and only time I arrive late for a shift. Studs Terkel has died, and I'm coming from a memorial service held at Cooper Union. A distinguished lineup of authors and activists spoke at the service, but I record the words of historian Howard Zinn, paraphrasing Terkel's introduction to his book *Working*: "To write about work is to write about violence—violence to the body and violence to the spirit."

When I arrive in the kitchen I see that the delivery counter is crowded with utensils from other areas. No time for pleasantries: I slide them all into the sink. I learn that no one worked the delivery day shift, so nothing is set up—the only item in place is the bowl of salt. Two delivery tickets are hanging from the shelf. The most recent one was just called in; the second order is already thirty minutes old. I check the order: chicken tacos, tortilla soup, and a double order of guacamole.

I spend ten minutes dashing around the kitchen, searching for our stolen utensils, filling the bowls of guacamole ingredients from the fridge, and snagging a molcajete from the restaurant floor. But after searching downstairs and in the prep area, I can't find a single avocado. I head back into the restaurant and ask one of the bus-boys where I can find some.

"*No hay,*" he says. There aren't any. I stop by each guacamole-making stand, but indeed everyone is out of avocados. Back in the kitchen Becky tells me she's asked someone to pick up a box at the store.

"But I've got an order that needs to go out now."

"What's going on?" asks one of the restaurant managers, who is passing through the kitchen.

"I've got this order that's already late and it needs a double guac, but there's no avocados in the entire restaurant. Why don't we just call her and tell her we're out? Then I can at least run the rest out before it gets too late."

"No, we are *not* running that out without guac," one of them says. "Hold on a minute and we'll figure something out." While they're figuring I grab the tacos from the counter and pack them in a bag and ladle out a tortilla soup, which I place on the counter. (I've learned to pack soups last, because the containers have a tendency to leak, and I want them on top where I can keep my eye on them as I'm riding.)

After a few minutes Becky is finally able to dig up two sickly looking avocados. As I mix up the guacamole, one of the bartenders comes up to me. "Is that the order with double guac? That lady's been waiting for like an hour at the bar."

"I thought it was delivery."

"Nope. She's out there getting impatient." I explain about the avocado shortage, scoop the guacamole into a container, and toss it in the bag.

"Ready to go." The bartender takes the bag out.

While I'm putting together bags of chips, Rafael walks up holding a container of tortilla soup. "Was this for an order?" Oh shit.

Rafael jogs to the bar, but the woman has already left. She's going to be *pissed*.

As I continue to scoop out chips, Rafael takes the bullet for me, calling the customer and informing her of the error. "She freaked out on me," is how he describes the conversation. "They want me to run a whole new order out to her."

Rafael disappears and is replaced by a manager. "Hey, what happened with the tortilla soup?" he asks accusingly.

"I don't know—it just didn't get packed?" I say, adopting the passive voice.

"Yeah, but who packed it?"

"I did—I just missed the soup."

"So what happened?"

I don't know what more to say. "I just missed it—there isn't some long story that I can come up with." He shakes his head and walks away.

After the tortilla soup fiasco, we eventually receive a batch of avocados. By eight o'clock, orders stop coming in and the restaurant goes quiet. One of the runners, Isaac, preparing a meal of tacos for himself, stops by our counter to add ingredients from our guacamole station. I'm leaning against the salad counter, talking to Gloria as she makes tortillas, when Isaac turns to face me. "What are you guys doing?" he asks.

"Nothing. What are you doing?"

Rafael, standing next to Isaac, says, "What do you mean?"

"Armando, check this out." Isaac picks up the salt container. During my training, Guillermo told me that there were two types of salt at the restaurant; we were to use the less granular version. Still, this doesn't seem like all that big a deal. Isaac dips his finger into the salt, tastes it, and begins to laugh. Armando tastes it, too, but he looks angry.

"What's up?" Rafael asks.

"What the fuck are you guys doing?" shouts Armando. "Don't you know you're supposed to taste the food to make sure everything is okay? This is fucking sugar!"

The entire kitchen erupts in laughter. Fortunately, none of the managers are around at the moment. Despite the cackles and cries of "*¡Azúcar!*" from the cooks and runners, Armando seems determined to remain angry. Finally, however, a slight smile crosses his face. I do a quick mental review: So far, we've sent out at least eight orders of sugary guacamole. "Armando, we've delivered a bunch of these and no one has called to complain," I say. "They must like what we've been doing. It's a new delivery invention."

"Whatever," he says, dumping the sugar into the trash. "Just don't ever do it again."

AT THE BEGINNING of the next shift, while I'm getting together supplies, Greg asks me to follow him outside. "So what happened yesterday?"

I'm going to assume that he isn't talking about our experiment in sweet guacamole. "You mean the tortilla soup?"

"Yes, the tortilla soup."

I explain that between the general chaos in the delivery area and the search for avocados, I had somehow forgotten the soup.

As he listens to my defense, Greg's face remains grave. He actually looks like he might fire me, and I really don't want to get fired *again*. Instead, he decides to let me off with a lecture. "I hired you to be a leader in delivery, but you have been more of a follower." He takes a deep breath. "I know maybe you don't want more responsibilities, but you need to remember that with more responsibility comes more money."

I remain silent and nod in agreement. He's right that I don't want more responsibility; I've been clear about that from the very beginning. And the truth is that I'm not the leader. Guillermo is the leader. He's been here longer and makes guacamole faster and can have an entire meal packed while I'm still trying to recall whether an order of enchiladas comes with a side of rice and beans. What I can do is bike fast. But the natural hierarchy that has developed is evidently hard for Greg to realize. I'm white, after all, and he expects more from me.

A WEEK LATER, nearing my two-month mark at the restaurant, I arrive early on a Sunday evening to find several tickets—all from Seamless Web—hanging from the shelf. I pack and take out the deliveries, noting again that each customer has tacked on a low tip. By now I've concluded that Seamless Web creates a great deal more work for us, with only marginally more pay. When I return, though it's not yet 6:00 p.m., there are already five more tickets hanging, and no one has shown up to assist. While I scramble to assemble the orders, Rolando, an Ecuadorian who started several weeks ago, clocks in and starts making orders of guacamole. We agree that I'll do the deliveries while he packs.

I dash out with the five deliveries while Rolando starts working on three more that have just been ordered through Seamless Web. The deliveries are all over the place, from Murray Hill to Chelsea to the West Village. I pedal furiously through the five-mile loop and return sweating and out of breath.

Back in the kitchen, the delivery area is unlike anything I've seen. Five orders are lined up on the dessert and salad counter, another dozen tickets are hanging in no discernible order, and Rolando stands frozen in place, his forehead glistening with perspiration as he tries to figure out his next move. Claudia has moved up from downstairs and is taking an order over the phone, but is having trouble hearing because a robotic voice keeps repeating "Seamless Web order," signaling that the machine is out of printing paper.

"Fucking shut up," Claudia screams at the machine. I add paper and three new orders print out. Other than deliveries, it's a very slow night in the restaurant, and the line cooks and runners are standing around gawking at the system overload.

"This is insane," Rolando tells me as I gather five more bags and head out the door. For weeks, Greg has promised us that with Seamless Web we're going to get slammed, and it's finally happening.

I make four quick deliveries, but no one answers the door at the last building, near Union Square. I call the number on the ticket and get a recording, which identifies the customer as an employee with the Blackstone Group, a multibillion dollar private equity firm. I leave a message and knock louder. Finally, just when I'm preparing to leave, a young man opens the door. "Oh, you're out here?" he asks, sounding not the least bit apologetic. I hand over the food and receive a two dollar tip, visions of class war dancing in my head.

On the way back to Azteca, as I'm entering an intersection, a cab driver on my left makes a right turn—right into me. By now I've grown accustomed to fending off drivers who make blind turns, usually by beating on their cars with my hand until they back down and allow me to cross, but this driver catches me unaware, and I ram the left side of my body against his passenger-side door. Thankfully, I am somehow able to stay on my bike by bouncing off the vehicle and changing directions. He slams on the brakes and comes to a stop, but I keep riding without even looking back. Hopefully he'll look next time.

Back at the restaurant, as I lean the bike against the wall, one of the managers walks by. "Hey, you're going to need to start working faster on getting those deliveries out," he says. I ignore him, but a thought pops into my head: I don't want to do this anymore.

That thought receives confirmation when I make it to the kitchen. There are now seven bags on the counter, four more tickets hanging, and the printer is again out of paper. I set a personal record by carrying out all seven orders—three on each handlebar and one in my right hand. As I'm leaving the kitchen, I see my first restaurant rat, which scurries under a large sink and disappears around a corner.

The rest of the evening is a blur. Each time I return to the kitchen, there are rows of orders waiting on the counter, and I'm in and out without even taking off my helmet. Several customers complain about the long wait when they open the door, to which I shrug and simply hand over the food. The only clear thought I remember, after being told a second time that I need to work faster, is that I'm out of here once the shift is over. Rolando and I finally cash out at 10:30 p.m., having delivered more than forty meals and earned $80 apiece.

A white server sitting in the office, also waiting to cash out, is upset by the news.

"What? The delivery boys made more than us?" he says aloud to no one in particular.

I turn to him. "We should. Our job is much harder than yours."

He doesn't say anything to that.

Rolando and I go out for beer to celebrate our survival. Afterwards, when I hop on my bike and head south, it seems like the city has gone to bed early—even the bars on the Lower East Side are subdued. The ride over the Manhattan Bridge is dark and eerily silent; as I pedal up the incline the only sound I hear is my breathing. Coasting down the descending half of the bridge, the wind whipping at my face, I pass a Latino man heading slowly in the other direction on a rickety mountain bike. He is wearing jeans and a flannel shirt and looks fresh. I imagine he's heading into Manhattan to work the night shift. As for me, I'm done.

CONCLUSION

ON ESPECIALLY COOL mornings in Yuma we would arrive at the fields and be forced to wait for the sun to thaw the frost from the lettuce. During this unpaid time—which could last more than an hour—an enterprising middle-aged woman from another crew walked among the workers selling lollipops and other candies. One morning, after I purchased two chocolates wrapped in tinfoil, she asked me what I was doing in the fields. I told her I was learning how to cut lettuce.

"*Es bueno,*" she said—That's good. "But after you're done, the next thing you must do is tell your friends what it's like to do this work. More Americans should know."

She continued on down the edge of the field in her search for customers, having succinctly captured the purpose of this book: to cast light on the hidden work done by a hidden workforce. I've come to think of this project as filling in the details of a backstory, one in which we all play a role but usually at the very end as a participant in a transaction that is stripped of context. Now, when I see heads of lettuce stacked in the produce aisle of a grocery store, I remember sweat and dirt and throbbing backs. Watching a KFC commercial full of smiling customers, I think of missing teeth and carpal tunnel syndrome and sleep deprivation. At restaurants my thoughts turn to the kitchen; when I order delivery, I leave big tips.

Of course, when I laid out my plans in the fall of 2007, I had no idea that they would coincide with such a momentous year, both for immigrants and the economy. In 2006, the Bush administration arrested and deported more than 4,000 undocumented immigrants at worksites, four times the number the previous year. The dramatic increase in workplace raids was seen as a means to shore up support for national immigration reform by demonstrating to conservative members of Congress that legalization could be coupled with enforcement.

The strategy didn't work, as Congress failed to pass immigration reform legislation two years in a row. Still, the Bush administration continued its policy of increasingly harsh enforcement and detention, culminating in 2008 with the highest number of workplace raids in American history. In Postville, Iowa, $5.2 million of taxpayer money was spent to apprehend 389 undocumented immigrants working at a kosher slaughterhouse, a cost of more than $13,000 per person. For good measure, many were charged with identity theft and sentenced in hasty court proceedings to five months in prison. Just a few months later, an even larger raid led to the apprehension of 595 immigrants at a transformer plant in Laurel, Mississippi. In all, more than 6,000 undocumented immigrants were arrested in workplace raids and either deported or imprisoned—a tenfold increase over the figure five years earlier. Families were separated, small towns like Postville upended, and immigrants were handcuffed and sentenced to prison terms for the crime of working long hours for low wages. After years of bemoaning the threat undocumented workers posed to our financial system, hard-line anti-immigrant forces cheered the developments.

Meanwhile, the economy was in free fall, brought on by the reckless business decisions and risky investment schemes of Wall Street executives and enabled by weak government oversight. Banks collapsed, outrage grew over CEO bonuses, and multibillion-dollar Ponzi schemes that had been ignored for years were finally exposed.* By the summer of 2009, about $4 trillion in taxpayer dollars had been spent to bail out institu-

---

* Pilgrim's Pride also suffered from unwise business decisions. With the purchase of Gold Kist and the rise in the cost of chicken feed, the company's debt load eventually soared to $2.7 billion. In December 2008, two years after triumphantly announcing the acquisition of Gold Kist, the company filed for bankruptcy protection under Chapter 11. Although they have closed or idled a number of processing plants, to date the Russellville plant remains open.

tions and attempt to stabilize the economy. As the dust began to settle, there was less oxygen in the room to argue that undocumented immigrants were doing our economy grievous harm by harvesting our lettuce or processing our chicken.

WHAT THE ECONOMIC collapse and my yearlong project make perfectly clear is that executives and bosses will do whatever they can get away with, whether they run investment banks, insurance firms, poultry companies, or the restaurant on the corner. Without vigorous union organizing, companies like Pilgrim's Pride have no reason to pay their workers anything but poverty-level wages. Without fear of worker complaint, Tony and Helen at the flower shop felt no need to offer their employees breaks. Not expecting an inspection from the government, restaurant owners had no incentive to pay delivery workers—who risk their life and limb daily—even the miserly $4.60-an-hour wage owed to them. The most satisfied workers I found were at Dole, but this is in large measure explained by their unique circumstances as commuting guestworkers earning high wages by Mexican standards.

Undocumented immigrants suffer disproportionate abuse on the job, but it is a mistake to pretend that their plight is unrelated to that of American workers. Their experiences reveal the ways in which many businesses, when unfettered by labor unions and given free rein by the government, prefer to treat their employees: as cheap and disposable. The work they do can be unbelievably punishing—I've never faced a greater physical challenge than surviving my eight weeks in the lettuce fields—and they face frequent abuse from management. But these are not simply "immigrant" problems—the same impulse to wrest more from workers is occurring across the board to the American workforce, and has been going on for some time. As Steven Greenhouse writes in *The Big Squeeze*, "Since 1979, hourly earnings for 80 percent of American workers (those in private-sector, nonsupervisory jobs) have risen by just 1 percent, after inflation . . . Worker productivity, meanwhile, has climbed 60 percent."[1] The increasing number of immigrant employees isn't what caused poultry work to become poorly paid and dangerous. It was a treacherous job paying poverty wages when African Americans dominated the industry in the 1970s and '80s. Farmwork is another industry that has always been backbreaking and exploitative—for American citizens as well as immigrants—as anyone who has read *The Grapes of Wrath* can recall. And if you think workplaces that demand long hours for low pay is a problem unique to undocumented workers, then you've never worked at Wal-Mart.

There are no easy solutions, but there are remedies that have as their goal honoring the dignity of labor—no matter who is doing the work. At the very least, workers who do some of the most difficult jobs should earn a living wage and be protected from hazards on the job. Living wages will vary based on location—it ought to be higher in New York City, for example, than Russellville—but should allow for a family to support itself comfortably and not be in a constant state of financial panic. (Kyle wasn't the only person I met in Russellville who never had reason to open a bank account.) Anyone who has worked in a lettuce field or poultry plant would find it hard to argue that the effort deserved anything less than a beginning wage of $15 an hour.

We already know how to achieve this: protecting the rights of workers to unionize, raising the minimum wage, and more vigorously enforcing labor and safety laws. All of these, of course, are huge tasks—and the real work is not identifying the goals but doing the exhausting work of turning these goals into reality. To organize the increasingly diverse workforces in the American South, unions will have to better engage immigrant workers and serve to build links between American and immigrant employees— not as an afterthought but as a central component of the organizing drives. It might seem like a daunting proposition, but in Russellville I found a surprising amount of curiosity and camaraderie among workers, and general dissatisfaction with working conditions and wages.

In workplaces that typically have not been targets of unions, such as the restaurants of New York City, innovative organizing is occurring among worker centers and grassroots coalitions like Justice Will Be Served. These groups are nimble, media-savvy, and have deep ties to immigrant communities. High-profile boycotts and lawsuits have thus far netted millions of dollars in back pay and damages for immigrant workers. Along with the $4.6 million awarded to delivery workers at Saigon Grill, the New York State Labor Department announced in 2009 a record $2.3 million settlement for back wages for workers at nine restaurants owned by Tsu Yue Wang, whose workers had also been organized by Justice Will Be Served. This sort of aggressive organizing can clean up industries. But it will take time, and won't be easy: As I discovered, for virtually all delivery workers, the minimum wage remains out of reach.

There is also a burgeoning food movement sweeping the country concerned with how and where our food is grown and whether or not it is organic. At the moment, many of the issues being raised are centered on the consumer: Is the food safe for my children? How far did it travel to get to my grocery store? We should expand these concerns, demanding that the foods are produced in a way that is not only safe for consumers and environmentally sustainable, but also safe and sustainable for workers. This, in turn, demands that we rethink our notions of the benefits of cheap food, because much of the pressure driving down wages comes from companies in competition with each other for contracts with national chains. Pilgrim's Pride and Tyson are in a race to the bottom to supply the cheapest chicken possible to places like KFC and McDonald's, and so efforts to improve wages will also need to pressure restaurant chains to use suppliers who respect their workers. An order of twenty hot wings for less than $10 might seem like a great deal, but the hidden costs are borne by workers in places like Russellville.

There is also the pressing need for immigration reform. Though many undocumented immigrants have played key roles in drives to improve working conditions, millions more are afraid to exercise their rights on the job, fearing deportation if they speak up. Their understandable fear about reporting workplace abuses effects a downward trend on working conditions, wages, and benefits for everyone. Such workers will not be deported en masse—to do so would be logistically impossible, prohibitively expensive, and immoral. Workplace raids have the ability to terrorize workers, separate families, and wreak general havoc on entire towns—but they certainly won't fix our immigration problem. It's worth repeating that the wide-scale raids in 2008 led to the arrest of 6,000 individuals, which might seem like a substantial number until one remembers that there are an estimated 12 million undocumented immigrants in the country. Raids are little more than public relations stunts—in the words of professor Jennifer Gordon, "good theater" for politicians seeking to look "tough on immigration"—doing nothing to improve working conditions or hold abusive employers accountable. If anything, they create a climate of fear that drives immigrants further underground to seek work in ever more abusive conditions.

Far more beneficial would be the introduction of a system that would allow immigrants a path to legalization, drawing them out of the shadows. This is an ambitious agenda, which the Obama administration promises to pursue, and is certain to meet stiff resistance. It will need the efforts of thousands of grassroots organizers and activists to be successful. It will also need to unearth stories that highlight the many unseen benefits that undocumented immigrants bring to this country, such as revitalizing countless towns like Russellville.

FOR A YEAR of hard labor, I have a surprising number of positive memories. I remember my lettuce crew singing songs and sharing food and stretching their limbs as the sun rose. I think of my coworkers on the poultry line shouting jokes over the din and covering for one another when taking forbidden bathroom breaks. In the kitchen, I recall the pride we took in preparing and making deliveries quickly, and the nonstop, lighthearted insults that were tossed around with such frequency that I considered them background music.

Perhaps the most surprising discovery was how willingly many of my coworkers helped me when my energy level flagged, or offered words of encouragement when they saw that my morale was low. I found that a strong ethos of cooperation among workers was more often the rule than the exception, even when engaged in the most arduous or mind-numbing activities. I never heard anyone utter those magical words, *worker solidarity*, but I saw it displayed countless times—and more often than not, I was the beneficiary. It's now time for all of us, the beneficiaries of so much invisible labor, to demonstrate our own solidarity by taking steps to make the lives of low-wage workers—undocumented immigrants and U.S. citizens alike—more stable and more safe.

NOTES

INTRODUCTION

1. Steven Greenhouse, "Crackdown Upends Slaughterhouse's Workforce," *New York Times*, October 12, 2007.

PART ONE

1. Daniel Gonzalez, "Shortage of Workers Imperils Yuma Crops," *Arizona Republic*, November 21, 2006. Also see Faye Bowers, "Along US-Mexico Border, Not Enough Hands for the Harvest," *Christian Science Monitor*, February 22, 2007.

2. Philip L. Martin, *Promise Unfulfilled: Unions, Immigration, and the Farm Workers* (Ithaca: Cornell University Press, 2003), 193–194.

3. Daniel Rothenberg, *With These Hands: The Hidden World of Migrant Farmworkers Today* (Berkeley: University of California Press, 2000), xxii.

4. Data on farmworkers is taken from a U.S. Department of Labor publication, "Findings from the National Agricultural Workers Survey (NAWS 2001–2002), March 2005.

5. Julia Preston, "White House Moves to Ease Guest Worker Program," *New York Times*, February 7, 2008.

6. Data on farmworkers' place of residence taken from a 2006–2007 survey conducted by the University of Arizona.

7. For bracero data, I relied on Philip L. Martin, *Promise Unfulfilled: Unions, Immigration, and the Farm Workers* (Ithaca: Cornell University Press, 2003), 47.

8. Jacques E. Levy, *Cesar Chavez: Autobiography of La Causa* (Minneapolis: University of Minnesota Press, 2007), 130.

9. Southern Poverty Law Center, "Close to Slavery: Guestworker Programs in the United States," 2007, 11. The report can be downloaded from *www.splcenter.org/pdf/static/SPLCguestworker.pdf* (accessed April 3, 2009).

10. Cited in Steven W. Bender, *Greasers and Gringos: Latinos, Law, and the American Imagination* (New York: NYU Press, 2005), 138.

11. United States General Accounting Office, "Pesticides: Improvement Needed to Ensure the Safety of Farmworkers and Their Children," March 2000, p. 12.

PART TWO

1. Peter Singer and Karen Dawn, "Echoes of Abu Ghraib in Chicken Slaughterhouse," *Los Angeles Times*, July 25, 2004.

2. Tara McKelvey, "A Soldier's Tale: Lynndie England," *Marie Claire*, November 2006.

3. Quotes and data from the April 19, 1989, and June 4, 1989, issues of the *Franklin County Times*.

4. In thinking about economic development in the South, I relied upon Eve S. Weinbaum's book *To Move a Mountain: The Global Economy in Appalachia* (New York: The New Press, 2004). See especially Chapter 2, "Selling Poverty: The Politics of Economic Development in the South," 16–66.

5. Patricia Thorpe, "VF Jeanswear Shutting Doors on Employees," *Franklin County Times*, November 16, 2001.

6. Gene Baur, *Farm Sanctuary: Changing Hearts and Minds About Animals and Food* (New York: Touchstone, 2008), 158.

7. Barbara Ehrenreich, *Nickel and Dimed: On (Not) Getting By in America* (New York: Owl Books, 2002), 214.

8. Héctor Tobar, *Translation Nation: Defining a New American Identity in the Spanish-Speaking United States* (New York: Riverhead Books, 2005), 94.

9. Trevor Stokes, "Franklin County Home to Highest Proportion of Hispanics in State," *Times Daily*, August 10, 2008.

10. Steven Greenhouse, "Union Organizers at Poultry Plants in South Find Newly Sympathetic Ears," *New York Times*, September 6, 2005.

11. Steve Striffler, *Chicken: The Dangerous Transformation of America's Favorite Food* (New Haven, CT: Yale University Press, 2005), 44–45.

12. Study overview and findings available at www.dukehealth.org/HealthLibrary/News/10176 (accessed April 3, 2009).

13. The entire series is available at www.charlotteobserver.com/poultry/ (accessed April 3, 2009).

PART THREE

1. Brennan Center for Justice, "Unregulated Work in the Global City," iii. The report is available at www.brennancenter.org/page/-/d/download_file_49436.pdf (accessed April 3, 2009).

2. Restaurant Opportunities Center of New York and the New York City Restaurant Industry Coalition, "Behind the Kitchen Door," 2005, ii. The report is available at www.urbanjustice.org/pdf/publications/BKDFinalReport.pdf (accessed July 26, 2009).

3. BikeSnob NYC, http://bikesnobnyc.blogspot.com/2007/08/cycling-in-nyc-know-your-enemy.html.

CONCLUSION

1. Steven Greenhouse, *The Big Squeeze: Tough Times for the American Worker* (New York: Knopf, 2008), 5.

ACKNOWLEDGMENTS

My first and largest debt of gratitude goes to the dozens of people I worked with throughout the year. I showed up in strange places without knowing a soul, and yet was immediately befriended by people who shared meals in lettuce fields and gave me rides to the poultry plant. Thank you—*Gracias*. You all made this a very special year for me.

In Yuma, special thanks to Janice Wasserman for providing a quiet place to sleep and eat, and to Kurt Nolte for his patience and thoroughness in explaining my many questions about agriculture.

That I ended up in Russellville was due to David Holthouse of the Southern Poverty Law Center, who suggested that I might want to check out the chicken plant. I'll be forever grateful for the advice, and once in town I was fortunate to meet Sabrina at Mama's Kitchen, who hooked me up with a trailer and fed me countless orders of *huevos a la mexicana*. Deborah Barnett of the Russellville Public Library and John Hicks of the Franklin Free Press also made my time in Alabama a pleasure. Along with sharing his thoughts about the town, Hicks, a remarkable reporter, treated me to a wonderful dinner beyond the county line, where we enjoyed Mexican food, beer, and tequila. Also helpful in Russellville was Chris Ozbirn, the director of the Franklin County Archives and Research Center, who assisted me in locating documents and even prepared sandwiches for me during breaks (try finding that sort of hospitality in New York City).

I was extremely fortunate to receive the Richard J. Margolis Award at the precise moment I shifted from working to writing. For offering quiet places to write at critical points, I'm grateful to Jim and Elana Ponet, Jesse Werthman and Alessandra De Almeida, and the town of

Montauk. A word of thanks is due to Steven Greenhouse, the dogged labor reporter for the *New York Times*, who wrote the article that gave me the idea for this book. Artemio Guerra generously allowed me to use him as a fictitious work reference for each job—no one ever did call him—and regaled me with stories about his own experiences working in a poultry plant in Georgia. Thanks, too, to Debbie Nathan, who helped me think through this project and connected me to various resources.

On the business end, thanks to Carl Bromley for his early enthusiasm, to Ruth Baldwin for her astute editorial suggestions, to Nancy King for her meticulous copyediting, to Laura Esterman for holding everything together, and to Michael Bourret for providing first-class representation.

As always, I could count on the support of Sandra Hietala, Jim Thompson, Ralph and Ivy Hietala, and Marjorie Bjerkager. *Gracias, mi familia.* And the newest official member of the family, Daniella Ponet, to whom this book is dedicated. Reporting this book placed significant burdens on our relationship—months spent in far-off places doing strange jobs can do that—and Daniella made many sacrifices during the year for my benefit. I'm eternally grateful, for both her understanding and her love.